Edwardian Beauty
Lily Elsie
&
The Merry Widow

By
David Slattery-Christy

Published by Christyplays 2022

United Kingdom
All Rights Reserved
4th Edition - Hardback 2021
3rd Edition – August 2014 – 2017 – 2018 compilation
Previous Editions:
1st Edition – 2009 & 2nd Edition – 2011
AuthorHouse

Hardback Edition 2022

ISBN-13: 9781838136536

www.christyplays.co.uk

Edwardian Beauty
Lily Elsie & The Merry Widow

This special edition features the previously published biography
by David Slattery-Christy

Anything But Merry!
The Life and Times of Lily Elsie

Plus a special feature for this edition is the inclusion of the
TV/Drama Screenplay

The Last Edwardian Star

By

David Slattery-Christy
Edited by Allan Bardsley

All Rights Reserved 2009/2014/2021

Edwardian Beauty
Lily Elsie & The Merry Widow

This book [Anthing But Merry! The Life and Times of Lily Elsie] and screenplay [The Last Edwardian Star] are fully protected under the copyright laws of the United Kingdom, the United States of America and all other territories. David Slattery-Christy is identified as the author of this work and has been asserted so in accordance with the Copyright, Designs and Patents Act 1988.

It is an infringement of the copyright to give any public performance or reading of this book or screenplay either in its entirety or in the form of excerpts without the prior consent of the copyright owners. No part of this publication may be transmitted, stored in a retrieval system, or reproduced in any form or by any means, electronic, mechanical, or by means known or unknown, or hereafter invented, without the prior permission of the copyright owners.

Permission to perform this work by professional or amateur companies must be obtained from the playwright by contacting slatterychristy@aol.co.uk or through the author's Literary Agent, Robert Smith Literary Agency, London, England.

Registered at The British Library, London.
Library Deposit Service

Blue Plaque

On a warm August day in 2019 I was delighted and excited to gather outside the former London Home of Lily Elsie at Stanhope House, Stanhope Place, Hyde Park W1, with invited guests including Roy Hudd OBE (President of the British Music Hall Society), his wife Debbie and the West End singer and actress Rosemary Ashe who had agreed very kindly to say a few words to unveil the blue plaque in Elsie's honour. It had been a long and frustrating road, that lasted over several years, to get this blue plaque erected. All the relevant permission one needs for it to be possible from Westminster Council to the Church of England authorities, the Hyde Park Estate, and by no means least the owner of the building, Dimitri Paleocrassas. They were all so very helpful and encouraging and I cannot thank them all enough.

It was a wonderful sunny morning and we were joined by several other Lily Elsie fans and friends including Mrs Sonia Berry's daughter Victoria and granddaughter, Flora. Once the plaque was unveiled by Rosemary we all enjoyed a champagne lunch nearby at the Services Club. It was a fitting tribute to a star of London theatre and the honour of a plaque was long overdue. I thank all those who donated towards the cost and made this possible.

David Slattery-Christy, Rosemary Ashe and Roy Hudd OBE
Unveiling the Blue Plaque in memory of Lily Elsie August 2019

Unveiling Lily Elsie's Blue Plaque, August 2019

Reflections On A Journey!

The development of this book, from first having the desire to create a biography of Lily Elsie, whilst researching the life of her most famous fan and great friend Ivor Novello, has been an interesting journey with many twists and turns. As a writer this process of evolution has added someting extra special to the experience and the end result – especially as I am now writing this new foreword for the compilation edition that includes both the biography and the screenplay. The first edition of 'Anything But Merry!' was published in 2009. To arrive at that first draft I had to write the book without the input of a living-link to colour Elsie' story.

As the pre-eminent Edwradian actress it seemed almost unbelieveable to me that no biography existed of her prior to this. She died in 1962, and her legacy had slowly disolved away and she was forgotten by all but a handful – mostly collectors of post cards from the Edwardian period that captured a youthful, smiling or coy Elsie smiling out. Her talent and achievements long forgotten.

At the height of her fame, she was courted by the likes of Harry Selfridge, who paid her handsomely to endorse the beauty products for sale in his Oxford Street store when it opened its doors in 1909 – and the fashionable clothes and hats made popular by famous designer Lucille, admired by those aristocratic ladies as depicted in Downton Abbey. Lucille found her mass market because she designed the costumes and hats for Elsie to wear in Lehar's hit operetta The Merry Widow at London's Daly's Theatre in 1907. The style then became the height of fashion and must have couture for Edwardian women of all classes. Indeed Elsie was the first celebrity to create a mass, hysterical following that we would recognise today. Everything she wore, every hat that adorned her, the cosmetics she used, every hairstyle and every piece of jewelry was copied and immediately became the most wanted item. She was also very beautiful.

It is why I took on this daunting task that others had abandoned or dismissed as impossible. Perhaps that was the spur – I always feel more determined when a task seems impossible to others. I was also determined to honour Elsie's legacy and make sure her achievements were recorded for future generations.

A few months after the first edition was published I was contacted by Sonia Berry. She lived in Bath and she wanted to tell me how much she had enjoyed the book because Elsie had been a great friend of her mother's, and also acted as an 'aunt' to her when she was a young girl. I had found my living-link to Elsie and we arranged to meet. Sonia was remarkable in that she was able to give me so much information from a personal, informal angle. She also very kindly allowed me to use some family photographs of her with Elsie, and also her mother with Elsie, for a new edition of the book I decided was imperative in light of this new information. In addition to this Sonia agreed to write a foreword for the book.

Meeting Sonia was special for me because she was able to fill in so many little gaps in Elsie's story. In addition she was able to confirm that I had managed to get so much of Elsie's story correct. In the three short years I knew her, I was delighted to have been able to call her a friend. Through her I was also able to see so many of Elsie's wonderful possessions that she still lived with and enjoyed every day at her home in the crescent at Bath.

Sonia was able to see the new edition when it was published in 2011 before she sadly passed away. There was a further twist to the story because Sonia also had another friend from childhood that she cherished and was very proud of. Although she was very discreet and private about it. Her father was a doctor and a leading authority on x-ray diagnosis, and as such became a specialist to the Royal Household for George V and Queen Mary. As a result of this connection Sonia, a child at the time, had been chosen by the then Princess Elizabeth, now Queen Elizabeth II, to be her friend. They remained friends for life. After Sonia's passing, during Her Majesty's Diamond Jubilee celebrations, I decided to send the Queen a copy of the book in memory of Sonia. I was delighted to receive a letter back thanking me and also expressing the Queen's delight that Sonia had been able to pass on the information about Elsie for the book. Sonia's friendship with the Queen is documented in a new book, Royal Childhood: A Souvenier Album, published by the Royal Collection Trust 2014.

From such humble beginnings then, Elsie's story had reached further than I could ever have hoped. Once admired and befriended by Edward VII, and later by Geroge V and Queen Mary. Photographed by Cecil Beaton. Elsie's achievements, life story and place in theatre history now secure for future generations. She was the one and only Merry Widow in Lehar's still popular operetta.

The next stage was to create a screenplay for a drama documentary of Elsie's life based on the book I had written about her. My late friend Allan Bardsley edited and suggested rewrites for the script. I also felt that it would be an opportunity to face and address her mental health problems that are, even today, still a taboo subject for many. I had done this in the book and even Sonia had vivid memories of how her mother helped Elsie when she had terrible depressions and mental breakdowns. It is still a subject that is cloaked in shame and seen as something to fear. The recent passing of the actor and comedian Robin Williams testament to that. My hope is that by honestly depicting the problems suffered by Elsie, and dealing with them openly, those suffering with mental health issues will feel more secure about seeking help and support rather than suffering in fear and silence. If Elsie's story can also help in some way, it would be another part of her legacy. One I feel she would be equally proud of.

This compilation edition is published in memory of Sonia Berry (1925-2012) – acknoweldging her help and friendship – and her trust in me to tell Esie's story.

David Slattery-Christy

Princess Elisabeth & Sonia in the 1930s

Sonia Berry (1925-2012)

BUCKINGHAM PALACE

21st May, 2012

Dear Mr Slattery-Christy,

    The Queen wishes me to write and thank you for your recent letter and warm words of congratulations, and for enclosing a gift of your book, *Anything But Merry!*, for Her Majesty on the occasion of her Diamond Jubilee.

    The Queen was touched that you took the time and trouble to send her this present, and pleased to hear of the contribution Mrs Sonia Berry gave you in recalling her, and her mother's, memories of Lily Elsie.

    Her Majesty has been deeply moved by the loyalty and support she has received throughout her long reign and letters such as yours give The Queen great pleasure and encouragement.

    I am to thank you, once again, for your letter and good wishes in this, Her Majesty's Diamond Jubilee year.

Yours Sincerely,

Lady-in-Waiting

Mr D Slattery-Christy

Reviews

"David Slattery-Christy is a writer very much in tune with British society during the first half of the last century...it has served him brilliantly with his two well-researched biographies. David has an amazing gift for bringing back to life the bustle and allure of London's West End in the days of Daly's, The Gaiety and beyond

The adolescent Novello was a huge fan of Lily Elsie who made her name as Lehar's `Merry Widow' in 1907, going on to star also in A Waltz Dream, The Dollar Princess and The Count of Luxemburg. She later appeared opposite him in his play The Truth Game (1928). Older by then, but still very attractive, it was to be her final stage appearance.

You'd have thought such an incandescent performer would have been blessed with a fulfilling life. But she was riddled with demons, tormented by stage fright and even her hoped-for happily-ever-after with a handsome, wealthy husband, ended in tatters. In the 1950s she had a lobotomy in an attempt to save her fragile mental health, but it only helped destroy her personality further. Nevertheless, Anything But Merry! successfully evokes the world of the Edwardian operettas and musical comedies, and reminds us of the life of one of its glittering, yet sadly forgotten performers - and the sometimes incalculable price of fame."

Raymond Langford-Jones -
Sardines Theatre Magazine

"It looked as though the London premiere of Franz Lehar's operetta, The Merry Widow, was going to flop. Its producer, George Edwardes, was running out of money and his critics damned him for choosing Lily Elsie as the star. A fragile actress seized with stage fright, Elsie herself believed her voice was not strong enough for the role. In the event, The Merry Widow was a roaring success, which transformed Elsie's career. It ran for 778 performances, admirers showered her with jewellery and she was asked to promote everything from face cream to toothpaste. So, why is her first biography called Anything But Merry?

Firstly, the show made her ill, both physically and mentally. Secondly, men scared her. Her marriage, which was deeply unhappy, ended in divorce. Thirdly, as time went by, her mental health broke down completely, resulting in a dubious operation on her brain. She became a recluse and, in 1962, she died alone.

David Slattery-Christy has researched his work diligently. He tells Lily's story clearly and dispassionately. He has added mini-biographies about the most significant people in her life, notes about the theatres she played and a list of the shows she appeared in.

His book is an important contribution to our understanding of Edwardes and the Gaiety Girls, one of the most glittering periods of London's theatre history."

Richard Anthony Baker
The Stage Newspaper

Special Thanks to David Brown, Allan Bardsley, and my agent Robert Smith for their continued support, help and encouragement.

Dedicated to the memory of:

Graham Greenwood *(1953-2021)*

Roy Hudd OBE *(1936-2020)*

Also available in paperback and hardback editions:

In Search of Ruritania
The life and times of Ivor Novello
By
David Slattery-Christy

"[A] biography which is the result of extensive research . . . I found this an intriguing reappraisal of a former theatre idol whom I had tended to dismiss.."
Tom Howard—Rogues & Vagabonds

"The writer often uses a compelling style—the description of his first visit to Redroofs is akin to something out of 'Rebecca', and the tension is also built up during his work in the archives of Drury Lane . . . this revealing biography is a useful and well-researched addition to other books on Ivor Novello: one which is not afraid to cover all areas of his life."

David Wheeler—The Gaiety Magazine."

Further information at: www.christyplays.com

Edwardian Beauty

Lily Elsie & The Merry Widow

by

David Slattery-Christy

AuthorHouse™ UK Ltd.
500 Avebury Boulevard
Central Milton Keynes, MK9 2BE
www.authorhouse.co.uk
Phone: 08001974150

©2011 David Slattery-Christy. All rights reserved.

No part of this book may be reproduced, stored in a retrieval system, or transmitted by any means without the written permission of the author.

First published by AuthorHouse   11/14/2011

ISBN 13: 978-1-5006-6289-9)
ISBN 10: 1-5006-6289-5)

Printed in the United States of America
Bloomington, Indiana

This book is printed on acid-free paper.

WITH GRATEFUL THANKS TO:

Cecil Beaton Archive
Sonia Berry
The Actors'Church
Susan Crabtree
John Culme
Daniel Creasey
Graham Greenwood
St John's College Library, Cambridge University
Matthew Lloyd
Richard Mangan
Mander & Mitchenson Theatre Collection
Lynn Nortcliff
Martin Phillips
Rosy Runciman
Rob Sedman
Templeman Library, University of Kent
Theatre Museum (V&A)
Paul Taylor

Special thanks to Sonia Berry for sharing her memories of Elsie with me, and my friend and editor *Lynn Nortcliff* for her honesty, patience and invaluable help during the creation of this manuscript. *Rosy Runciman* for information which clarified the history of London's various *Strand* theatres, the *Novello Theatre* history and information regarding *George Edwardes*. *Rob Sedman*, *Matthew Lloyd* and *John Culme* for their willingness to help with information and images of Elsie. All those at the *Theatre Museum (V&A)*, *Samuel French Ltd*, *Mander & Mitchenson Theatre Collection* and the *Templeman Library, Kent University*, for their help and last, but by no means least, *Daniel Creasey* for assisting with research for this project.

Elsie & *Sonia* at her 10th Birthday party, 1935.

"Aunt Elsie"

Looking back on my childhood during the 1920s' and 1930s, "Aunt Elsie" as I called her, played a large part in my life, not that we were related, but she was a great friend of my mother's and, as such, they met quite often, and sometimes I went with them.

I remember Elsie as an enormously glamorous figure. Beautiful, elegant, not like a 'pop star' of today, but dignified although recognised wherever she went. In those days, when women used little make-up, it was their bone-structure and features that counted, and there were few who passed the test. But Lily Elsie did, and her public worshipped her from afar, for essentially she was a very private person who, although she had no need, lacked self-confidence and was plagued by breakdowns. Yet as a child I remember her as a loving companion who was warm and funny, and made us all laugh.

As a family we spent several summer holidays with Elsie, in Kent at St Margaret's Bay at a local hotel, at a rented house at Thurlestone in Devon when I was six years old, and twice in France, once in Biarritz and at another time in Le Touquet where we were joined by a couple of her friends, The Malcolms—Lady Malcolm was the daughter of Lily Langtry.

When World War II was declared she left London and stayed with various friends in the country, in Berkshire and Sussex. I saw her quite often still, but petrol rationing prevented much visiting which one would now take for granted. When the war ended she returned to London and stayed for a while at the Connought Hotel, it was while she was there that she had a final major breakdown.

I was named Sonia after her 'Merry Widow' character, because my mother had seen her in the operetta and longed (unsuccessfully!) for a beautiful daughter.

Sonia Berry
February 2011

Foreword

Elsie's **story has been a joy to recreate**, certainly full of surprises but also tinged with sadness. Her heyday in the years prior to WWI are hard for us to imagine today. From the slums of Victorian England to the glittering Edwardian age anything was possible and life was to be enjoyed to the full—even if it meant overindulgence and excess for those fortunate enough to be able to afford it. The theatre of that Edwardian time was also full of excess and extravagance, where *George Edwardes* established his 'musical comedy' vision at the *Gaiety Theatre* and *Daly's Theatre* in London's West End. They became shining beacons of excellence, and an elegant alternative to the coarseness of the music halls, under his unique style and management where *Gertie Millar* was the queen of the *Gaiety*, along with the sophistication, beauty and elegance personified in *Edwardes' 'Gaiety girls'*. *Daly's* would become the home of operetta with the most famous of that genre's composers *Franz Lehar* at the helm. In a foreword to her biography on *Edwardes* in the 1940s *Ursula Bloom* said of those times:

"This was most certainly the era of entertainment, and all the Edwardians availed themselves of it whensoever they could. The music halls were well established. On their stages fat-thighed young women with breasts like St. Paul's dome, and emphatic hips, disclosed themselves in spangles, to sing lewd songs in a gin-in-a-fog voice. Comic turns rattled off inviting choruses, to be taken up lustily by the audiences who had come to enjoy themselves and enjoy themselves they would . . . then came *George Edwardes*, and what he did for the musical play! What first night was there after 1914 compared with *The Merry Widow*? Indeed it was a merry world. It was far happier than the period which came after 1914, and although the modern young things may not see it in that light, it is only because they do not now recognise the tremendous attractions which it had to offer . . ."

During my initial research for this biography I was frustrated at times because I could discover no living link to Elsie, a link that would help me to flavour her story with small, intimate personal details. In spite of this I felt after time that I began to get a real sense of Elsie and her character, and even began to feel I had created a posthumous friendship with her. At times she was still shrouded in a misty haze, but it became clearer at times, only to then envelop her again. This experience, I now realize, was not dissimilar to what it would have been like to know her during her life.

Some months after the first edition was published I received a letter, which literally stopped me in my tracks and filled me with joy. The letter in question was from a most charming lady, Mrs. Sonia Berry. Sonia's mother met Elsie in the 1920s whilst undertaking charity work together and became a life-long friend. I was delighted when Sonia agreed to write an introduction for this new edition of Elsie's biography. The information she has shared with me has helped to fill some gaps and also to clear up some of the mystery, which surrounded Elsie's final years and what happened after her death in 1962.

In addition to this I was also contacted by an archivist at St John's College Library, Cambridge University, who sent me copies of many hand written letters either by Elsie or those who worked with her. Cecil Beaton was a great admirer and friend to Elsie and there are some personal letters, which give a real flavour of her relationship with him. There are also some which offer a tragic insight into Elsie's mental health problems. I would like to thank them all for their help and for the opportunity to create this new edition.

"David Slattery-Christy has researched his work diligently. He tells Elsie's story clearly and dispassionately . . . his book is an important contribution to our understanding of Edwardes and the Gaiety Girls, one of the most glittering periods of London's theatre history."
Richard Anthony Baker—The Stage

"This is not a formal footnoted biography . . . [Elsie's] life is written like a very well researched novel for the reader . . . it shines a light on a lady whose postcards from the height of her fame fascinate even now . . ."
K. Maxwell (Sydney, Australia)

CONTENTS

Chapter1. 1886 1
Chapter2. Love or Marriage? 7
Chapter3. New Beginnings 15
Chapter4. Little Elsie 23
Chapter5. Destiny & The Guv'nor 45
Chapter6. A Chinese Honeymoon! 55
Chapter7. Slings & Arrows! 65
Chapter8. Franz Lehar & Reconciliation 75
Chapter9. What Price Success? 103
Chapter10. A Reluctant Widow &Her Prince. 115
Chapter11. Mrs Bullough. 133
Chapter12. The Last Edwardian Waltz 167
Chapter13. Comeback &The 1920s 179
Chapter14. The Last Act: Room 34 191
Chapter15. Tempus Fugit Semper Amici
(Time flies but love remains) *197*

Reference Section 211
Biographies 214
Theatres.. 238
Productions 244
INDEX Anything But Merry! 275

"To that gracious lady 'The Merry Widow' who entranced us,
the 'Sonia' who captured our hearts and who waltzes
forever in our memories
Lily Elsie."

W. Macqueen-Pope
Theatre Historian

1886

"The boy I love is up in the gallery/The boy I love is looking down at me/ There he is, can't you see?/Waving his handkerchief/As merry as a robin that sings in a tree."

NELLY POWER

Lottie screamed in pain, sucked in her breath sharply and felt the beads of sweat trickling down her forehead. She was not naïve to the process of giving birth, but she hadn't expected this and the little bugger was proving difficult seeming not to want to come into the world; at least not alive. At this rate they'd both end up dead. Bellowing again like some deranged demon she contracted her muscles and felt the stabbing pain shoot up her back, silencing her momentarily. Her thought at that moment was that she really was going to die; sure her heart had stopped for an instant as a result of the increasing pain. For the first time since she could remember she uttered a silent prayer to God. In her terror she could see the midwife looking at her with what she perceived as fear etched across her face. In the distance the face of her erstwhile lover, Bert Hodder, looked on with what she could only describe as disinterest in her plight. He was after all responsible for her conceiving this baby; or was he? Some things she just couldn't be sure about and Billy Cotton was also a contender. Bert had no thought of the consequences when he'd downed a few beers; all he cared about in those moments was his own pleasure. At first his loving was thrilling but eventually she would just lie there unresponsive and hating him for being drunk and not caring about her feelings. She hated him more than ever at this moment. If she died she would bloody well come back and haunt the bastard whether he was the father or not. But if she didn't die, and this baby survived, it would be a bloody mouth to feed and worry about. Billy on the other hand had been so loyal and caring, which at times was less than exciting and at others bloody irritating. Maybe she'd been foolish to turn her back on the stability he offered her. At least Billy adored her in his own way.

In that moment the squalid rooms of the theatre digs came into sharp focus. She could see every shabby detail, every cobweb, every patch of damp which stained the walls and ceiling. Every creak of the rough floorboards came back to haunt her and remind her of the poverty they lived in. It wasn't living, it was existing. Usually you only had to put up with these places for a week or two whilst on tour, but since she had run off with Bert and found herself pregnant it had grounded her for a while. She had never liked Leeds, its dingy dark alleys and squalid streets with the claustrophobic throb of its sweaty, unwashed inhabitants. How she longed for the fresh air and countryside of Lancashire. At least living in Manchester had enabled her to escape the gloom of city living on occasions. In that moment she decided she would bugger off back to Lancashire and take the baby with her. Sod Bert, he could stop in Leeds and rot for all she cared.

She felt the scream rising up her throat and expelled it with the force of a whistling steam train. It shattered the silence in the room, reverberated through the house and was heard along the street if truth be known. The midwife noticed the colour drain from Bert's face and smiled to herself as he hastily left the room. She concluded long ago that men had no stomach for childbirth. It was the ferocity of the scream and the accompanying push that allowed the baby to poke its head into the world for the first time. The child's body slithered out with relative ease and within a moment it was screaming its heart out. If nothing else, the child had a good set of lungs, but looked quite feeble physically. Relieved the ordeal was over, Lottie waved away the chance to hold her new born and instead slipped, exhausted, into a deep sleep. Her first in nearly two days. As she drifted into unconsciousness, she could hear the child's screams fading into the distance. Within moments she was oblivious to everything.

The midwife looked at the now sleeping Lottie with anything but sympathy and shook her head, an indication of her irritation to anyone that knew her. Holding the new born infant, she couldn't help but admire the feisty little girl who was, after exhausting herself in the initial moments of life by screaming, still determined to continue exercising her lungs in spite of her tiny body deciding otherwise. Wrapping the child in a shawl, she gently placed her in the old drawer her mother had prepared for the purpose; one which the midwife was pleased to see had been lined with a rough blanket to offer some kind of comfort. She suddenly found herself startled by the intense look the child gave her, then just as quickly the child closed her eyes and drifted into sleep. She crossed to the small fireplace and poked the fire as the room was rather chilly, replaced the guttering candle on the dresser with a new one, then added a couple of lumps of coal onto the fire to keep it burning and adjusted the damper to prevent it burning itself out again too quickly. Busying herself with these tasks she found herself thinking how the child stood a chance of surviving because it was early April, therefore the warmer weather was approaching. The bitter winters in Yorkshire killed more babies than she cared to think about. She should know, she'd delivered enough of them. Looking across at the child she hoped that this would be the case, she was a pretty little thing and seemed to have real features and smooth skin, unlike most babies who had crumpled red blotched faces for the first few hours of their life. Looking at Lottie she couldn't help feeling irritated again. She was a strange box of tricks indeed. Seemed to have ideas above her station in life, with an unhealthy "grand attitude" as if she were somehow superior to the rest of them. An actress indeed! It would be wise to keep that kind of fancy to herself if she wanted to avoid the workhouse; or worse, end up being mistaken for an immoral woman. She'd learn, and probably the hard way. Some women, for all their supposed experience of life, never seemed to learn that romantic love and airy-fairy ways didn't get you very far! Men were all the same and cared little for anything but their own needs. Love usually didn't come into it. All that mattered was finding the money to survive and keep a roof over your head and food in your mouth; however frugal the existence. You can be as "grand" as you please when you're rich, but it gets you no where when you are poor. At least that was her own mother's philosophy, and nothing she had yet witnessed had made her hold a different opinion.

At this moment Bert walked back into the room and slammed the door. The baby flinched but didn't wake. Lottie muttered something unintelligible and turned over. He glared at the midwife and took a swig from his beer bottle. As their eyes met she held his gaze for a second or two. She had seen the likes of this one too many times before. He was handsome and broad shouldered, but they always were, and she knew the type. Charm the drawers off anyone to get his own way. She had heard about theatre Johnnies and their ways. Well he needn't look at her. The smell of drink and the slight aroma of stale sweat invaded her nostrils. He sneered at her as if he had read her mind, then sat himself down in the chair next to the fire without saying a word and began pulling his boots off. Wrinkling her nose in disgust she gathered her few belongings and threw them into her carpetbag, pulled her shawl tightly around her shoulders and walked to the door. He held out his clenched hand towards her, then slowly opened it to reveal a sixpence laying in his palm. She crossed to him to take her fee, which unusually had slipped her mind, and as she did he grabbed her hand and held it tightly. She tried to pull away as he laughed and her panic rose when he stood up and pulled her closer and grabbed her round the waist with powerful hands. She felt his rough stubble scratching the side of her face as he tried to kiss her and his hand groping her behind. As suddenly as it started he released his grip and, slightly breathless but not wanting to show him her dignity had been displaced, she hurriedly put the sixpence in her pocket and scurried across the room relieved to reach the door. With her heart pounding she opened the door and glanced back to see him grinning at her as he sat again in the chair by the fire. Closing the door behind herself, she knew there was no happiness there. She would be glad to get out of the house; she had always distrusted theatricals, and nothing she had experienced tonight had made her change her mind.

Lottie had quickly learned that life for those working the music halls was anything but glamorous. It was a tough transient life, which offered little by way of security to those involved. Those working back stage like herself earned very little and had no guarantee of work; the managers and owners of the halls were powerful and vindictive and she was definitely at the bottom of the heap. She had witnessed the treatment meted out to those who complained or attempted to get a decent wage. She had seen how they were blacklisted throughout the country and left destitute. It was an incestuous business reigned over mostly by ruthless employers. That said, it was preferable to working in the cotton mills, factories or the mines and most of those fortunate to get their foot in the door, like she had, were prepared to put up with anything. Yes, Charlotte Elisabeth Barret, known to her friends as Lottie, had been lucky enough to find an opening to allow her to escape from the Lancashire cotton mill she and her mother had toiled in for several years. All because she had a talent for dress making and had been fortunate to cross the path of Nelly Power, the famous singer in the music halls.

Lottie was in awe of Nelly as she was the undisputed queen of the halls since the 1870s and had a big hit with the song written especially for her by George Ware titled "*The Boy I love Is Up In The Gallery*". Lottie loved this song and knew it by heart, indeed she had seen Nelly perform it many times during her visits to local halls and never dreamt she would one day meet her. Fate played its part in bringing them together in 1885. Nelly was appearing as part of her national tour of the halls at the *Prince of Wales Theatre*, Salford. On her arrival at the theatre she discovered her costume trunks had been damaged during their train journey from London. Her silk dress had been torn in several places and with no suitable replacement she feared her performance would have to be cancelled or delayed. William Charles Cotton, known to his friends and Lottie as Billy, was the theatre baggage handler, who had met Lottie at the stage door one night asking for work. He remembered she mentioned her abilities as a dressmaker. Luckily, as he had liked her he had jotted down her address, he was able to send a stage boy to find her and bring her back to the theatre as quickly as possible. Lottie duly arrived and swiftly and enthusiastically repaired Nelly's costume. Lottie knew her work was faultless, and it was almost impossible to see where any damage had been inflicted to the fine silk. Nelly was grateful and very impressed at Lottie's skill with a needle. Billy was also grateful and found himself quite taken with her. So it was by chance that Lottie found her way out of the cotton mills and would meet the man who would play a large part in her future. Nelly had also employed her as her dressmaker and dresser for the duration of her current tour. At first it was a glamorous and exciting life and she had loved travelling the country and meeting new people. The work was hard, money scarce but in spite of the crummy digs it beat the cotton mills hands down. Lottie couldn't believe her luck.

Her luck wasn't that great at the moment. As she lay there with her baby girl she wondered what on earth she was going to do. Remembering the events which had brought her to this moment caused her to shudder. One thing was certain, she had chosen the name Elsie for her daughter, for no other reason than she liked the sound of it and in a strange way it suited the child. Looking across at Bert sleeping in the chair by the fire she couldn't help wondering what had made her so foolish where men were concerned. In the stillness of the night and with the glow of the fading firelight it seemed such a cosy little place. You could be mistaken for thinking they were a happy little family. Even Bert looked like the man she had first been attracted to once again. No one could deny he was handsome and charming and all those things which bewitch the heart. Working as a fly man in the theatre, hauling ropes and lifting heavy scenery in and out, day and night, had made him physically strong. But sometimes his strength frightened her, especially when combined with his drinking. He was dangerous and unpredictable, everything Billy wasn't, which is why she was initially so attracted to him she supposed. She was suddenly aware of Elsie staring at her, the child's eyes trying to focus to catch a look at her mother for the first time. Lottie felt a tear trickle down her face and found herself whispering to her "bugger them blokes eh? It'll be just you, little Elsie, just you and me—we'll be alright, won't we? You just wait and see . . ." Lottie drifted into a deep sleep with little Elsie cradled in her arms. For a short while they were warm and content in each other's company. But it wouldn't last for long.

Love or Marriage?

*"Now if I were a Duchess and I had a lot of money/
I'd give it to the boy that's going to marry me."*
NELLY POWER

Billy Cotton was nobody's fool, or so he thought. He had decided from an early age that the only person he could truly rely on in this life was himself. For several years he had happily worked the halls as a stagehand. Slowly he had worked himself up the ladder, such as it was, and impressed the owners of various halls with his dedication and increasing skill in all areas. He was also shrewd enough to make himself invaluable to them and he was now respected among them. He loved organising things and was now in charge of the tour arrangements for Nelly Power, one of the most famous performers doing the halls. She had been impressed with the way he had handled the crisis at Salford, when her costumes were damaged, and had requested his release from his job at the *Prince of Wales Theatre*, taking him on as her personal organiser and luggage handler. Old Mr Moss wasn't too pleased but had little choice. When Nelly wanted something, she got it. That was over a year ago, and apart from one unpleasant incident with Lottie he had no regrets.

As he watched Nelly performing from the wings of Manchester's Queen's Theatre, he felt nervous about the conversation he knew he had to have with her later that night. Made more nervous because it involved Lottie. She had thrown him a broadside when she ran off with that fly man six months ago. Made worse because she infuriated Nelly by walking out. He had to use every ounce of his charm and diplomatic skills to calm those waters because nobody walked out on Nelly Power. But he didn't care about Nelly's thoughts on the subject when it came to Lottie; all he cared about was finding her. He had searched high and low for months and questioned every contact he had in the halls. It all came to nothing, until today. He smiled to himself and reasoned that if he was smart he'd forget about Lottie and concentrate on the one person he could rely on—himself. The simple truth was, he couldn't. Lottie had literally stolen his heart—even made him realise he had one! Damn the troublesome creature and all her charms. He couldn't believe he was admitting, even to himself, that he loved the wretched girl and he wanted her back at whatever cost.

By chance and a stroke of luck he had discovered that Lottie was living in theatre digs in a less than salubrious district of Leeds with Bert the fly man. His informant, the manager of *Thornton's Music Hall* had also told him that Bert had been a bit too handy with his fists on occasions and was liable to be violent; not just to Lottie but anyone who crossed him when he'd had a few beers. As a result he'd been sacked and blacklisted from all but the most disreputable halls in Leeds. The one he was now working in, *Princess Palace of Varieties*, in spite of its grand title, was nothing more than a rowdy brothel where drink and casual sex were top of the bill. As worrying as this was it was the next piece of information which had completely knocked the wind out of him better than any well placed left hook could: Lottie was pregnant. At first he just couldn't believe it, couldn't believe that she would have run away knowing she was expecting. But maybe that is why she ran away? His mind was in turmoil and brimming with questions that were impossible to answer. Only one person could answer them and that was Lottie. The question he tried hard not to contemplate was who the child's father was. Somewhere in his mind he wanted it to be him, but equally he couldn't bear the thought it might be that drunken bastard, Bert. He chose to push the question away whenever he found it had crept back to the forefront of his mind. It was literally too painful.

Waiting back stage in Nelly's dressing room he was impatient to tell her the news and that he was going to Leeds tonight on the mail train to find Lottie and resolve this impossible situation once and for all. She may well be happy with Bert and tell him to bugger off and leave her alone. Whatever the outcome, at least he would know where he stood in her life. Catching sight of himself in the mirror, he realised he was trembling slightly and beads of perspiration were glistening on his forehead. He wasn't a bad looking chap, and only just thirty-years-old. He had seen worse than the reflection staring back at him. He had always had a stocky, well built physique as a result of his love of sport and running. He found that running helped him to cope with the pressures of life; allowed him to vent his frustrations before it turned to anger. His father had been an angry man and he had witnessed the beatings his mother endured as a result. It was why he had no time for drink. He had seen first hand how it can change the personality of those in its grip. One thing he had never been, or could ever be described as, was handsome. His face was too round and chubby, and his red hair was no match for those men blessed with more dark swarthy looks that women seemed to swoon over. No, he was definitely not the kind to be swooned over, but he had other qualities that were not immediately obvious. He was, and always had been, a kind and sensitive man and hated seeing anyone harmed or downtrodden. He could be tough when required but as he'd said many times "he was nobody's fool" and never would be. Lottie was the only girl who had ever really got beyond his protective shield; there had been other girls, but just ones where they enjoyed mutual fun whilst spooning and perhaps sex. Smiling at his reflection he blushed slightly as he remembered having more than enough fun in that department, and usually in the weirdest places—theatres really did hold some secrets of those who worked in them and visited them for entertainment. His thoughts were interrupted abruptly as Nelly came bustling through the door. She looked at him and noticed he was blushing, which accentuated the redness of his hair. He didn't have to say a word for her to know this had something to do with Lottie. He cleared his throat to speak, and she sat at her dressing table and looked at his reflection expectantly in the mirror.

Nelly found her mind wandering as she watched Billy convey the news about Lottie and how he had found her whereabouts at last. She was angry with the girl for leaving without any kind of explanation but on hearing she was pregnant she could understand why the girl had bolted. In spite of her initial anger with Lottie, Nelly was fond of her—whatever she had done. She also knew that Billy was more than enamoured with her and had been pining for her since she ran off. He was so courteous and professional and probably no one else noticed the slight change in him. He had acquired what she could only describe as a wistful look when he thought no one was looking at him. Whatever he wanted to do, she was happy for him to do it. Hopefully, she reasoned, it would sort out the muddle and she would be able to have them both back in her life. How a child would affect that she didn't yet know, if indeed a child would be involved; there was nothing to say if Lottie had carried full term or even if the child survived the birth? All she hoped was that Billy would not end up disappointed and find Lottie had moved on or, more importantly, that he should find out the child wasn't his. No, she was happy for him to go and sort things out, and said so. The sooner he did, the sooner she would get her efficient Billy back on track. As the door closed behind him, her thoughts turned to her work. It was proving to be a busy and demanding tour and, much as she hated to admit it even to herself, she was finding her nightly performances exhausting; more so in the northern halls because the audiences, although just as appreciative of her in their own way, were much more tumultuous, harder to work and easily distracted. Her eye was caught by the sight of her name on a page of the Manchester Herald, which Billy had left for her attention. As she read the article, she smiled at the irony:

"Miss Nelly Power proved a very sprightly interpretress of the lively puns in one of her hit songs '*The City Toff*'. She has a good voice; her style of singing was superior to the ordinary requisites of burlesque, and her energy and spirits were unflagging. Having forsaken the legitimate stage for the music halls, she has contented herself with the laurels she has achieved by singing as a finale the publics favourite '*The Boy I Love Is Up In The Gallery*' to which her rapt audience at the *Queen's Theatre* last night roared its approval . . ."

She couldn't help but read again how her "energy and spirits were unflagging" and sighed to herself. If only they knew how she really felt. In truth she was terribly tired, and it seemed to be getting worse as each week passed. Perhaps she should confide in her husband and mother? She dismissed this as she didn't want them to fuss over her anymore than they did already. Maybe she could confide in Billy? The fact she even had this thought surprised her, but then he was someone she could trust to keep it to himself. Shrugging her shoulders in an attempt to lift herself out of the gloom that descended upon her when she dwelt on such matters, she began to remove her stage makeup. She decided she must get a grip of herself—after all she was thirty-two-years-old and, although she said it herself, had never looked better; at least with her make-up on.

Besides, she had other, more urgent, things to think about. It had been brought to her attention by Alec Hurley, a promising young coster singer on the tour, that a new girl in London was using her number *The Boy I Love Is Up In The Gallery*. Every act knew it was an unwritten law that you never use another artiste's song, unless they either sell it to you or agree to it being used. It would seem this girl needed a lesson as to how things worked, and the consequences if you chose to ignore the rules. To make matters worse it seemed she had made quite an impact with the song; which if she was honest, had annoyed her more. She needed to arrange with Billy to try and check out a performance of this Marie Lloyd girl and find out if it was indeed true. According to Hurley, Miss Lloyd had made a name for herself and worked her way out of the east end halls. As a result, she was now appearing in the more legitimate halls on the Tottenham Court Road. Nelly admired ambition and tenacity—it had always served her well—but she needed to see this girl and determined to organise the visit with Billy as soon as he returned. Her thoughts were interrupted by a knock at her dressing room door and her husband entered, reflected in her mirror. As she smiled at him she prayed he wouldn't notice how pale and exhausted she really looked.

Lottie sat in the chair by the fire silently crying. She was desperately unhappy and afraid to wake little Elsie who was sleeping peacefully in her arms. Elsie had been a perfect baby for her first day of life and had made no demands on her mother apart from wanting to be fed. Lottie hadn't known what to expect, or even how she would feel, once the baby had arrived, but now Elsie was here she wouldn't part with her for anything. She was just so tiny and Lottie worried and wondered whether she had the strength to survive at all. But then Elsie would look at her with those big expressive eyes, and in those moments it was as if she was reassuring her mother that everything would be alright and that she understood everything. Sitting there with the firelight flickering in the room it felt peaceful, peaceful but somehow empty. Lottie knew that in a few days she would have no choice but to leave this place. Where she would go she had no idea. Bert had decided he didn't want the responsibility of a baby and be obliged to provide for a woman he no longer cared about. Lottie wasn't surprised really, Bert always had been, and probably always would be, a fly by night more interested in his drink and a quick thrill. There were plenty of stupid girls out there like her who would be willing to fall on their back for his charms. In that moment, holding onto that thought, she found herself hoping that Billy was the father of Elsie—better him than Bert. It was impossible to be sure. Ironically she had loved Bert, but accepted he had never really loved her. Billy she liked, liked a lot, but it was a different kind of feeling. Maybe the child would grow to resemble one or the other in time. For now she just wanted to sleep, she would face up to her reality tomorrow. Suddenly aware that Elsie was staring up at her with those big knowing eyes, she smiled at her and began to sing softly:

The boy I love is up in the gallery,
The boy I love is looking down at me,
There he is,
Can't you see?
Waving with his handkerchief,
As merry as a robin that sings in a tree.

Billy huddled under his heavy coat in the corner of the train compartment. It was a cold night. He had been amazed at how easy it was to persuade Nelly to let him have a couple of days off; more so because she seemed quite supportive of his quest to find Lottie and sort things out. Even more surprised when she asked him to tell Lottie she could have her old job back if she wanted it. He had expected a big scene about the whole thing, but none had ensued and for that he was grateful. The mail train was notoriously slow, stopping at every station—it would take all night at this rate to arrive in Leeds. Drawing on his cigarette, as much for the warmth it afforded as the pleasure of smoking, he inhaled deeply savouring the taste of the tobacco before exhaling with a sigh. He had no idea what he might find, and even less idea what he was going to say to her. And what if Bert was there? How would he deal with him? The man who had been sleeping with Lottie behind his back whilst she was sharing his own bed. He decided he would see what happened in the moment. Supposing he found her at all. As he sat there cold, tired and anxious about what was to come just one thought kept his spirits buoyant: he would ask Lottie to marry him. Even if she did have a child and even if it wasn't his (tho' he hoped it was), he would treat it as his own. As long as he had Lottie he didn't much care.

Bert had been sitting quietly in the public house thinking about Lottie and the child. He had heard through gossip that Billy Cotton was looking for them, and from what he had heard it was a persistent campaign to find out any kind of information. That could only mean one thing, the dope was in love with the girl; and after the way she had treated him he was a bigger fool than he thought. He smirked as he recalled how Lottie had almost begged him to sleep with her as soon as Billy's back was turned, and he also recalled the night he had her right under his nose—well, under the stage at least while Billy stood in the wings above. According to Lottie's chatter Billy was a bit lacklustre in the bedroom department so it was little wonder that she was all over him. Her and a hundred other stupid girls—problem was all that fun had come at a cost, and the cost was the reason for his silent contemplation of his current pint of ale. Bloody women had given him a dose and according to the doctor there was a fair chance he might even have syphilis. He'd been feeling a bit off for a few weeks, which had frightened him. He'd given the quack a back hander, more than he could afford, and he'd given him some bloody awful mercury stuff to take. So all he could do now was hope. Then it occurred to him: perhaps he could cover this expense, and any future ones, by capitalising on Billy's obsession with Lottie. Maybe there was some money to be made. That Lottie loved him and not Billy was undisputed, so if he offered the dope a deal, to leave her and the kid alone, he just might take it. Yes, he just might take it.

Little Elsie lay in her makeshift crib, her eyes drawn to the candle light dancing across the ceiling. She was oblivious to everything but the sound of her mother's breathing. Nearly three hundred miles away a young girl called Marie Lloyd began singing the last chorus of her new song to resounding cheers at London's Caledonia Music Hall, Tottenham Court Road.

The boy I love is up in the gallery,
The boy I love is looking down at me,
There he is,
Can't you see?
Waving with his handkerchief,
As merry as a robin that sings in a tree.

New Beginnings

"*My old man said follow the van/ And don't dilly-dally on the way.*"

MARIE LLOYD

Lottie had learnt some hard lessons and decided never again to allow herself to be beguiled by men like Bert Hodder. By nature, she reasoned, she was an emotional person and although far from perfect had done little to deserve the treatment he had inflicted upon her. She had wisely omitted to tell Billy all the details of her time with Bert, but she remembered the bruises left by his drunken rages. She never wanted to experience that again. The resulting emotional scars had left her with a nervous disposition and severe melancholia. At these times she realised she could be unbearable and difficult, and was prone to weep for hours for no apparent reason; at least no reason she could think of or explain to anyone even herself. Deciding her heart was fragile in the extreme, she was determined not to rush into another relationship too hastily. Billy had understood and told her he was prepared to take things slowly. How could she refuse? Billy was a kind and considerate man and, in spite of her treatment of him in the past, had happily forgiven her everything. That fact alone took her breath away and made her realise that although she didn't love him in the true sense he indeed loved her above everything else. He was also beguiled by little Elsie, and was a true father to her; unflinching in his support both emotionally and financially. Thank God this man had come into her life and had the determination to find her in Leeds. If he hadn't, she shuddered to think what might have happened to her and Elsie.

Billy had rented a small terrace house on Liverpool Road in Salford for them. It was a typical red brick two up and two down with an outside privy and enough draughty windows and doors to aid the dusting side of housework. The neighbours were nice enough but all factory or mill workers with whom they had little in common. In truth it was a bit grey and bleak but Lottie had managed to furnish the house so it had a cosy feel. Once the fire was lit and the door closed it was a calm and safe little world for them.

It was also just a few minutes walk to the *Prince of Wales Theatre* where she had met Billy, and they had crossed the path of Nelly Power. Nelly had intended they would both return to work for her but as Elsie was just a baby, they had decided that some stability was needed; it would have been impossible to traipse around the country with a baby in tow. She had discussed it with Billy and they both regretted having to let Nelly down as she had been so good to them. How could they tell her? In the end it didn't matter because Nelly died suddenly on 20th January 1887 at the age of thirty-three. Lottie remembered how distraught Billy had been and how it had upset her more than she thought it would. To die at such a young age and so unexpectedly was horrible and made Lottie realise that life was indeed to be cherished. Her death was due to a "disorder of the blood" according to her doctor.

Billy, ever practical even whilst truly grief stricken went to see old Mr Moss at the *Prince of Wales Theatre*. He explained how his employer had died and that he had a wife and child to support—even though they weren't as yet married—and wondered if he could perhaps have his old job back. Mr Moss took him back without question, and was glad to do so because since Billy's departure things never been run quite as smoothly and some of the acts at the bottom of the bill needed a firm hand—or so he declared. Thus their life centred around the Salford music halls and they were content for the time being. Elsie also took Billy's name and became known as Elsie Cotton. Lottie was, she had to admit, happy for probably the first time in her life.

The full facts of his meeting with Bert had been kept from Lottie. Billy reasoned there was no point in hurting her by laying out the full scope of Bert's betrayal. In the end she was just a commodity to him, a commodity worth a few quid which he could drink himself into oblivion with. The man was not worth scraping off his shoe, Billy had decided. Bert was waiting outside that hovel in Leeds they were living in when he arrived. He was told the full story and was aghast when Bert asked for money in return for not keeping hold of Lottie and the baby. He would let him take them without hindrance for a fee. Billy recalled how stunned and disgusted he was by the man and his proposition. For the first time in his life he had behaved like his father, but this time it was Bert Hodder receiving the punches and not his mother. His strength and the depth of his anger frightened Billy, and frightened him still when he thought about it. He could have happily killed him, beat him to death, indeed had a passing stranger not intervened that's probably what would have happened. He shuddered at the thought of what might have been. Spending the rest of his days in prison over that man would not have been worth it. He might never have seen Lottie again, or experienced the joy of his daughter little Elsie; for he was convinced she was his daughter, nobody so sweet natured and pretty could have sprung from the loins of Bert Hodder. If he never saw or heard from him again it would be too soon.

Nelly had also confided in him that she had started to feel tired and unwell. Having sworn him to secrecy he had told no one, not even Lottie. He had urged her to seek some medical advice, but she had been outraged at the cost some doctors charged, put it from her mind and just carried on hoping things would get better. He would always remember her the way she was the night they went to see the competition; especially the errant Marie Lloyd who was blatantly using her song. When confronted by Nelly back stage after the performance Ms Lloyd had apologised and feigned innocence; and Billy shrewdly realised there was little in the way of "innocence" in her character. Nelly had graciously accepted her apology. Cute as ninepence that one, as far as Billy was concerned, and he'd told Nelly so in no uncertain terms. To his amazement she agreed and demonstrated another trait which was not often visible to those who didn't know her well. Nelly had been so impressed with Ms Lloyd and her talent that she had decided to forgive her—deciding she would eventually allow her to use the song. As it turned out, there was no need. Nelly's death allowed Marie Lloyd to claim the song as her own. For Billy, it would forever remind him of Nelly and he would rather hear Nelly perform it every time; and ten times better than Marie Lloyd could ever hope to at that.

The next few years passed quickly enough and Billy turned out to be a very supportive partner for Lottie; he especially doted on little Elsie, indeed she felt loved and protected, if not worshipped, because of his kind and gentle ways. The relationship, although they were still unmarried, worked very well and to the rest of the world they seemed a happy little family unit. By 1891 Lottie had relaxed and finally agreed to marry Billy. He had asked her so many times only to be rejected with her desire to "wait and see how things go" that finally she concluded that "things" couldn't really go any better than they had. Besides, she was aware that Elsie adored him and to all intents and purposes was her father; indeed his name had been recorded on Elsie's birth certificate. The matter of Elsie's actual paternity didn't worry her too much anymore. She would never say it to Billy but she did have doubts as to whether he was her real father; but then she couldn't bear to think that the other contender had passed on any of his less than desirable traits to her daughter. So yes, everything was well in their world and Billy deserved to become a legitimate husband and father to them both. And so he did on the 19th March 1891, at Chorlton on Medlock Register Office near Manchester. The wedding was a quiet affair with no guests and no fuss; witnesses were provided by registry office staff. Most people who knew them assumed they were already married and Billy didn't want to compromise her reputation when they had lived as husband and wife for so long. It would also serve to protect Elsie from the shadow of illegitimacy and the gossip and hurt it would eventually lead to among the more narrow minded in the community.

Elsie had begun to spend a lot of time with Billy and accompany him to the music hall in Salford and the grander *Queen's Theatre* in Manchester. Despite Billy's assurances that she would come to no harm under his protection, her mother was not entirely happy about encouraging such a young girl as Elsie into the theatrical milieu. Lottie, after all, knew from first hand experience some of the more disreputable characters that inhabited both sides of the footlights. Nevertheless, she privately admitted that she was at least partly to blame for the child's curiosity about the life of the theatre: she had taken Elsie to see a play and was taken aback when the child stood up and announced "I want to be an actress". For most eight year olds this might be considered merely precocious behaviour, but Elsie was mature beyond her years and knew her own mind.

Being with her father at the theatre was heaven to Elsie, and it was a welcome release from school which disagreed with her, more because she had so little in common with her class mates, and because of her innate shyness, than a lack of willingness to learn. It was also a break away from her mother who could be suffocating at times and seemed frightened to let her out of her sight. Billy had seen the way Lottie over protected her, so decided to organise these visits. Elsie would sit in the wings and watch all the acts, but her absolute favourite was always the singers. She would sit and watch, then start to imitate them as they performed before packed houses. One day Billy caught sight of her singing along during a matinee performance. She was oblivious to his presence and as he watched and listened to her he was amazed to discover she had perfect pitch; her voice was strong and very pretty to boot. She was also a gifted mimic for one so young, effortlessly copying the graceful movements of the singers on stage. He decided to say nothing at the moment but to keep an eye on her encouraging her to sing for him when he would be able to judge her ability a little better. Elsie loved her trips with her father to the halls and was entranced by everything she saw. She had no idea that by learning their songs and imitating their performance she was in fact learning from them; for the moment she had no idea this would lead her away from her secret place, hidden in the wings, where she could forget everything and indulge in her own little world of make believe.

By chance a young comedian, George Graves, was booked at her father's hall in Salford at short notice. He didn't much like travelling up north, preferring to stay within the London circuit, but he had been asked as a favour by Billy whom he had met several times and very much respected, so he relented and made the journey north glad it was only for a week or two. He had been working steadily in the halls as a comedian but rather than be himself on stage he preferred to invent a character to do the performing. In common with many artistes he was shy and still insecure of his abilities. His ambition was to shift from the halls to the more "legitimate" stage; although he was the first to admit his talents in terms of acting were limited as yet, but one thing he did possess was determination. During the course of his engagement at Salford he began to notice a very pretty child hiding away in the shadows of the wings who would mimic and sing along with the various singers. When opportunity arose he would stand a few paces away and listen to her sing, enchanted by what he heard. The voice was pretty and strong. Thus he became instrumental in making Elsie take those few strides from the darkened wings and into the limelight.

During his second week, prior to a matinee performance, a terrible thunderstorm had erupted over the streets of Salford followed by sheets of torrential rain. Transport had suffered due to the flash floods and the general chaos that ensued. As a result several of the acts were unable to get to the theatre; those that did manage to navigate the chaotic scenes outside arrived at the stage door wet and bedraggled. But the show had to go on. The house was far from full but under no circumstances would Billy cancel a performance and lose the revenue. Amidst all this, Billy also realised they had anything but a full complement of acts and so persuaded those who had arrived to do extra time and fill in with whatever they thought would work. Listening to Billy's anxious pleading, George made a suggestion: why not give Elsie a chance and let her sing a song? Elsie who was standing beside her father looked fearful but also glanced towards the stage as if imagining herself up there singing. Billy at first dismissed the idea, but he too saw the way Elsie looked towards the stage. What harm would it do? After all the child had a lovely voice why not let her have a shot at it. Elsie grabbed her father's hand and, with a pleading look beyond her ten years, she persuaded him to let her do it. Elsie smiled at George, a smile he would never forget and one that would come back to dazzle him in years to come.

So it was that on a cold and stormy Wednesday afternoon in the *Prince of Wales Theatre*, Salford, that "Little Elsie", as she would soon be known in the profession, made her debut singing a ballad titled *Dear*

Heart which stopped the show. Billy looked on with pride tinged with uneasiness, even fear. He loved Elsie and wanted the best for her, but he wondered if he had done the right thing allowing her to acquire a taste for the halls by bringing her here and now letting her perform. No one knew better than he did how the theatre can destroy those who fall under its spell; how it can take over the life of those who enter its doors. She had always been his little Elsie, but now the chances were she would become everyone's "Little Elsie". He smiled as her voice soared for the final bars of the song, then wondered how on earth he was going to explain this to Lottie. His instinct told him she would be less than pleased.

George listened transfixed to Elsie performing the song. It was hard to believe a girl so young could have such maturity of feeling and wisdom in her rendition of the song. Her phrasing of the lyrics was delightful, the voice strong and clear as a bell with near perfect diction. Even in the gallery they could hear every word. He decided there and then that she had "something", some quality that was hard to define. It made the hairs on the back of his neck stand on end. One day the world would hear about "Little Elsie" and he had a feeling it would not be in the music halls of the land.

Little Elsie

"I sang ballads. Some friends were flattering enough
To call me the infant Patti."

LILY ELSIE

As it turned out, Billy didn't have to break the news of Elsie's singing debut to Lottie. Arriving home late after a busy evening at the theatre Billy was greeted with silence and no supper. The latter he could deal with, it was the former which unnerved him. He knew immediately that somebody must have said something to Lottie about Elsie, and although he didn't know who that might be as yet he cursed them just the same under his breath. He waited for the onslaught, and he couldn't blame Lottie for being mad; he deserved everything she might throw at him because he had procrastinated about telling her mainly because he didn't know how to without worrying her, in truth he had avoided the task for which he now admonished himself more harshly than she ever could. Lottie said not a word, just slammed a copy of the evening paper on the dining table. Glancing at it he let out an expletive, which made Lottie wince, as she disliked him cursing, because the article in the paper had the heading "Little Elsie" in large type at the head of the story that read:

"The *Prince of Wales Theatre*, Salford, was charmed by a new child singer this week; Little Elsie. She has a sweet voice and delighted the audience with a rendition of the popular song Dear Heart, singing the highest of notes with ease, and performing the exacting song with good articulation and perfectly in tune, whilst the audience listened with rapt attention."

Furious as she was, she couldn't help but be pleased that Elsie had done so well. She had to admit when she heard her sing around the house it seemed she possessed a natural and effortless talent. She was also amused and touched at Billy's evident pride at their daughter's success, although he would be the last to know it as she was still annoyed that he hadn't told her. They shared everything and never had secrets from each other, which made it even harder for her to understand why he'd avoided telling her. She didn't like secrets, they led to deceit and the gradual erosion of a relationship—if nothing else she had learned that lesson as a result of her time with Bert. She had also witnessed first hand her parents' disastrous marriage and didn't want that for herself and Billy.

Elsie had begun to take much more notice of the details of their daily lives and had become aware of her mother's odd mood swings and periods of tearful silence. She found her behaviour upsetting and confusing, not knowing why she behaved in such an odd way. It made the time she spent with her father even more enjoyable and always eagerly anticipated. She loved the atmosphere of the theatre and found most of those she encountered there friendly and willing to spend time with her, especially Albert the head musician and piano player. Listening to him rehearsing the musicians always kept her attention. There was something about hiding in the shadows and watching that she found thrilling. Sometimes Albert would sit alone in the dimly lit auditorium and play the piano quietly to himself. She tried to imagine what he was thinking about at such times, mainly because the piece he was playing seemed to have a sadness attached to it. If he spotted her he would call her over and get her to sing the latest song—he knew she had learned it word and note perfect because sometimes out of the corner of his eye he would see her in the wings from his vantage point in the orchestra pit during a performance. Since she had performed for the first time Albert had started to rehearse songs with her nearly every day. She enjoyed the attention but couldn't help feeling that perhaps being hidden in the shadows had been a little more exciting because she could also dream there. Those shadowy dreams which only had to please her. She had also felt more comfortable being hidden from view, stepping into the limelight had been scary and now there was no going back; especially now her mother knew about it.

Elsie's life suddenly became a frantic whirl of activity because her mother had decided to capitalise on her new found fame, even if she felt perhaps it might not be what Elsie wanted after all. At first all the attention had been nice but there were times now when it frightened her. Even at such a young age she realised it was all consuming. Lottie and Billy had furious arguments over it all. He felt that Elsie was far too young to embark on the rigours of the professional circuit, but Lottie was having none of it. She had decided to seek work as an actress for sketches and such like and that way she could accompany Elsie. Billy worried that Lottie was vicariously living her own lost dreams through their daughter, and seriously wondered whether Lottie was cut out to be an actress of any sort. Suddenly by allowing Elsie to perform at the *Prince of Wales Theatre* he found their whole world had been turned upside down. Lottie for her part was glad to throw off the shackles of domesticity which had confined her for the last few years.

The first few engagements were as a direct result of the review Elsie received in the local Manchester press. She performed concerts at the *London and North Western Hotel*, Cross Lane, Salford, and had been mesmerised at the sheer size and grandeur of such places, not to mention the elegantly dressed men and women and their exotic perfumes. Later that week she found herself a star attraction at Salford's *Regent Theatre* on Cross Lane, more familiar to her as it was a music hall with a lavish interior, all red velvet and gold carvings of angels and cupids with enormous chandeliers sparkling like oversized jewels. It was a heady but tiring experience for Elsie, one which she enjoyed in spite of her reservations and her mother's obsessive determination.

She began to notice the tension between her mother and father. Late at night she would lie in bed and listen to their arguments. The shouting and banging frightened her and she would try to block out the sound by burying her head under the bed covers but it never worked. Once the shouting had subsided she would hear her father's footsteps clomping up the stairs and the bang of the door to their bedroom. Then there would be an awful silence usually followed by the sound of her mother sobbing quietly in the distance. On one occasion she was convinced she heard her father crying too. She loved them both so much and was confused as to why they should suddenly start to behave this way. Was it something she had done; was it somehow her fault? All these thoughts swirled around in her mind. Elsie just wanted them to be happy again. Perhaps it would all be alright again if she told them she wanted to return to the shadows, to stand in the wings and just watch as she used to do.

The next day her mother announced that she would be taking Elsie for an audition to Manchester's *Queen's Theatre*. They were casting for a new show. Elsie was confused at first and had to ask what an "audition" was. Her mother explained and revealed they were looking for a child actress and singer to play *Princess Mirza* in *The Arabian Nights*. It sounded terribly exotic and Elsie was intrigued. They duly arrived outside the theatre and Elsie couldn't believe the size of it, holding onto her mother's hand they walked down the side alley to the stage door entrance and registered with the keeper. An assistant led them to a waiting area along vast corridors that smelt a little of disinfectant. Eventually they arrived at a dressing room where the assistant asked if they had brought some piano music, was assured they had, and then left with instructions to wait quietly until they were called. Elsie looked at her hands and realised they were trembling. For the first time she felt anxious and afraid and wished her father would come and take them home. Wondering why all adults seemed to be cross and difficult at times, she suddenly felt as if she would be sick right there and probably all over her mother's nice coat. Taking a few deep breaths, she was just going to ask her mother to take her home when the assistant popped his head round the door and asked them to follow him.

Leading the way the assistant took the sheet music from Lottie and instructed her to stay in the wings and be quiet. Elsie was told to go and stand centre stage. Nothing prepared her for the sight and size of the stage and auditorium: compared to other theatres she had seen it seemed a hundred times bigger and more. The walk from the wings to the centre of the stage felt like a long, long journey. Elsie was aware of her mother, watching anxiously from the wings, and of the cleaners up in the gallery who looked from this distance like ants. At that moment she wished she could be part of the shadows once again, but it was too late . . .

Miraculously, as soon as she began to read from the script she didn't feel nervous at all; indeed she felt exhilarated and loved to hear the sound of her voice echo in the vast auditorium as she spoke the words. Once she had finished there was a silence followed by whispering from way back in the stalls. The voice then asked kindly if she would sing her song. As she began to sing she felt like she was a different person and found the experience quite thrilling. Her voice seemed to have something extra when she sang in this theatre. Lottie, standing in the wings, was delighted. The acoustics in this theatre were good and Elsie's voice was strong enough to fill the auditorium; she had also read from the script with an assurance she didn't realise the child had. Where Elsie had acquired this ability was a mystery to her, but she had it and deserved the best chance of using it to her benefit. Lottie, in spite of Billy's reservations, decided she would do everything in her power to make sure Elsie had every opportunity.

Once Elsie had finished the song there was more whispering at the back of the auditorium. Finally a man's voice asked them to wait at the stage door. Once there, and after only a few minutes, the assistant appeared and informed Elsie she had been cast as *Princess Mirza*. Rehearsals started in one week and a script and music would be sent to her the next day.

Rehearsals were fun and very busy. Elsie found she thrived in this new world and loved every minute of it. Everyone was so determined and committed to having a good show. Sadly it was not a great success and managed only a few performances but the press had a kind word or two for "Little Elsie" describing her as "delightful" with a voice which was "as fresh and bright as morning dew," in the opinion of the Manchester Globe. "The Arabian Nights would not," opined the Manchester Herald, "have been half as exotic without Little Elsie as Princess Mirza".

It was more than Elsie could have wished and within a few days of closing she had been offered and was rehearsing for the title role in *Little Red Riding Hood* again at Manchester's *Queen's Theatre*. Far more successful than the previous show, this one played for six weeks and then went on tour for a further six weeks. Again her reviews, this time in the Manchester Guardian, were encouraging and made comment on her developing "ability as an actress" describing her scenes as "beguiling" and expressing astonishment at her ability for one of such "tender years".

Towards the end of the tour it happened suddenly. Her mother and father had drifted apart even further since they embarked on the tour of *Little Red Riding Hood*. Her mother accompanied Elsie and Billy stayed in Salford at the *Prince of Wales*. On the rare occasion they found themselves at home, the arguments and tears grew increasingly volatile. Lottie felt Billy was trying to destroy Elsie's chances of making a success of her career, and Billy felt Lottie was pushing the child too much and robbing her of her childhood; not to mention her schooling. Elsie just wanted them to be happy again. Secretly she blamed herself and, whilst listening to their arguments from the safety of her bed, she noticed how her hands would shake, shake so much she couldn't stop them. She decided she would have to be strong for them both, and never let them see the tears she cried whilst alone in bed. Her pain was for them all. Never in her wildest dreams, or even as an invention of her fertile imagination, could she have foreseen the tragic resolution to her parents' problems. Her father died of a heart attack. One minute he was alive and well, the next his life was snuffed out. And never had he suffered a days illness in his life.

Elsie was numb with shock. Lottie was distraught and couldn't cope. For the first time in her life Elsie felt pain she couldn't bear and her heart was broken. Her mother seemed like a lost and wounded child. His funeral was arranged by Mr Moss at the *Prince of Wales Theatre* and so many people were wonderful to them and made the awful process bearable. All Elsie could remember about the day of the funeral was the huge black feathers bobbing above the shiny black horses drawing the hearse, the undertakers with their sombre expressions and tall, black, shiny top hats, and how everywhere she looked people were in tones of black or grey. The weather contributed to the sadness by providing sheets of fine misty drizzle, the kind which soaks through heavy coats making them oppressive with extra weight; not unlike the weight of sadness that bears down on the heart of those who are bereaved. She couldn't equate the grey miserable event with her father who had always been like a ray of sunshine in her life. His face always kind and smiling and jolly. None of the faces she saw that day were remotely jolly—they were grim and lacked life.

That day Elsie was also aware of a man and a woman who looked on herself and her mother with more than the usual interest which such events create. She noticed they were there in the background for most of the proceedings. They registered with Elsie more because every time she looked away from her mother, they seemed to smile knowingly if she caught their eye. Why she didn't know, but Elsie had the odd feeling that they knew her more than she knew them; for she was sure she didn't know them or had ever seen them before. On the way back from the cemetery in the carriage she found herself listening mournfully to the clip clop of the horses as they manoeuvred through the busy streets. As they approached the *Prince of Wales Theatre* she asked her mother about the man and woman who had been staring at her so. Elsie was shocked to discover that they were in fact her mother's brother and sister! And she didn't even know her mother had siblings. They were not on speaking terms and hadn't been for many years, and Lottie wanted nothing to do with them still. Sometimes her mother puzzled her and, despite her own curiosity—she had never experienced the feeling of actually having an aunt and uncle—she decided to put it from her mind for her mother's sake. The last thing she wanted to was exacerbate her mother's melancholy and create any more upset in their life. One day though, she decided silently, she would find out more about them.

Reflecting back on that time in years to come, Elsie realised that this was the moment the role between mother and daughter reversed. From this point on she became the adult and started to look after her mother. Life without her father was beyond comprehension, but instinct told Elsie you either sank or you swam. Billy would have wanted her to not only swim but soar. So she did, for him, because she had loved him. She also decided that "Little Elsie" was not quite such an appropriate stage name now she was getting older. From this point she would be known as "Lily Elsie"

Nelly Power circa 1879
(Courtesy of John Culme's Footlight Notes Collection)

Photograph of *Lily Elsie's* friends *Phyllis* and *Zena Dare* with their parents and brother circa 1905.

(DSC)

A popular post card image of *Lily Elsie* circa 1908.
(Courtesy of Rob Sedman)

A popular post card image of *Lily Elsie* circa 1908.
(Courtesy of Rob Sedman)

Gertie Millar and her husband Lionel Monckton. After his death in the 1920s Millar married the Earl of Dudley.
(Courtesy of Rob Sedman)

Popular post card image of *Lily Elsie* circa 1912.
(Courtesy of Rob Sedman)

London' famous *Gaiety Theatre* (now demolished) in a photograph taken from the *Strand* circa 1907. To the left of the *Gaiety* is the *Novello* (formerly *Strand*) and *Aldwych Theatres*.
(*Courtesy of Matthew Lloyd*)

Lily Elsie poses in a fashionable *Merry Widow* hat, 1907
(DSC)

George Edwardes. Edwardian theatre impressario and founder of the *Gaiety Theatre* and *Daly's Theatre*, London.

(DSC)

Lily Elsie and her mother, *Lottie* circa 1903.
(Courtesy of John Culme's Footlight Notes Collection)

Gabrielle Ray at about the time of her appearances in *The Little Cherub* circa 1906.
(Courtesy of John Culme's Footlight Notes Collection)

Gertie Millar in a popular post card circa 1912.

(DSC)

Marie Lloyd circa 1912
(Courtesy of John Culme's Footlight Notes Collection)

Gertie Millar in a popular post card circa 1912. *(DSC)*

Destiny & The Guv'nor

"She has a sweet voice and delighted the audience . . . singing the highest of notes with ease . . ."
MANCHESTER HERALD

B y the dawn of the new century Elsie had moved to London with her mother in an attempt to get a foothold in the West End. At least her mother had decided she should. Elsie as ever was unsure and more than a little reticent; as much as she loved being involved in the theatre she had never lost that feeling of self doubt about her own abilities. The atmosphere that greeted them in London was one of optimism, an optimism that followed in the wake of Queen Victoria's sad death in January of 1901. A few months later spring had come and with it the sense that everything was going to be alright after all—that the world wouldn't stop because the old Queen was dead. Edward VII had ascended the throne of England and the Empire and a freer and more liberated society began to slowly emerge from the loosening of the social corsets imposed by Victoria.

But Elsie argued, mostly with herself, as her mother would hear nothing against it, that having success in Manchester and on tour in the provinces was no guarantee she would be good enough for the wildly exacting and sophisticated standards demanded by the West

End theatre. Up to this point her career had progressed remarkably and, if she were honest, surprised nobody more than herself. That said she had made the decision that perhaps it would be prudent to move away from the halls and cross over into the more legitimate theatre; or at least a half way house which was the light musical stage. It was not, and would never be, equal to the true legitimate theatre which was of the classics, but it had a sophistication the halls would never have with their coarse and vulgar elements. In addition it was just a little more sophisticated and acceptable to society generally; perhaps! Her singing voice was good enough for some modest productions and operetta, but again she would never be able to possibly compete at an operatic level; neither did she have the desire to do so.

London exhausted her in those initial weeks. The clatter of carriages and hansoms and the overpowering smell of horses was at times unbearable. Never had she seen so many people crammed into one place, all busily moving to and from goodness knows where. She wondered what they all had to do and why they were all in such a hurry to get to their destinations. If she were honest it frightened her. Never had she seen so many dubious looking characters milling about, and on hot days the smell of perspiring people and horses was more than she could bear. The expensive rents had forced her to find suitable accommodation for herself and her mother in Lambeth. The streets were dark and crammed with houses and she determined that as soon as possible, when with luck her fortunes were a little better, they could move to more central accommodation across the river, on hand for the West End theatres. Her mother was supportive and helpful but tended to leave the responsibility to her daughter. It caused some friction, but they always managed to resolve these petty issues and focus on Elsie's career. For a girl of fifteen she had the maturity and responsibilities of someone much older.

For the last couple of years she had found her place in pantomime which, with its disciplines and multiple daily performances, allowed her to develop her stage technique away from the more burlesque skills required in the halls. Burlesque was, she decided wisely, not really her forte: she was naturally shy and still struggled to summon up confidence whilst preparing to go on stage. It was odd really because once she had stepped from the wings she felt truly alive and in control; but sometimes that single step was torture to her and made her long to run and hide in the shadows she had so happily occupied in the wings as a child. Pantomime also allowed her to develop her acting and timing for dialogue, which was all an attempt on her part to move away from the halls and into the more legitimate musical comedy stage—if indeed it would have her.

Having been engaged as *Aerielle*, a fairy, at the *Brittania Theatre*, Hoxton, in a musical revue titled *King Klondike* she had made her mark on the London managements. The audiences had like her too, which was thrilling—and she always found it difficult to read what had been written about her in the newspapers. It was whilst appearing at Hoxton that she watched a performance by Marie Lloyd. Her mother had told her about the song she had stolen from Nelly Power and how Nelly had forgiven her before she tragically died. Elsie was entranced watching her performance and delighted in hearing Lloyd's rendition of *My Old Man Said Follow The Van* which, with her skill and timing, had the audience rolling in the aisles with laughter, the next minute she would sing *The Boy I Love* and have them sobbing into their handkerchiefs. Elsie went back stage to congratulate her and was surprised to find Marie was also complimentary about her and wished she "had the grace and style" that Elsie possessed. Even more surprising, she discovered that Marie had seen her perform a couple of times and told her in no uncertain terms to look beyond the halls as she was too good for them.

For all their differences, and despite some of the adverse publicity that Marie received, Elsie had liked her and sensed her vulnerability under the bravado. She had guts and took no nonsense from anyone, trusting people even less. She did it to protect herself. All the flashiness, bottles of champagne and unsuitable young men that surrounded her was in part a way to protect herself. She worked hard and lived life to the full in a way that Elsie never could. The one story that epitomised Marie, and fascinated Elsie, was when the Royal Household asked that her appearance at the Royal Variety Show be cancelled because it had become common knowledge she was having an affair with the young jockey who'd won the Derby. The hypocrisy of the situation stunned and angered Marie. So she defiantly hired the *Alhambra Theatre*, Leicester Square, with her own money, on the same night as the Royal Variety, and had packed it to the rafters with fans. This is where she performed her new song *My Old Man Said Follow The Van* for the first time and, to her delight, it was sung or whistled by everyone, everywhere on the streets and became her biggest ever hit. Elsie always believed that this incident summed up Marie's courage and determination even in the face of such adversity and overt snobbery.

So Elsie's performances at Hoxton had led her to the offer of a part in *The Silver Slipper* for which she was just about to start rehearsals. Billed as an "extravaganza", ("whatever on earth that was" as she had declared to her mother) it had music by Owen Nares and seemed to be perfect for her to progress her acting and singing abilities. The best part of the engagement was that it would be staged at the *Lyric Theatre* on Shaftesbury Avenue. She would be making her West End debut—and nobody was more surprised than she. It worried her that perhaps this opportunity had come too easily, or even that perhaps she was not yet ready for such a stage, but her mother chided her and made her push all such thoughts from her mind. Silently she would seek the counsel of her late father, Billy. She would often chat with him and sometimes she could hear his reply as clear as anything. It was nearly as good as actually having him with her.

The Silver Slipper opened on the 1st June 1901 at the *Lyric Theatre* and was a great success. Elsie was really just a chorus member but it was a great learning experience. She found it strangely comforting to fade into the background and not have to be the centre of attention, whilst still being able to enjoy the experience of being on stage and performing. She found her dreaded nerves were indeed much better and she felt more relaxed and assured. Her immediate future was also assured as she had been booked to go on tour with *The Silver Slipper* until the late autumn, and then she was booked to play in pantomime, *Dick Whittington*, at the *Camden Theatre*, for Christmas of that year. During the run of *The Silver Slipper* she met a man who was destined to play a crucial role in her life and career. She would find him charming, intriguing, utterly frustrating but most of all a shrewd judge of her character and abilities as a performer. His name was George Edwardes.

Edwardes had seen *The Silver Slipper* on two occasions. Both times he had been intrigued by a young girl in the chorus who had enchanted him; something that rarely occurred as he never allowed his emotions to cloud his judgement when it came to theatrical productions or people. But there was something about this young girl which drew his eye, and it mattered not if fifty people were on stage, he could only see her. His curiosity aroused, he decided to initiate a meeting to see if she was as fascinating up close as she was from a distance. Neither realised it at the time, but it was a meeting which would change both their lives and that of the light comedy musical stage.

By the time his path crossed that of Elsie, Edwardes was satisfied he had established himself as the creator of light musical comedy productions and as the leading impresario of London's West End. Those who worked with him and for him called him "The Guv'nor" out of respect. It was not a title he initiated but one that developed slowly among his peers. It was, he told himself often, a reflection of the respect they had for him; a respect he had worked hard for and earned in spades.

It never ceased to amuse him that some considered him to be a formidable and ruthless character and that he ran his empire with efficient organisation. The latter was true, but it was borne out of years of determination to create something new for a potential audience for London's theatres he calculated was an untapped market. Since he had put his vision into practice, first at the *Gaiety Theatre* and, of late, also at *Daly's Theatre*, his formula, once considered eccentric by the knockers of theatre land, had been proved right. The productions, every aspect of which had flourished, had attracted that untapped market in their droves and had made these the most famous theatres in London. He had also managed to create a respectability for his theatres the halls could never hope to have: from his early days he had decided he wanted to move away from the more vulgar music hall and burlesque entertainments and create something which would attract a more refined and well behaved audience. In this, he thought with great satisfaction, he had succeeded.

He often reflected on the experiences that had brought him to this point in his life and was thankful for everything they taught him along the way. Having served his time working with Gilbert & Sullivan at the *Savoy Theatre* he slowly developed his knowledge of all aspects of producing and staging productions. His primary objective always, and one he reminded himself about whenever he was about to mount a new production, was to emulate the quality and high production standards he had witnessed at the Savoy. This approach had its downside because it was so expensive, but never afraid to put his head on the line (and, he thought with a shudder, his finances and those of the investors who trusted him) he would still always gamble on his productions financially. On many occasions he would come perilously close to disaster and ruin, but fate had been kind and his luck had held good. It was all down to quality and having the best; this was paramount and the basis on which he built his reputation. If he was unable to mount productions this way and had to resort to penny pinching he would probably go mad—or give up the business altogether.

As far as he was concerned imposing these exacting standards on the way his theatres were run, also added to the overall quality of the venues and the public's perception of them. It was all part of creating a respectable and welcoming environment for all—whether they originate from the east-end or Mayfair.

This innovative approach and his shrewd understanding of public taste enabled him to develop a new genre of theatre: "musical comedy". This idea was influenced by the Gilbert & Sullivan operettas he had seen and, crucially, how they had a developing storyline and consistent characters with the songs being relevant to the story and plot. Although he felt that this was something he could build his own style on, he had realised that the Gilbert & Sullivan format and style had alienated a section of the audience whom he thought of as the "middle ground". His special ingredient was the glorification of elegant and glamorous women.

The *Gaiety Theatre* had given him his start and from that theatre he had introduced his musical comedy style to the public. It still retained elements of burlesque style but he made sure it also personified the elegance he was determined to achieve. His chorus girls, which he hand picked for their grace and style, became a necessary ingredient in the success of his musical comedy presentations. The plots of these presentations were often, at least initially, somewhat threadbare but Edwardes considered it absolutely vital that character development and interaction would carry the story and keep the audience involved. He congratulated himself that he had been proved right when one witty critic wrote how "cartloads of money" were flowing into his theatre. Little did the critic realise how necessary that flow of money was: had it not arrived then the world would probably never have heard of George Edwardes.

The subjects of his productions tended towards boy meets girl—mutual misunderstandings and difficulties leading to estrangement—eventually reunited in a happy ending. The emphasis was on strong female characters in particular; the storyline invariably wrapped around the current vogue for far-flung and exotic locations in the Far East or China, the comic elements of the story arising from the 'foreign' characters whose treatment reflected the imperialistic attitudes of the day. Edwardes insisted on employing different writers to develop book, music and lyrics, many of whom continued to work exclusively for him over the years. This was much discussed—and in some cases criticised—through the business although the reaction bewildered Edwardes who considered that collaboration was always preferable to dealing with a single ego. It was undeniably the case, he argued, that composers had little knowledge of writing a book, with effective story and dialogue, just as a good book writer could not necessarily compose music to the highest standard. Similarly, a good lyricist's talent may not produce the finest music.

Once established he had to make sure the resulting production satisfied the expectations of the public; that it would be, in their words "*a Gaiety show*" or "*a Daly's show*". The audience's opinion mattered to him above all else. Those working for him he exasperated at times and he would hear them mutter, when they thought he was out of earshot, that he was "too strict" or even that he was arrogant. Maybe he was but as long as he received loyalty from his stable of performers and creative team he didn't care what they said under their breath. One of his biggest stars, a star he had groomed and aided with her career, was his gorgeous Gertie Millar. She had starred in many of his productions at the *Gaiety Theatre*, and he would hazard a guess that such had been her impact on London audiences that her fame would be forever linked to that theatre. He sighed to himself at this thought, resigned to the fact that a hundred years from now he would be long forgotten and Gertie would have her place in the history of the *Gaiety*; for he was sure it would still be a beacon of the West End even then.

Popularity and success had come at a price, and he had to admit to himself it was a cost he hadn't bargained for, and one that had nothing to do with money: too many of his "*Gaiety girls*", as they had become affectionately known, were courted by wealthy clients and the nobility of the land. This had become such a problem for him and the productions that he insisted on a "nuptial clause" being inserted in all the girls' contracts to prevent them from leaving during the run of a production; he was also shrewd enough to realise it allowed him to control them indefinitely—because he made sure the contracts stated they were engaged for "the run of the production". What else could he do? He'd been left with little choice because those girls who had married gentlemen of the nobility were expected by their new husbands to give up their stage career and conform to polite society's (as well as their aristocratic family's) expectations. He had to smile at the thought of all those elderly countesses and duchesses fainting upon their chaise longues on hearing the news that the young son and heir wanted to marry a *Gaiety girl*. The older generation at least still regarded all theatre people as vagabonds—the women in particular were classed as little better than common prostitutes—and Edwardes was thankful that there was at least some signs of times and attitudes changing for the better.

Since he had acquired *Daly's Theatre*, Leicester Square, he was determined to develop what he had established at the *Gaiety*. However, his intention was to take it to another level and thus further refine his light musical comedy style with the productions he planned to present at *Daly's*. They would, he hoped, have an appeal all of their own and gain an even more respectable reputation in terms of how he hoped the public would perceive them. Where most society women, and some men, would rather be seen dead than in the audience at the *Gaiety*, he wanted them to feel comfortable attending a performance at *Daly's*. He was determined he would get the countesses and the elderly duchesses into his theatre, and give them reason to enjoy the experience. His plan for *Daly's* was operetta, and he intended to import the shows developed and performed in Germany for this purpose. The translation of the book and lyrics of these productions would be undertaken by his own stable of creative personnel, only the music composed for the original would survive his tinkering; although even that was not sacred if he felt it could be improved! That said, he knew that he had to develop a positive creative relationship with the composers and librettists and involve them wherever possible in the translations from German to English.

Unfortunately he had struggled to find the right production for *Daly's* and to date he had not had the financial success he'd hoped for: in spite of the money he lavished on the sets and costumes he hadn't had a big hit, at least not one where the revenues were arriving by "the cartload". As he entered the stage box at The *Lyric Theatre* the house lights were dimming. He decided to reposition his chair so that instead of looking predominantly at the audience, which he liked to do to assess the effect of the production on them, he could catch sight of this chorus girl who was intriguing him so.

Unbeknown to Elsie, she had confounded him and try as he might his eye would wander to the curious chorus girl in *The Silver Slipper*. He was mildly irritated to find himself expectantly waiting for her reappearance on stage. He decided that he should try her out in something, and decided there and then she would be perhaps suitable for *A Chinese Honeymoon*. This new production was being financed by Frank Curzon and himself and, after an initial tour, was opening at the *Royal Strand Theatre*.

A Chinese Honeymoon!

"I knew at first sight that I loved her . . ."
LILY ELSIE ON SEEING THE CHARACTER
PRINCESS SOO SOO.

Edwardes had approached Elsie and discussed the idea of her appearing in *A Chinese Honeymoon*, but had been irritated at her cool attitude towards the suggestion. Most girls would consider themselves to be highly honoured by such an offer from Edwardes. But to her credit he realised she was concerned because she was not only committed to her contract for *The Silver Slipper* but also to appearing in pantomime that coming Christmas, for which she had already signed a contract. His offer to negotiate her release had been met with a firm "no thank you" from Elsie. He understood and respected her loyalty and resigned himself to having to wait until she was free.

Elsie in turn had been extremely flattered to be asked by Edwardes to appear in his production. The trouble was she felt obliged to honour her current contracts, however tempting the offer had been; and if she were honest with herself, the prospect frightened her for reasons she couldn't fathom. The boys and girls in the cast, as well as her mother, had told her in no uncertain terms she was mad to turn him down, convinced that another offer would never be forthcoming from such a powerful man. Elsie stood her ground and, out of curiosity, went to see the production at the *Royal Strand Theatre*.

She found *A Chinese Honeymoon* to be an enchanting, if slightly ridiculous, production in terms of its characters and their exploits in a far-flung land. Their very British attitudes when faced with the quaint Chinese customs provided the comedy aspects of the show and the music was delightful. *Princess Soo Soo* was played by Beatrice Edwards, and Elsie immediately found herself captivated both by the character and Beatrice's performance. Initially the full force of her insecurities came to the fore, but after some reflection, and her mother's positive encouragement she realised that perhaps she would like an opportunity to play the character after all. Beatrice had played the role with some gusto but Elsie found herself wondering how she could make the character more believable as a Chinese princess. The plot was really a trifle ridiculous and involved a sea captain being entrusted with finding a suitable bride for the Emperor at which he fails miserably. Being China, the punishment for failure is the death penalty which the sea captain does everything he can to avoid with hilarious results in true musical comedy fashion. He is aided by a cockney salesman and his jealous wife, the latter accompanied by her bridesmaids. A pair of star struck young lovers on their honeymoon who break the kissing laws complete the cast. All embroiled in entirely imaginary Chinese customs.

During the months she remained on tour with *The Silver Slipper*, and then performing in pantomime, Elsie was constantly working out how she would make the role of *Princess Soo Soo* her own. She had never taken over a role created by somebody else and felt it important to attempt something original in her portrayal. As much as she had admired Beatrice's performance and her lovely rendition of the songs, she couldn't help feeling that something was missing. Beatrice was a very experienced singer and had used the part mainly to showcase the talent for which she was chiefly admired; and there was nothing wrong with that at all, indeed it was most sensible of her. Elsie also decided that she felt less nervous whilst performing if she created a character rather than just being herself on the stage. The dreaded nerves had come back to haunt her and as much as she felt fine once on stage, those dreaded moments standing in the wings waiting for her cue had paralysed her with fright. She imagined in such moments that she would forget everything and stand there looking a fool, even thinking about it made her eyes fill with tears and her palms sweat terribly. It never ceased to amaze her how that little voice in her head would calm her and rationalise her fears enough so that she could take that first step from the shadows and into the limelight.

George Edwardes she had found to be polite and very patient with her. There were times when she was convinced he would just give up and cast somebody else in the role. But after an initial fractious period when he realised she was determined to fulfil her contractual agreements with others, he signed her to take over the role in early 1903. Her mother had advised her to allow Edwardes to negotiate her release at least from her pantomime contract, but Elsie was determined to remain loyal. Edwardes was a powerful man but Elsie reckoned that if he really wanted her then he would wait until she was available. The fact he actually did wait gave Elsie a confidence boost she needed and was grateful for.

Elsie and her mother continued to support one another and had at last managed to find suitable accommodation nearer the theatres of the West End. Lambeth had been a temporary location and one that Elsie was glad to see the back of. Not that they had been completely unhappy there, it was just such a long trek across the river into the West End, and she had found the cramped streets almost suffocating and unbearable at times. The atmosphere in Lambeth had also worsened her mother's melancholy making her irascible and difficult to keep happy. Elsie was constantly worried about her and the interminable gloomy silences she sank into; it seemed increasingly that these silences were a part of a terrible change in her mother's personality, a change that meant Elsie scarcely recognised her anymore. In these dark moments she would take refuge in secret conversations with her dead father, asking for his assistance—assuming, that is, that he was out there somewhere looking for her. She couldn't help but think how differently their lives would have turned out is he hadn't died so suddenly and left her alone to look after them both; he, she thought, would know so much better what would be best for her mother. Elsie would be overcome by the desire to be loved and protected by her father's presence once more—and then she would be angry with him for leaving her to shoulder all this responsibility alone.

There were even times when she wished he had not allowed her to go on stage in Salford: she could have had a proper childhood and remained anonymous for the rest of her life. After these moments of anger she would be stricken with guilt and lie in bed weeping silently for her disloyalty to her beloved, lost father. There was no one with whom she could share such feelings, and especially not with her mother who now relied on Elsie completely as she became increasingly fragile. Nevertheless, Elsie was no fool and knew well that her mother was living her dreams vicariously through her and her achievements. She had no choice but to be strong for both of them.

George Edwardes had made such an impression on her because he reminded her in some ways of her father and his manner towards her was almost fatherly so that she felt comfortable in his presence. After such an eventful young life she had to remind herself that she was just seventeen years old, never mind that at times it felt as if she was seventy!

Her mother on the other hand had become even more dependent on her since she had secured some level of steady employment, if not overwhelming success, on the West End stage. Since she had been taken under the wing of Edwardes Elsie did feel a little more secure; enough to have found comfortable rooms for herself and her mother in Portland Place. The accommodation was less than spacious but had a slightly faded elegance which added to their charm, and at least there was enough room to have a bedroom each and a comfortable drawing room. They had no live-in servants, which was just as well, Elsie reminded herself, because she was nothing if not practical when it came to financial matters. Her one concession was to employ a daily maid to come in and help her mother. She had noticed that her mother had recently affected a slightly 'grand' demeanour when dealing with others on a daily basis and had also started to rewrite their life history when discussing the past with her friends and acquaintances—even the tradesmen. Whilst Elsie didn't object too much to her mother's fantasies—she knew the poverty and hardship she had experienced and perhaps these delusions made her feel better when recalling the past—she nevertheless felt slightly uneasy. She felt sure there were elements of Lottie's past she was not privy to; Elsie had not forgotten those grim faces at her father's funeral and her shock at discovering the siblings her mother had never before mentioned. On occasion she had tried to broach the subject with Lottie, but had quickly retreated when her mother simply clammed up, her face ashen and thunderous.

The only scrap of information she had gleaned was regarding Lottie's sister who, it turned out, used to be a costume maker for Gilbert & Sullivan at the *Savoy Theatre*. Elsie knew she was the elder of the sisters and that her mother had learned her dressmaking skills from her, but as to the cause of the rift which was still so raw even now, she had no idea. Perhaps one day all these secrets of her mother's past would finally be revealed.

Her immediate worries concerned her mother's increasing health problems with more frequent and severe bouts of anxiety and melancholy. Her fantasies were also, she felt, part and parcel of the same problems. Fearing for her mother's well-being and continued acceptance in society, she decided they had to be covered up as best they could. It would not take much for them to be ostracised if anyone suspected her mother was mentally unstable; for indeed there were times when Elsie feared this was the case. If it made her feel better to pretend they had come from a more refined background than Salford's music halls, then that was how it would have to be. Elsie was the first to realise that without her mother, she would be a lot worse off than she was.

Lottie would gaze across the room at her daughter and catch her profile in the firelight. Moments like that reminded her of the time she was born and how she would gaze at her new-born in the firelight and wonder what on earth would become of them. Had she only known what life had in store for them both, and how this child in so many ways had been her saviour. Even in her blackest, bleakest moments of melancholy she never once regretted having Elsie. She couldn't help recall the time prior to her birth when she had considered giving her away, how her thoughts were all selfish about not wanting the responsibility of a child to tie her down. It made her shudder. What thoughts were now going through her daughter's mind she wondered? If only she knew the truth of how she had behaved with Bert and Billy and what a fool she had been. Billy had ensured that Elsie was spared the shame of illegitimacy, and indeed had he not it would have seriously affected her chances of success now. She never wanted Elsie to know the details of that sordid past; a past she had now buried away forever. She was glad that Elsie considered Billy as her father and glad that she had nothing but happy memories of him. That is how it must remain Lottie decided, although she knew in her heart there was a good chance that Billy was not her real father. She shuddered again. Elsie looked across at her and smiled. Both sensed their individual thoughts were somehow connected, but nothing was said.

Rehearsals for *A Chinese Honeymoon* had been much more fun than Elsie could have hoped for. It had been hard work, as rehearsals always are, but she had been made so welcome by the cast and Beatrice was delightful considering she was replacing her. Elsie had worried she might resent her but as it turned out she was glad to be leaving the show as it had served its purpose in elevating her profile and establishing her as a singer of note in the West End. Beatrice had laughed at Elsie when she first told her she wanted to characterise *Princess Soo Soo* and give her a believable Chinese demeanour and costume. Beatrice told her it was a sweet thing to consider but nobody would care, or notice, because all they were interested in was how prettily she sang the songs. Elsie disagreed but said nothing and did it her way. Surprisingly, Edwardes had been delighted at her suggestions and proceeded to aid her in every way possible, even to spending large amounts on new costumes. Elsie pored over any books she could lay her hands on regarding Chinese etiquette and, most importantly, fashions and hairstyles which she could emulate in some way. She was determined that she would bring to life the character of *Princess Soo Soo* for the audience. When she had seen the production it was, to her, the way she could make this her own. It would be so simple to just step into Beatrice's shoes and play it for the songs, but that way she would not be noticed. At least her way there was a chance that she could make it her own and breathe new life into the show.

Her opening night had approached so quickly it left her breathless. Breathless and scared. She had stood in the empty auditorium of that elegant theatre during the afternoon of her opening and so many ghosts of the past came to wish her luck. Her father she could see in her mind's eye smiling and bursting with pride. All the characters she encountered as a child in the music halls were also at the forefront of her mind and wishing her well. As she entered the pass door to the backstage area she was drawn to the shadows in the wings and remembered the little girl she had been hiding there and emulating all the performers she witnessed from her secret hiding place. There was no hiding now; she had stepped into the limelight and it seemed the limelight was determined to keep her in its beam. She made her way to her dressing room and began to prepare for her debut in *A Chinese Honeymoon*. Time would tell if her instincts had served her well: her costumes were authentic in style, as was her hair, emulating the pictures she had discovered in the course of her researches. Her biggest fear, a symptom of her deep-seated lack of confidence, was that the audience would not take her seriously.

Edwardes never considered himself sentimental nor likely to be blinded by charm and beauty. Nevertheless, as he sat unnoticed at the back of the grand circle and watched Elsie walk down the aisle to the orchestra stalls, it was as if he had been hypnotised by this lovely girl. Sensing that she was apprehensive about her first performance tonight, he remained silent, not wanting to intrude into her private thoughts and happy merely to observe her poise and beauty. The fact that she seemed entirely unaware of her power only added to the effect, he thought. He had been astonished at her preparation for taking over this role and her determination to bring authenticity to her characterisation of *Princess Soo Soo*; in fact, her enthusiasm had beguiled him so much that he had spent far too much money in bringing her ideas to fruition. What the audiences would make of it only time would tell, but he was confident that her voice would make their spines tingle—just as it did his.

As these thoughts drifted through his mind, he realised that he had already taken the decision to make this girl a star; whatever happened, whether her debut in *A Chinese Honeymoon* was successful or not, somehow he would make her a star! It occurred to him that perhaps he was even a little in love with Elsie, but he quickly shrugged off the uncharacteristic idea: George Edwardes loved women for their beauty and their talent, but he wasn't the one to fall in love where business was concerned. With the possible exception of Gertie, women were a commodity to him; they adorned his productions, providing the elegance and grace to attract audiences to the *Gaiety*, *Daly's* and the *Royal Strand* in their droves. He almost laughed out loud at the direction his thoughts had taken him, but quickly stifled the rising laughter lest Elsie should hear him and realise she was being watched. Luckily she had already disappeared backstage and was blissfully unaware of the effect she had had upon her unseen admirer.

In truth Edwardes was irritated at being led—or so it seemed—into a part of himself that he hid so carefully from the world at large. Lily Elsie was a damnably infuriating girl! He felt as if she could wrap him round her little finger and yet she was quite unaware of this fact despite being strong-willed and knowing her own mind to the point of being headstrong. They were in many ways two of a kind and only time would tell if they would thrive as an artistic partnership or if it would all turn into a nightmare. He fervently hoped it would be the former but prudently decided to wait and see.

Within twenty-four hours of her first appearance in *A Chinese Honeymoon*, Elsie knew her instincts had been right. Her portrayal of *Princess Soo Soo*, and her attempt to be authentic in that portrayal had caused a sensation; in equal measure to that of her vocal rendition of the part. The newspapers were full of what they perceived as Elsie's innovation. Elsie couldn't see what all the fuss was about. To her way of thinking it was just common sense. She was flattered by the kind comments in the reviews and Edwardes had been over the moon, mainly because all the fuss meant a rush of bookings which resulted in full houses for some weeks to come. *The Era's* critic declared she "dazzled with oriental grace and charm," adding effusively that, "her elegance and purity of voice ensured every audience would be captivated." At best Elsie was more embarrassed by the attention in the newspapers than pleased by it. She instantly worried that other members of the company might resent her and the attention she received; if so she couldn't blame them as they had all worked so hard for weeks before she appeared on the scene. To her delight the opposite had in fact been the case, and before a week was up she noticed a concerted effort on behalf of other cast members to adopt similar oriental appearance and mannerisms in their own roles.

Edwardes was equally delighted with the reception that Elsie had received in the production. He wasn't entirely sure how the public would react to her, but now he had no doubt of her natural abilities to become the focus of the audiences' attention, and her skill as an actress was admirable in one so young. She had brought a fresh perspective to the production with her characterisation of *Princess Soo Soo*; so much so that it had cost him a considerable sum in new costumes and wigs to balance the other characters in line with her. But that didn't matter because Elsie had also ensured healthy box office receipts for some weeks to come. He read again the article dated 16th March, 1903, in the London News:

"Miss Lily Elsie enchanted the audience last night with her portrayal of Princess Soo Soo in George Edwardes oriental fantasy farce at the Royal Strand Theatre. On her first entrance the audience were heard to audibly gasp not only at Miss Elsie's beauty but also her acting and singing. The fact she packaged her talents and presented herself with an oriental fashion added to the delight. Her rendition of the song 'But Yesterday' drew more gasps as the silver lined notes soared up to the gods effortlessly. Her predecessor in the role was Beatrice Edwards, Beatrice who? The only name on the lips of patrons as they left the theatre for their carriages was Lily Elsie."

There was little which surprised Edwardes when it came to actresses, or actors for that matter, but he had to admit he was impressed with the way Elsie had been careful not to dominate the production to the detriment of the other performers. Princess Soo Soo was a secondary character in the story and it would have been easy for Elsie to up stage and overplay the role. This, Edwardes decided, was one of the main reasons he was so impressed with Elsie, and it was a trait that many would never realise about her. He was convinced that with the right production, and the right part, he could make her a star. He would bear it in mind but say nothing to anyone, especially Elsie, if or until the right opportunity presented itself. He felt a little sorry for Beatrice—he knew she had been upset by some remarks in the newspapers—but to her eternal credit she had at the earliest opportunity presented herself at Elsie's dressing room and declared herself delighted at the success Elsie had achieved with the role. Those who expected fireworks or any kind of bitchiness were disappointed.

Lottie savoured the attention and delighted in the subsequent newspaper articles. She enjoyed sitting in the auditorium and watching the performances, as much for the opportunity it gave her to dress in her best and be seen in the box her daughter arranged for her. During one of these occasions she was casually glancing around the audience during the intermission and waving to and acknowledging those known to her—if she were honest with herself she enjoyed this element of the evening more than the performance—until one evening, glancing up towards the gods, her eyes met those of a man and flickered with recognition. Looking away, she felt her heart miss a beat and the colour drain from her face. A moment later she glanced back to where he had been sitting but he was gone. It seemed impossible, but Lottie was sure she had just looked into the eyes of Bert Hodder once again. As the performance started she could hear the song which always made her laugh, but there was no laughter that night for Lottie. All she could think about was Bert Hodder and what he might want from her—or Elsie. Ripples of laughter intruded on her anxious thoughts as the song came to its climax:

'I want to have an evening dress that opens down to there,
And wear a great big diamond ta-ra-ra in my hair;
And when I to the playhouse go, I want to do the grand
With a wreath of flowers on my breast, and a bucket in my hand.
I want to be a lidy, and have a private box,
I want to wag a great big fan, and shake my golden locks,
I want to hiss the villain, and cheer the maid forlorn,
So that folks will know, when I say "Bravo!"
I'm a lidy bred and born
I want to learn to patter French, just like a parlez-vous,
And call my servants "garçons" and my letters "billy-doos,"
And when I go a-visiting, and on my friends I drop,
I want to say "Pardon, Mamselle, I hope I'm not de trop . . ."'

Slings & Arrows!

"I'm always rude to men. The ruder I am, the more they like me!"

LILY ELSIE TO HER FRIEND LUCILLE

After her successful appearance in *A Chinese Honeymoon*, it was decided to send the production on a short tour of the provinces where the show and Elsie were equally well received. Edwardes was relieved because it gave him time to think about what he would do with Elsie next. She was a conundrum to him in many ways. She didn't really fit in with the more burlesque style of musical comedy he was presenting with Gertie Millar at the Gaiety Theatre. Not that he would ever say as much to Gertie, but Elsie was what he would define as elegant and refined. There was a grace and charm about her demeanour on stage as well as off. Gertie on the other hand was much more of a 'slap my thigh' girl in her style of performing. Naughty but nice as Edwardes liked to describe it. Nothing vulgar as he wouldn't stand that; after all he had fought hard to eradicate the coarseness of the halls from his shows. No, Elsie was a real problem in some ways but one thing he was sure of: now he had got her he wasn't about to let some other management poach her from under his nose. From the first night of *A Chinese Honeymoon* he'd put her under a permanent contract. At least in that respect he felt secure.

He was also concerned that Elsie might allow this initial success to turn her head, although instinct told him that she was more astute than to let this happen. Nevertheless, he wanted to make sure that he wouldn't end up with a troublesome, demanding actress on his hands—the last thing he needed was to have to cope with a diva. He had more or less decided to keep her grounded by placing her in the chorus for his next production; it wouldn't do any harm to remind her that it takes more than one show to achieve success and it would also give him time to find a suitable vehicle for her unique talents.

Edwardes also had other problems to worry about. To his horror, and try as he might, he had failed to present anything at *Daly's* which had the money, via the box office, "arriving by the cart load". In truth he had suffered a series of flops and non-starters. *Daly's* had proved to be a difficult theatre for him. He thanked his lucky stars he had the *Gaiety*, which in many ways was subsidising *Daly's*. The one area he refused to compromise on was the quality of the productions: he lavished money on the sets and costumes because those values were what made his reputation. Against his accountants' and advisers' advice he had continued to spend lavishly. Luckily there had always been an "eleventh hour", as his grandmother used to say, and he scraped by yet another potential financial catastrophe relatively unscathed. But ever mindful of such things, he knew his luck wouldn't hold out forever. Elsie, he believed, was key to that future success. He wasn't sure how, but was sure all the same.

Elsie was relieved to return home from the tour, not least because it meant she could again keep a close eye on her mother's health. Lottie had accompanied her on the initial part of the tour but the week before they were due in Manchester she declared that she was unwell and wished to return to their flat in London. Elsie agreed to this despite her concern and, indeed, disappointment. She had hoped that she would be able to persuade her mother to accompany her on a visit to Salford and her father's grave; only after she had waved her off on the London-bound train did it occur to her that Lottie had simply found the prospect of facing her memories too overwhelming.

Elsie was acutely aware that her mother's bouts of melancholy had increased considerably since she had been performing in *A Chinese*

Honeymoon. Her unstable behaviour was all the more trying for Elsie as she had no one she could confide in about the problem. She was sure that something must have triggered this decline, but as to what it could be she was mystified. The irony was more acute because for the first time she could remember they didn't have to constantly worry where the money was coming from to pay the next bill. Being under a permanent contract to Edwardes was a blessing and a curse perhaps, but it gave Elsie one less thing to worry about—money. As much as she had tried to get her mother to talk about her problems it always resulted in hours of silence, and worse, the sound of her sobbing quietly to herself in the night. This was torture to Elsie as it reminded her of other unhappy times when her father and mother were at odds over her career. At other times Elsie would find her mother hiding behind the lace curtains and constantly looking out the window as if she were searching for someone. But what could she do? Exposing Lottie's condition to the medical profession would certainly result in her being ostracised, and she couldn't allow that to happen. She had always been there for her, they were there for each other no matter what. That is how it would remain.

Edwardes hadn't yet informed Elsie what she would be doing next. Frank Curzon and George Dance from the *Royal Strand Theatre* had called to see her to ask her to be in a new show they were planning. To say they were furious when they discovered that Edwardes had put her under an exclusive contract was an understatement. Elsie liked them and was truly sorry; after all they had co-produced *A Chinese Honeymoon* with Edwardes so her success was partly due to them. But there was little she could do about it: a contract was a contract. Besides, had they acted as swiftly as Edwardes, perhaps things would have been different. Elsie tried not to think about it too much because such machinations and power struggles upset her. The less she knew about such things the better. She decided she would never have a tough enough character to deal with business matters; matters which, if she were honest with herself, she had little understanding of. Curzon and Dance left somewhat forlornly and wished her well, adding quickly that if anything changed to please let them know.

Edwardes finally contacted her and told her he was placing her in *Lady Madcap*, taking over the role of *Gwenny Holden*, a minor role, really a glorified chorus part, at the *Prince of Wales Theatre*. She was puzzled at first because her role was nothing more than standing looking pretty in the chorus; although she did have some lines of dialogue it was nothing like *Princess Soo Soo*. Edwardes assured her this was just a stop gap until he found the right vehicle for her. An explanation she accepted with good grace and a certain relief not to have the pressure of a main character. Her stage fright was ever present and with her worries over her mother at the forefront of her mind it would allow her time to regain her strength and also rest her voice. Singing as part of the chorus required less effort and was in some ways tantamount to a rest. Her mother balked at her being relegated to the chorus especially since she had made such a success with *Princess Soo Soo*, but her reaction was more to do with her own feelings than Elsie's. Her mother's problems coupled with her increasing tendency to act grand and superior towards others baffled Elsie, but she put it down to her mental state and allowed her to carry on in spite of her own misgivings. Of late she had noticed that the daily maid and the tradesmen had started to address her mother as "Ma'm" or "Mistress Charlotte". Although she was quite aware that this was her mother's proper name Elsie still wondered why "Lottie" had suddenly been abandoned. When she raised this her mother had told her bluntly that they now "had a position in society to maintain" and she intended to do just that. Elsie gave up the argument and told herself that it could do no harm for her mother to continue with this charade of pursuing respectability

Lottie meanwhile had decided to eradicate all thoughts of her past: it was all too upsetting and unnerved her terribly. Even to remember how she had behaved with Billy and Bert Hodder made her cringe inwardly with the shame of it and the thought of Elsie discovering this sordid episode was more than she could bear. Convinced that she had indeed looked into the eyes of Bert that night at the theatre she had suffered nightmares and had found herself waiting for him to appear out of the shadows one day, even worse, to call at their home and reveal the awful truth to Elsie. The shame would kill Lottie and ruin her daughter's career. Then again, if it had really been Bert Hodder why had he made no attempt to contact her? What could he want from her? The possibility of him telling Elsie of her illegitimacy was unthinkable and, not for the first time these past weeks, Lottie cursed him under her breath. She had not been able to cope with the strain on tour with her daughter and her panic attacks had worsened at the thought of going to Manchester and Salford—places too full of the ghosts of her past—so feigning illness and returning to London were her way of escaping. It seemed, however, that Bert Hodder was determined to give her no peace.

Whilst on tour Elsie had visited Manchester where *A Chinese Honeymoon* had played a week at the city's *Queen's Theatre*. It was strange to be back on that stage. She remembered the first time she had walked across it for an audition when she was a child. It had seemed so huge and the auditorium so cavernous and forbidding. She was surprised at how much smaller it was, but decided it was most likely because she'd become an adult during the intervening years. More strange was something which occurred just before she made her first entrance during the first night of the performance. She sensed someone right behind her in the wings and, naturally assuming it was another cast member, turned to smile at them. But no-one was there. Turning back to the stage her eye was drawn to the opposite wing, from the shadows of which stepped her father as large as life and clear as day. He smiled at her and winked affectionately then just as quickly vanished into thin air. She had been rooted to the spot and could feel her heart beating furiously. But then, she reasoned, this theatre had been such a big part of her father's life. He had worked here many times with Nelly Power, if she was going to see him anywhere it would be here. Convinced her mind and imagination were just playing tricks, she smiled to herself and decided she was glad they were. It was reassuring to see her father again even if it meant she missed him even more acutely. For the rest of the week she sensed him several times but wasn't concerned at all. In fact she found herself hoping he really was there—it reassured her to think he might be watching over her.

During this time she found herself cast in several other productions including *The Little Cherub and Little Michus*. Both produced by Edwardes in London and on tour which turned out to be just as much fun. Elsie had slotted into the chorus of various productions with ease and thoroughly enjoyed not being centre of attention. Indeed it was in this production she found herself becoming firm friends with four other chorus girls. Phyllis Dare and her sister Zena had carved out their individual careers and were renowned for their beauty rather than any extraordinary talent in terms of singing or acting. Any production they adorned would guarantee gasps of delight from male members of the audience and, much to their dismay, they were always described as the *"Dare Sisters"*. Zena would make Elsie laugh by declaring loudly to anyone who could hear that "anyone would think they were either joined at the hip, Siamese twins, or about to jump off a cliff together!" Although Phyllis was not working in this production with her sister, she was always back stage haunting their dressing room. In addition to Zena, Elsie was enchanted by Gabrielle Ray and Grace Pinder. *The Little Cherub* was flimsy in plot and narrative, but it was suitably lavish, as audiences had come to expect of a George Edwardes production. For all the characters love inevitably found a way and Elsie enjoyed herself in the minor role of *Lady Agnes Congress* as well as delighting in her new found friends. They all found themselves being frequently moved between *The Little Cherub* and a very similar production at *Daly's*, *The Lady Madcap*. Zena declared herself utterly confused and challenged Edwardes with "Am I a lady or a cherub tonight, George?" Elsie loved being in the company of the sisters and she had to admit that she hadn't laughed so much in a long time, if ever.

Elsie now found herself thinking about men in a way she never had before: she wondered if she would ever have an admirer, other than those she saw on the other side of the footlights. She was fascinated by the handsome men who would call to collect her new found girlfriends from the stage door after the evening's performance and the next day would listen in wonder to the tales of candle-lit dinners at the *Savoy* or the *Ritz*. Vivid comparisons of the men's various abilities at kissing would make her gasp, as would the reported value of the gifts bestowed on the objects of their desire. As much as she enjoyed hearing about the exploits of Zena, Gabrielle and Grace, she confessed in all honesty that she would be far too scared and wouldn't have a clue what to do in such a situation. The girls in their turn were astounded when Elsie told them how many ardent requests she had, with the help of various stage door keepers, declined. She stated how some men would approach her in the street as she left the stage door and how, as much from fear as anything else, she would abruptly turn down their invitations. Trouble was, she said, that the more rude her refusal the more keen they became! This, she declared, was something she would never understand about men.

Unfortunately the laughter the girls enjoyed created a situation which none of them could have anticipated. Zena was a skilled mimic and had taken to making Elsie corpse and giggle during the performance; aided by Gabrielle who was wicked when it came to making Elsie laugh on stage. It was unprofessional behaviour and would have sent Edwardes into a fury if it came to his notice. Zena, as full of mischief as her sister, dared Elsie to pat a balloon at the most handsome man in the stalls during a chorus sequence. Edwardes happened to be standing at the back of the stalls at *Daly's* during this matinee performance, saw Elsie giggle—and the final straw was her apparently flirting with a male member of the audience. He was outraged by her behaviour and, whilst giving her a dressing down, pointed out that such behaviour might have been acceptable in the music halls of Salford but it was not acceptable in his theatre. He could lose his licence to operate if there was any hint of immoral behaviour by the girls in the cast and he therefore had no choice but to make an example of her and dismiss her without notice. She should collect her belongings from the dressing room and vacate the premises immediately. He never wanted to see her again.

Elsie fled from the theatre in floods of tears and ran home as fast as she could. Angry and humiliated she just wanted to hide herself away. Gabrielle and Zena had also been admonished by Edwardes but had escaped being sacked. Elsie was distraught, convinced her career, everything she had worked so hard for, was over. What would she do for money? Who would look after her mother? It was all too much to think about. She realised she had been childish, foolish, unprofessional and deserved everything that had happened. It was then it struck her. Yes she had been childish in enjoying laughing with the girls, giggling at silly things, because she had never done it when she was a child. She couldn't remember a time when she hadn't been free of responsibility. 1905 was not ending well; she could only hope that 1906 would perhaps be a better year for her.

In the weeks that passed since her dismissal, Elsie had been thankful for her prudence and her savings. This had enabled her to meet the household expenses without too much concern. However she was aware that her meagre savings wouldn't last forever. As Christmas had approached she had been kept busy nursing her mother through a bad bout of flu, and as a result had been tied to their apartment. Zena and other friends had been to visit and attempt to raise her spirits but, as she told them, she was busy looking after her mother and actually quite enjoying being a little melancholy. Gertie Millar had insisted on taking her for tea at the new *Waldorf Hotel* and to see London's newest theatres. As her mother was tucked up in bed, and the daily maid promised to keep her eye on her, Elsie agreed to go, although she told Gertie she didn't want to meet at the new *Gaiety Theatre* in case she bumped into Edwardes.

And so it was that on the 31st December 1905, Elsie found herself in the company of Gertie in the Palm Court of the new *Waldorf Hotel* on the Aldwych sipping tea and chatting. They had also looked at the two new theatres built at either side of the hotel, *The Waldorf Theatre* and *The Aldwych Theatre*. Elsie felt sad the old *Royal Strand Theatre* across the street, where she had played *Princess Soo Soo*, had been demolished as part of the area's redevelopment to make way for the new *Aldwych Underground Station*, but agreed with Gertie that the new theatres and the hotel had splendid facades. Gertie informed Elsie she was having supper with Edwardes that very night and did she want her to perhaps try and smooth things over to somehow resolve this dispute? Elsie thanked Gertie but declined her kind offer. It didn't seem so important anymore, and maybe it was for the best. Performing placed such a strain on her nerves, so perhaps it was better this way. Maybe she was not destined to have a career in the theatre after all. At this moment, her main concern was her mother's health and well-being.

Later that evening, Elsie stood at her window and waited to hear the chimes of Big Ben. What would 1906 bring to her life she wondered? In a few months she would be twenty-years-old. Suddenly feeling so alone she began to cry. She hated self pity in others and disliked it even more intensely in herself. But she had to admit she felt better for shedding a few tears. Whatever happened, whatever she decided to do with her life, she would make sure they survived. Perhaps they could go and live in the country where the air would be better for her mother. Big Ben began to strike the first chimes of midnight and Elsie laughed at the feeling of optimism it gave her. Drying her eyes and blowing her nose she sat in the chair by the fire and drifted into a much-needed sleep.

Several hundred miles away at the *Theater an der Wien* in Vienna, Franz Lehar was celebrating the success of the first performance of his operetta *Die Lustige Witwe*; which had reached the stage with all the odds stacked against it. Within eighteen months his operetta would have a lavish London production and become famous all over the world as *The Merry Widow*. Although, on this rather cold, bleak December evening he was unaware what fate had in store—as were Elsie and George Edwardes, who would also be drawn into the clutches of this fascinating Widow.

Franz Lehar & Reconciliation

"Lehar knows nothing about waltzes!"
RICHARD HEUBERGER—VIENNA COMPOSER

L istening to the screams of *"Bravo!" "Bravo!"* from the first night audience Lehar could allow himself a moment of self-satisfaction. His critics had been fierce in their opposition to his operetta and, against the constant efforts to derail the production and countless pessimistic comments, he had been triumphant in the face of such adversity. He reminded himself that moments such as this are very rare in life and should be savoured. With a sense of concealed delight he watched as the directors of Vienna's famous *Theater an der Wien*, Walner and Karczag, strolled stage centre puffing themselves up like peacocks to announce their delight at the success and how they always knew the show would be well received. Lehar smiled to himself at their hypocrisy.

When he had been approached to compose the music for this production he remembered well his reaction at first reading the libretto handed to him by Victor Leon and his partner Leo Stein. Instantly captivated by the story of the widow he had practically begged to be allowed to compose the score. Leon had informed him that another composer had attempted a score but his efforts were deemed lacklustre. The eminent Vienna composer Heuberger had finally admitted defeat, with reluctance, and withdrawn from the project. Hearing Heuberger's name made Lehar more determined than ever to undertake this task, for it had been the same man who had prevented him from being employed by the *Vienna State Orchestra* as conductor and composer with the scathing criticism that he "knew nothing about waltzes!" Nothing indeed! Lehar saw his chance to silence this rival and his critics once and for all.

Wallner and Karczag were less than impressed when they eventually heard Lehar's score for the operetta; indeed Karczag had even announced to Leon that "this is not music!" Although they had reluctantly agreed to mount the production they would provide only the meanest of budgets to cover sets and costumes. Fortunately, the cast were enthusiastic and agreed to rehearse after their evening performances, resulting in many nights of rehearsal starting at 11pm and finishing as late as 3 o'clock in the morning. Sets and costumes were scraped together from the contents of store rooms and necessitated much improvising yet, despite such haphazard production values, with characters dressed in odd Ruritanian folk costumes, the music and story captivated the first night audience.

Lehar realised that this was just the beginning, for now the operetta would get the respect and the money it truly deserved. His association with *The Merry Widow* had taken root and was about to blossom. The thought of a London production had not even entered his mind at this point.

London was cold, damp and bleak in January. Edwardes hated the cold, it seemed to affect him more as he got older. This January of 1906 seemed worse than any he could remember. Perhaps it was because he had so much on his mind: his meeting with Gertie on New Years Eve still vivid. He had been looking forward to dinner at the *Savoy* that night and usually enjoyed Gertie's company on such occasions. All had seemed well until, suddenly becoming serious, she began to talk to him about his treatment of Elsie. Gertie was very upset at the way he had treated her and, while she agreed that the girl had behaved inappropriately, she certainly did not deserve to be so cruelly banished. Furthermore, she was a young girl—barely twenty—who needed support and guidance, something she had probably never had in her young life. Besides, Elsie was a talented artiste and he should consider himself fortunate to have discovered her; if he was truly a man of substance he would make amends and sort things out as soon as possible. Having made her point, Gertie promptly exited amid the rustle of silk, the swish of fur and an exquisite haze of perfume that lingered in the air long after her departure.

Gertie's diatribe was still ringing in his ears two weeks later. He had been furious with her initially, but his fury soon abated because he knew she was right. Trust Gertie to see through his rigid façade and glimpse the fondness he carried for both her and Elsie. He decided Gertie's directness must be a trait in those born in Bradford! Yorkshire women were, he thought, nothing if not direct and fearless when it came to mere men. Women! Why did they have to be so infuriating; and why was it his fate to meet two of the most compelling and talented women of the modern age? It was a curse, but one he'd happily live with. In truth, his reaction to Elsie's behaviour had been upsetting for all concerned; his hostility towards her had come as a rather frightening surprise even to himself. After she had fled the theatre he had locked himself in his office not wanting anyone to see how affected he was by that dreadful scene. It was impossible for him to deny the fact that he cared for the girl and the strength of his emotion scared him. Even his affection for Gertie did not compare with the overpowering feelings he now recognised in his relationship with Elsie. She was after all little more than a child and he, a man now well past middle-age, should have offered support and the wisdom of his experience rather than send his protégé into undeserved exile. It was too easy to forget how young Elsie was. Mature beyond her years in many ways, Edwardes suspected she had not had a chance to enjoy her childhood, burdened as she was with the sole responsibility of breadwinner and nurse to her ailing mother. To his shame he had deliberately ignored the problem of Lottie in Elsie's life and the strain it must continue to be for her.

Walking into the wind down Charing Cross Road, he decided he would call and see Elsie and discuss the future; he still had her under an exclusive contract so she would be unable to work for any other management without his permission. He hated the wind, hated walking into it, and hated it even more when it was accompanied by sheeting rain. Feeling the wetness down the back of his neck and a rain drop gathering at the end of his nose he cursed the English weather in January. To add to his misery the traffic and steaming horses pulling their rattling carts created an unbearable cacophony of sounds, whilst other pedestrians exacerbated his bad humour by knocking into him without as much as an apology. Women and their damn hats would garrotte him before he was much older. Why wear such wide-brimmed creations on god-awful days like today? Crossing the road and heading into Leicester Square feeling decidedly grumpy, he rounded the corner towards *Daly's Theatre* looking forward to a stiff malt whiskey by the fire in his office. As this thought occurred to him, he crashed into a fellow pedestrian with a thud which knocked the wind from him. As he composed himself and adjusted his hat, he looked up to discover an equally breathless Elsie standing in front of him, very wet, and very sorry for herself.

Ellen's Tea Rooms on the opposite side of Leicester Square had always been a cosy and inviting establishment. Before he knew it, he had offered an invitation to Elsie to join him and they were seated in a little booth opposite a very welcome coal fire partaking of afternoon tea. He had walked past the tea shop on many occasions, but usually he had little time for such indulgence. Under the circumstances it was the perfect place to have this meeting with Elsie because none of his staff could distract him. Looking at her sipping her tea he couldn't help but smile to himself, she was so very striking and her complexion was faultless; he wasn't sure hers was a classic beauty but he had to admit something about her was mesmerising. It was her eyes that gave away how she was really feeling. There was a deep, deep sadness in those eyes which suddenly made the hairs on his arm stand on end. He wasn't sure he would ever be able to delve into the depths of this girl's character, but he would from this point make sure he did everything in his power to guide and protect as best he could. A paternalistic role would suit him very well, at least he imagined it would.

Elsie looked across at Edwardes and felt relief that at least they would be able to discuss things and she could explain what had actually occurred during that performance. If she told him honestly that she realised she had been unprofessional and was sincerely sorry to have upset him so, he might forgive her. He was a strange man in many ways. There was something about him that frightened her a little but she could also see great gentleness, even kindness, towards her in his eyes. Even that awful day when he had shouted at her so cruelly she could have sworn she saw a tear in his eye. Strange how she should collide with him today of all days. In spite of the rain she had decided to take a walk to get away from her mother and her ailments; which she was convinced were mainly a manifestation of her mother's imagination rather than anything real. Today was the anniversary of her father's death and she wanted time alone to remember him. She had sat a while in St Paul's Church in Covent Garden and said a little prayer for him. How she wished things could have been different and he could still be alive. Then a thought just popped into her head: take a walk through Leicester Square on the way home and have a look at *Daly's Theatre*? If she were honest with herself, which she had decided she must be more often, she missed the theatre and especially *Daly's*. It had such a magical atmosphere and was so beautifully decorated with its red velvet seats, shimmering chandeliers and gilded plasterwork. Back stage, especially the dressing rooms, was less than magnificent but what did that matter when you could look out into that auditorium of dreams. Her reverie was broken by Edwardes stirring his tea. The spoon clunked rather loudly as he vigorously tried to aid the dissolving of the sugar lumps. A middle-aged waitress walked by briskly and gave him a stern, disapproving look which made Elsie giggle. She saw him look at the waitress, then at her, and he also sort of laughed which came out as a loud snort, and as it was the first time she had ever seen him laugh this made her giggle even more.

Elsie would often think about that afternoon she spent with Edwardes. It was one of those moments in life where, through honest communication brought on by an argument that had caused them both unhappiness and distress, they viewed each other differently than before. Elsie had told him all her hopes and fears and the sadness of her father's passing and how she wished he were still alive. The worry over her mother which at times left her feeling helpless and frustrated at Lottie's increasing melancholy and bouts of tortured silence; silences which could go on for days on end and seemed to be getting worse. The next moment her mother would be full of the joys of spring and twice as lively. It was all so confusing and at times she felt like she couldn't go on any longer. Edwardes too had given her an honest perspective on her prospects and future career and on a personal note had confided in her his sadness at not having the inclination to spend more time with his wife and children. He hardly ever saw them and revealed that he spent more time with his valet, who he couldn't imagine being without. His children were a mystery to him but now, as they were nearing a similar age to Elsie, perhaps their maturity would help to lessen the distance that had grown between them. Elsie appreciated his frankness and guessed she was privileged to be given an insight into his private thoughts and intimate details of his life. From that time on their professional relationship would also have a friendship which gained an added dimension. Never overt in showing his feelings, a glance from Edwards would nevertheless offer her reassurance or understanding, an unspoken communication of friendship that lay always between them from this point in their relationship. He was, Elsie thought, almost a surrogate father to her and she determined to show her gratitude by never letting him down again. Most reassuringly, she knew she would have his support and advice if things worsened with her mother and, for the first time since her father's death, she began to feel a little more secure and much less alone.

Gertie was pleased her day had not gone as well as planned. She had intended to do some shopping on Bond Street that afternoon to cheer herself up after enduring a horrible bout of influenza. However the inclement weather had put a stop to that little outing. She loved shopping, but hated the rain more. As her carriage was in the West End when the rain became more persistent she decided it would be a shame to drive all the way back to Eaton Square, so asked her driver to make a stop at *Daly's Theatre*. She'd hoped to catch Edwardes in his office and find out if their little chat regarding Elsie had had the desired effect, and also to discuss plans for the following Christmas show at the *Gaiety*. Waiting in his office, which overlooked Leicester Square, she had seen them walk together through the gardens and into the tea shop opposite. Deciding there was no point in waiting, she wrapped herself up in her fur coat and decided to make her way home. She had done what she could, now it was up to them.

Within days Edwardes had sent Elsie the script of his new production that was in the planning stage. A comic opera in two acts titled *See See*. An odd title she thought, no doubt someone's idea of a comical way to allude to Chinese pronunciation? It would be presented at the *Prince of Wales Theatre* around the middle of June 1906 if all went well. Elsie was a little disappointed it wouldn't be produced at *Daly's Theatre*, but aside from that she was delighted to have another good role to work on. In many ways it reminded her of *A Chinese Honeymoon* in that it was set in China and involved cultural misunderstandings between the visiting British and the natives, all to great comic effect. The songs by Sidney Jones and Adrian Ross were pretty and she had two good solos. She also liked the name of her character: *Humming Bird*. As with all of Edwardes productions the sets and costumes would be lavish; and the initial design sketches she had seen left her in no doubt this production would be no less lavish. Having made such an impact with her previous oriental role, she was looking forward to creating her costumes and makeup for *Humming Bird*. With this in mind she began to research in great detail. All things oriental were the height of fashion and although Elsie was aware of the absurdity of how Chinese people were portrayed in a very British musical comedy way, it seemed not to matter because the public loved it. With only a few weeks until rehearsals began she had much to do and was determined to make her mark and give Edwardes no cause to regret giving her a second chance. The Dare Sisters and Gertie were delighted she was back in Edwardes' good books. Zena made her giggle by declaring to everyone that Elsie's career was progressing "from *Soo Soo* to *See See*!" adding mischievously "*When When* do you open, dear?" Elsie had also decided to send Gertie some flowers by way of a thank you. Gertie would never admit it, but Elsie was certain she had orchestrated the reconciliation between Edwardes and herself. She duly sent two dozen of Gertie's favourite pink roses with a little card that simply said: "*Thank you—Elsie.*"

Edwardes watched with some considerable satisfaction as Elsie began preparing for her role as *Humming Bird*. He had initially been attracted to this production as an opportunity for Elsie to develop her acting and vocal skills; he had blamed himself for not using her talents sufficiently after *A Chinese Honeymoon* and placing her in the chorus had been a mistake. With no responsibility, Elsie had relaxed and become distracted—too easily drawn into mischief by the other girls—but now she had plenty to think about and was attacking the role with zest. Her modesty never ceased to amaze him: she had been entirely responsible for the trend to realism in the depiction of characters, using design and makeup to add the depth of the character. She seemed, however, to be entirely unaware of her unique role in this innovation. The designers contracted by Edwardes for *See See*—Joseph Harker and Hawes Craven—were delighted at the interest Elsie showed in their designs, intriguing them further by disclosing that she had discussed with Molly Freedings, the costume designer, how complementary colours could be used.

Molly however took exception to this perceived interference. As a result there was friction between her and Elsie which Edwardes had to smooth over. For now the tension was relieved, but for how long? Edwardes didn't much care because as long as Elsie was happy, then so was he. He also had other more important things on his mind. He had been contacted out of the blue by his friend, and co director of *The Gaiety Theatre*, William Boosey. He assumed the music publishing world must be quiet at present and he had too much time on his hands. This thought was reinforced when Boosey told him to make arrangements for the following week because he wanted him to accompany him to Germany. On being asked why, he informed Edwardes that he needed to deal with some music publishing business, but he had also been informed that a new operetta might be worth taking a look at for a possible production in England, or the publishing rights for music sales at least. Edwardes declined his invitation, mainly because he hated sea travel, but Boosey persisted claiming he didn't want to travel alone and it would give them an opportunity to catch up. Besides, hadn't he asked him to keep his ear to the ground about any good German operettas that might translate well? After further consideration he decided he would go. Maybe this new operetta would be suitable for *Daly's* although he wasn't enamoured with the title: *A Fickle Duchess!* That would definitely have to go.

Lottie sat by the first floor drawing room window watching everyone who passed along Portland Place. Making sure she was concealed behind the lace curtains should anyone look up, she particularly scrutinised the men. Where was he? Why was he torturing her like this? Startled by a knock at the door she jumped and noticed her hands were shaking. The daily maid entered with her afternoon tea tray. Placing it on the table she bobbed a little curtsey and left. Lottie crossed to the chair by the fire and poured herself a cup of tea, adding a drop of brandy from her silver hip flask which she told herself was medicinal. Elsie would be home soon, she should try and pull herself together.

The last few months had been a terrible strain on her nerves and had left her exhausted. It had given her time to think and reflect on the past and also analyse her feelings at the shock of seeing Bert Hodder again. She had been through so much all those years ago that she decided she had to let it go. That she had loved Hodder was without question, but he hadn't deserved that love. From this day forward as far as she was concerned he simply didn't exist any longer; she was certainly not going to send herself to an early grave because of him. Her mood swings must have been a strain on Elsie who with her usual good grace took it all in her stride and continued to be patient and supportive. Lottie counted her blessings every day and her biggest blessing was her daughter. Realising her own selfishness she decided to make a concerted effort to support Elsie in whatever way possible. She had faced adversity with the same grace she faced everything in life. Now she had resolved the misunderstanding with Edwardes she seemed so much happier and more secure in her abilities again. Elsie was never going to be a supremely confident woman, it wasn't in her nature to be that way, but she could be determined and resolute. These qualities would always serve her well and help her face anything in this life.

She decided to be honest with Elsie and tell her about her family. She had asked so many times since that day at Bill's funeral; Lottie had been shocked because she hadn't laid eyes on either of her siblings for years until that day, and she certainly had no idea they would turn up without an invitation. For Lottie it had all been too painful, but now seemed a good time to release all the secrets she had held close for so long. They were both several years older than her. Her sister Grace was a seamstress who had worked as a costume designer and maker for the Gilbert & Sullivan operas; indeed it was ironic because she would have worked for Edwardes when he was at the *Savoy Theatre* all those years ago. Her brother Albert had always worked in banking. Both had left home at the earliest opportunity, mainly to get away from their aggressive father; they had all endured beatings at his hands as children. She guessed they also wanted to escape the drudgery of a life working in the cotton mills. Lottie couldn't forgive them for abandoning her and their mother to such a brutal and lonely fate. That they never contacted them or even attempted to see if she was alright was something she could never forgive. She was a child and they left her. Even after her parents were both dead there was still silence from both. Her guess was they suddenly appeared at Billy's funeral because they had seen articles in the newspapers about 'Little Elsie' and thought there might be money involved. Lottie sighed to herself and decided it was all giving her a headache, but for the last time. Perhaps she could find some forgiveness in her heart eventually but she would never forget. Elsie would understand, she was sure, but she was also entitled to know what had really happened. She could then make her own decisions.

Franz Lehar composer of *The Merry Widow*, 1907
(DSC)

The cover of the second souvenir for the London production of *The Merry Widow*, distributed at *Daly's Theatre*, London, 8 June 1909, to mark the second anniversary of the production - the protrait on the cover from an original watercoulour portrait of *Lily Elsie* by Talbot Hughes, published by William Heinemann, London, 1908/09.
(Courtesy of John Culme's Footlight Notes Collection)

Actor and singer *Bertram Wallis* who starred opposite *Lily Elsie* in *The Count of Luxembourg* at *Daly's Theatre*, London, 1911.
(DSC)

Gertie Millar as Lally in *The New Aladdin* circa 1906.
(Courtesy of John Culme's Footlight Notes Collection)

Daly's Theatre, Leicester Square, London, Circa 1907. The *Warner Multiplex Cinema* now stands on the site.
(Courtesy of Matthew Lloyd)

Publicity photograph of *Lily Elsie* as *Princess Soo Soo* and *Farren Soutar* as *Tom Hatherton* in *A Chinese Honeymoon*, the *Royal Strand Theatre*, London, 1903.

(DSC)

Lily Elsie and *Ian Bullough* on their wedding day,
November 1911.
(Courtesy of Rob Sedman)

Popular post card of *Lily Elsie* circa 1911.
(Courtesy of Rob Sedman)

Cover of *A Chinese Honeymoon* souvenir, London, 5 October 1903.
(Courtesy of John Culme's Footlight Notes Collection)

Lily Elsie as *Humming Bird* in the 1906 production of *See See* at *The Prince of Wales Theatre*, London.
(Courtesy of Rob Sedman)

Actress and dancer *Gabrielle Ray*, *Lily Elsie's* friend, in a popular post card image circa 1912.
(DSC)

The Gaiety Theatre (now demolished) on the corner of *Strand* and *Aldwych*.
(Courtesy of Matthew Lloyd)

Lily Elsie in a popular post card image circa 1914.
(Courtesy of Rob Sedman)

Actor *Owen Nares* who starred with *Lily Elsie* in *Pamela*, 1917.

(DSC)

Left to right: *Lily Elsie* and *Gertrude Glyn* with two companions at Biarritz - snapshot, circa 1907/08.
(Courtesy of John Culme's Footlight Notes Collection)

Play Pictorial cover with *Lily Elsie* and *Ivor Novello* to promote *The Truth Game*, 1928. Elsie's last public performances.
(Courtesy of Rob Sedman)

Gertie Millar, the most famous of the 'Gaiety girls' and *Elsie's* friend.

(DSC)

Gertie Millar in a popular post card image circa 1912.

(DSC)

What Price Success?

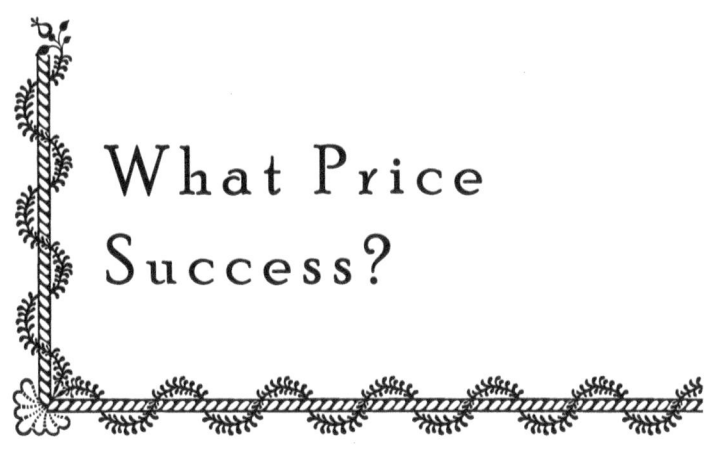

"Girls whom I know are continually asking me questions about the world of the stage, and they all want to know if it is easy to get on it!"
LILY ELSIE TO THE LONDON ILLUSTRATED AND
DRAMATIC NEWS

Elsie noticed the change in her mother immediately. It was if a large dark cloud had been lifted from her shoulders and she was transformed. As a result there was a lightness and joy to their daily life where her mother was supportive and even began to take on some of the responsibility for the running of their home. Elsie was able to concentrate fully on the preparations and rehearsals for *See See* and her character *Humming Bird*.

Her friendship with Gertie also blossomed during this time. They often went for afternoon tea at the *Waldorf Hotel* and even to a formal dinner at the *Savoy Hotel*. Elsie had always avoided such occasions but, in the company of Gertie, found she enjoyed dressing in her best evening wear and experiencing this side of London life. She was still terrified of men and found herself absolutely tongue-tied when they tried to engage her in conversation. Gertie would make her giggle and point out she didn't have to say a word, just sit there and look gorgeous.

Elsie couldn't see herself as anything like gorgeous, in fact she would look in the mirror and see nothing but plain.

Gertie also introduced her to the world of shopping and Bond Street in particular where her favourite dressmakers operated. Elsie was aghast at the amount of money Gertie would seemingly spend on a single gown and couldn't imagine ever being able to afford such indulgence. Whenever they went out in the evening Gertie would also be dripping in diamonds and especially sapphires, which were her favourite. Elsie asked her how on earth she afforded all this luxury, only to be met with gales of laughter from Gertie. She rarely paid for any of it, as the dressmakers were happy to provide her couture because it guaranteed dozens of orders from women wanting to emulate her. The jewels were loaned to her by the jewellers for the same reason. She was a walking advertisement for these establishments, and when the press interviewed her for gossip stories she would make sure they knew where her jewels and outfits came from. Elsie was amazed as she had no idea this kind of thing went on. She decided she had a lot to learn!

During one shopping expedition Elsie had dragged Gertie into a haberdashery shop on Oxford Street, and proceeded to baffle her by asking the assistant if they could look at the largest wooden knitting needles available. Gertie asked her in whisper what on earth she wanted knitting needles for? Elsie told her to wait and see. When the assistant returned she picked two large wooden needles and carefully began to stick them in her hair. The look on Gertie's face was priceless as she watched, fearful Elsie had gone temporarily mad. Elsie turned to face her and struck a pose as her character *Humming Bird* and it instantly made sense. She had wanted something to emulate a Chinese hairstyle and the knitting needles crossed through the back of her hair did exactly that. Gertie admired her determination to be different and really become her character using her unique approach. From this point they spent many happy hours together experimenting with Elsie's hair and make up to create just the look she had in mind. Gertie was also shrewd enough to realise this kind of dedication and attention to detail was the very thing that set Elsie apart from her contemporaries. She really had the desire to bring to life the characters she played in a way that no one else had ever done. The audience and their enjoyment really mattered to her. She admired that and decided she too could perhaps learn a thing or two from her friend. Her only slight worry was that Elsie was using all of this to give her something to hide behind.

For Elsie this was the part she enjoyed above everything else. The time she spent with Gertie and her other friends was precious to her. It allowed her to forget her nagging doubts and fears of being not good enough. She also had moments when she dreaded the thought of having to actually do a performance to a live audience. The rehearsal process and all the planning was a pleasure, but as soon as she was standing in the wings waiting to go on she would be overwhelmed with fear. Elsie was surprised to hear Gertie reassuring her by saying that she too had such moments of fear which made her feel wretched. It was normal because every performer had such moments, and usually the best performers suffered the worst! Elsie appreciated her reassurance but couldn't imagine Gertie feeling as bad as she did. She had seen Gertie perform at the *Gaiety* many times and she would marvel at her confidence and energy. She could never be that self-assured, ever.

As the opening night of *See See* approached they moved into the *Prince of Wales Theatre* to rehearse on the beautiful and colourful sets created for the production. It was a very happy company and there was a really positive and energetic atmosphere around the production. Edwardes had been delighted at Elsie's dedication to her part and watched rehearsals with pride. He loved to sit in the shadows at the back of the stalls, and would usually creep in so no one would know he was there. That way he would get a true sense of what was happening and it would also help him identify what problems had been encountered, and how best to resolve them. He had a good feeling about this production. There was a palpable excitement and anticipation in the pre production press reports which pleased him. Elsie was the focus of this attention and her popular appeal was certainly growing to the point where the opening night was awaited with bated breath. Her image was everywhere and she had become very popular on the post card circuit; all of which helped to make the pre box office sales healthy indeed.

His trip to Vienna with Boosey had resulted in a very positive outcome. An outcome he also had a good feeling about. On arriving in Vienna, after an horrendous channel crossing that had left him terribly sick, followed by an equally horrendous train journey, he was not in the best humour for a day or so. Boosey had dragged him to a performance of *The Fickle Duchess!* which had not lived up to expectations; he'd decided there were enough fickle duchesses to deal with in England without importing this one! The music was average and the story non-existent and most of the performers were barely amateur in ability. He'd left after the first act. He knew what he liked and what he wanted and this production was not it. Boosey feigned annoyance and said it would be rude to leave, if not disheartening for the cast and composer, but his protestations were borne more from embarrassment than a real desire to stay.

They had spent a couple of days seeing what else was on offer, which amounted to nothing of note, and were about to depart for home disillusioned at the waste of time and effort the trip had been. At the eleventh hour and by pure chance they were asked to take a look at a new operetta that might be what they were looking for. An associate of Boosey's had seen the first night of the production the previous New Years Eve and found himself captivated by the story of *The Merry Widow*. Having undertaken some research he discovered the story was based on the play *L'Attache* by the French farce-writer Henry Meilhac. The basis of the story was gleaned from this and turned into a libretto by Leon and Stein, with the score by Lehar. His enthusiasm was infectious. Edwardes asked him to explain the story of *The Merry Widow*, but he was reluctant to do so and insisted they went to see it for themselves. Edwardes and Boosey were irritated somewhat by this cloak and dagger approach but decided they had little to lose and everything to gain by seeing a performance.

Sitting in the stage box of the *Theater an der Wien* there was a ripple of excitement and anticipation from the audience as they entered the auditorium to take their seats. For Edwardes this was perhaps a good sign as word of mouth had created a buzz about the show. The anticipation was palpable and continued to grow until the house lights dimmed; which was also a good sign in its favour. As the music began, Edwardes found himself listening intently to the richness of the orchestra with Lehar as conductor.

Lehar was very aware of Edwardes and Boosey's presence in the stage box that night. His heart was beating furiously and he prayed they would like the production. Edwardes was the most famous London producer and the most powerful, his reputation pre-eminent all over Europe. Boosey was also a very powerful man and could transform a composer's fortunes by publishing his music all over the world. His worries melted away once the performance began as he became fully absorbed into the world of his merry widow.

The story was set in the mythical, and very Ruritanian, land of operetta make-believe, and revolved around the young widow *Sonia* who had inherited a vast fortune on the death of her husband. *Prince Danilo* is a handsome young man who once was in love with *Sonia* prior to her marriage. Enduring a self imposed exile in Paris, he is ordered by the government to marry the widow because if she marries a foreigner her inheritance would be removed from the country causing economic disaster. Informed the mysterious widow is in Paris he is instructed to attend an Embassy Ball that evening in her honour. Initially he agrees but on his arrival at the ball he is shocked to discover the widow is *Sonia*. He refuses to propose to her because he really does still love her but doesn't want her to think he wants her money. As a result he is aloof and arrogant when they meet and *Sonia* becomes upset because she thinks he no longer loves her as he once did. After much confusion, and laughter, and ludicrous court intrigues involving the other characters, the situation is resolved and they marry out of love and the country is saved from economic collapse. All to the strains of the *Merry Widow Waltz*.

Edwardes liked it but didn't fall hopelessly in love with *The Merry Widow*. He did like the score which was brilliantly constructed but felt the libretto would need some serious work to translate into English and make it palatable for a London audience. Boosey was also of the same opinion. They discussed it until the early hours of the morning aided by copious amounts of brandy and innumerable cigars. By the time they retired to bed they had reached the conclusion that perhaps it just wouldn't work in London. Having been offered first refusal for the rights of the show, Edwardes knew he had the unpleasant task of withdrawing his interest the next morning.

But by the following morning Edwardes had changed his mind. He had woken with numerous thoughts and ideas whirling around his mind; one of those inexplicable occasions when his mind seemed to work independently whilst he slept. The score was excellent and the main characters—*Sonia* as the widow, and *Prince Danilo* as the suitor—were strong. *Sonia* as played by Mitzi Gunther was agreeable in terms of her singing ability but she was an actress of middle age and her comedic talent was very German. Edwardes wondered if the dynamic of the central love story between *Sonia* and *Prince Danilo* might not be heightened if the widow was much younger and the comedy elements of the story balanced better with the romantic aspect. It occurred to him that with Elsie playing *Sonia*, his team in London rewriting the libretto, maybe it could work. The more he imagined Elsie as *The Merry Widow*, the more he could see the possibilities. By a strange coincidence Boosey had also had a change of heart and suggested they take an option on the rights anyway. Although both agreed they hadn't understood the full story in German, they had been captivated by the situation of the central characters and could see the potential. The title was also an issue as neither of them liked it, but time would allow them to think of something better. Edwardes considered the title could be simply *Sonia!*

Lehar was thrilled and disappointed in equal measure. On the one hand he had a very successful operetta and was pleased that Edwardes had bought the rights for a London production, and on the other hand he was worried because he hadn't liked the libretto and wanted his own team to work on it back in London. Lehar was concerned it wouldn't be just the libretto that would be changed by Edwardes, he feared that he would even consider a new composer for the English version. Lehar need not have worried because Edwardes had no intention of replacing him; but Lehar was unaware of this and continued to worry right up until the day he would be summoned to London for rehearsals. Until then he would have to wait patiently.

Edwardes had been obliged to purchase the rights of the show with money reserved for *Gaiety Theatre* productions. There was very little available in the *Daly's Theatre* account due to the run of bad luck with productions there. He realised that *The Merry Widow* had possible potential to be a *Daly's* production; but was equally convinced it would never work in any form at the *Gaiety!* Boosey agreed to the purchase using these funds and so they signed the deal. Edwardes decided he would bring Elsie to see the German production and gauge her reaction to *Sonia*.

Watching Elsie from his vantage point at the back of the stalls during rehearsals for *See See* at *The Prince of Wales Theatre* he had moments where he could picture her as *Sonia* very clearly. She was so graceful and elegant and could portray naivety and a feistiness which was endearing and rare for any actress. Her singing voice had developed and seemed much stronger and more assured. Pleased her confidence had improved he slipped quietly away and left them to their labours. He decided he wouldn't mention anything about *The Merry Widow* as yet, she had enough to think about with opening night getting ever closer.

Elsie always knew when Edwardes was around even if she couldn't see him. She could sense his presence in the atmosphere. Rehearsals had been going well for *See See* and she was, much to her surprise, looking forward to opening night. Usually she dreaded it but this time she felt at a point where she just wanted to get on and do the job. However she was concerned about the gossip she had heard regarding Edwardes financial situation. It was also rumoured he had gambled and lost a lot of money on his favourite hobby, horse racing. Not that she believed it, but some were saying he was struggling to keep *Daly's* afloat and desperately needed a hit show to replenish his finances. She truly hoped that *See See* would be a success for him.

The first night for *See See* on 19th June 1906 was a resounding success and a personal triumph for Elsie. The majority of the press remarked at her "authentic and charming" characterisation as *Humming Bird* noting that her voice was strong and carried her solo songs with "grace and elegance". Elsie was as usual embarrassed by the flattering remarks and wondered what all the fuss was about. All she could think about were the things that could have been better with her performance, and how she had fluffed some lines of dialogue which had caused problems for others in the cast. Her stage fright had returned to haunt her and she would physically tremble as she stood in the wings awaiting her entrance. She hid her fears well and none of the other cast members would particularly notice because once she was on stage invariably her fears vanished and she was able to perform satisfactorily. Her mother however would witness a very different Elsie once she had returned to the privacy of her dressing room: on one memorable occasion her daughter was so distraught she threw a perfume bottle across the room which shattered against the wall. Breaking down into sobs of unhappiness Elsie declared she never wanted to go on stage again. Lottie was aghast at this out of character behaviour, behaviour which troubled her more because Elsie would have these outbursts and within a blink of an eye would suddenly be calm and serene wondering how her perfume bottle had been broken. Lottie's concerns were exacerbated because she began to see her own melancholic, erratic behaviour mirrored in her daughters.

During the run of *See See* there were times when Elsie's mental struggle caused her to miss performances. Although the reason was always given as physical illness, Lottie was afraid that if it happened too often Edwardes would become suspicious. Whilst he had ensured there was always an understudy ready to take over, his patience with Elsie could start to wear thin. The production was just about limping along and not exactly making a fortune. That said, Edwardes was well aware that Elsie's presence in the production kept the box office buoyant.

Elsie felt exhausted when these bouts of stage fright seemed to take her over. She would shake uncontrollably in her dressing room when the half hour was called and invariably rush to the toilet and vomit. Cold and hot sweats would follow and at times her head would spin so much she imagined she would faint dead away. Her terror knew no bounds and she was convinced at times her wretchedness would completely swamp her. Usually at the last minute she would summon up all her reserves of strength and, composing herself, walk from the dressing room to the stage desperate that no one would realise how she was really feeling. Once in the wings she would focus her mind and literally at times will herself to take that first step. Agony as it was, exacerbated by the voice in her head telling her to turn and run, she would breathe deeply and walk on stage. Once on stage she became a different person and would sometimes think she could see that wretched girl she had left behind in the wings watching her on stage and marvelling at her confidence.

On a couple of occasions the fear and panic had overridden everything and she was rooted to the spot in her dressing room like a terrified wild animal looking into the barrel of a gun. She would vomit so violently that her body became exhausted and as a result she was unable to walk out of her dressing room. Her understudy was notified and Elsie was able to recover some of her composure before being taken home. Her mother was worried and chastised Elsie for eating so much prior to a performance: she felt this did not help and was perhaps the cause of the vomiting attacks.

Gertie too was worried about Elsie and, after discussing it with her husband Lionel Monckton, decided to confront her friend and attempt to help in any way she could. She had heard reports about her erratic behaviour back stage, and had noticed how frail Elsie looked at times. She wondered if her nervous bouts were because of overwork. She might even confide in Edwardes and see if he would allow Elsie a short holiday to recuperate. In the meantime she would try and keep a close eye on her and broach the subject next time they had afternoon tea together. On reflection, she decided that maybe it would also be worth having a chat with Elsie's mother before she mentioned anything to Edwardes. Lottie might be able to shed a little more light on the situation.

Edwardes had decided to arrange for Elsie to have a few days off from *See See* but not to allow her any kind of holiday. Still unaware of her anxiety attacks he informed her they would be taking a trip to Berlin to see a production of *The Merry Widow*. Elsie happily agreed as it would allow her a few days to relax and hopefully build her strength both physical and mental. But she was also intrigued by the stories Edwardes had told her about the production. She had never seen him so enthusiastic about anything and it crossed her mind that maybe he had plans for her with regard to this show. However, the role of a widow was not one she immediately supposed would be suitable for her. She was only twenty years old and far too young to play any kind of widow, or so she thought. Edwardes was more likely interested in her opinion and some company for the journey.

Lottie was relieved that Elsie had been given some time off from *See See* and hoped her trip to Berlin with Edwardes would allow her to recuperate sufficiently to enable her to resume her role in the production in a more positive state of mind. Her angry and tearful outbursts had worried her deeply. There was only so much she could hide from the other cast members and Lottie feared that Elsie's increasingly neurotic behaviour would start to be damaging to her career. Now that she had resolved things with Edwardes the last thing she wanted was for Elsie to undermine that important relationship by losing her nerve completely. Gertie had even broached the subject of Elsie's behaviour, but she had managed to reassure her that everything was well and that she shouldn't worry. She wasn't convinced that Gertie had wholeheartedly believed her, but felt she had defused what could potentially be a difficult situation.

In the last few months Lottie had done her utmost to present herself as rational and in control. She still fought her demons but had found that mostly she could control and disguise her own problems for the greater good of her daughter. She still had moments when she was convinced someone was following her or watching her, that Bert Hodder would leap out of the shadows one day and confront her. She shook off such thoughts as quickly as they entered her mind; it was the only way to stay in control of her nerves. If he ever did, she had decided she would deny everything. It would be his word against hers. Edwardes would protect Elsie's reputation and well-being if it came to it, she was too valuable a commodity to him. The last thing she wanted was for Elsie to now fall apart when things were going so well.

The trip to Germany had been an enjoyable one for Elsie. Edwardes had taken her to see an operetta by *Lehar* called *The Merry Widow*, which she had enjoyed very much in spite of her complete lack of German preventing her from fully understanding the plot. The love story between *Sonia* and *Prince Danilo* had been at its heart and was easily understood. Elsie had been very impressed with the soprano *Mizzi Gunther*, although the gusto with which she sang could at times be distracting. Edwardes had shocked her by asking her to play *Sonia* in his planned London production of *The Merry Widow* Her reply was instant and sincere: "I couldn't possibly!" Edwardes said no more about it other than asking her to think it over. As far as Elsie was concerned there was nothing to think about. She would never be able to sing the role of *Sonia* as it needed a trained opera voice and hers was far from that. Neither was she old enough or alluring enough to play the widow. The journey home gave her time to think and take stock of her life and career. The supreme irony was the countless questions and comments by girls of a similar age who all wanted desperately to be on the stage—she was genuinely baffled by their desire to emulate her—but they knew nothing of the sickness and terror she suffered. It struck her as odd that she had what they desired, but she had never wanted it as ardently as them. Maybe this life on the stage was her destiny? All they could see was what they perceived to be the glamour and excitement, but in reality there was precious little of either. "Is it easy to get on the stage" she would be asked countless times. Maybe it was, Elsie thought, but it was so much harder to stay on it—and she was convinced that attempting to play *Sonia* in Edwardes production of *The Merry Widow* would facilitate a speedy exit off it!

A Reluctant Widow & Her Prince.

"Oh, no, It couldn't possibly be for me—they must be applauding the costumes!"
ELSIE'S REPLY TO A FELLOW CAST MEMBER ON THE FIRST
NIGHT OF *THE MERRY WIDOW*

Edwardes was pondering the prospect of staging his production of *The Merry Widow* and as he gazed from his office window across Leicester Square he decided it had to be a *Daly's* show. If it worked it would help him establish a genre at the theatre which would hopefully prove as successful, and profitable, as the shows he'd similarly established at the *Gaiety*. He had serious reservations about *The Merry Widow's* chances of success but for now he would keep any doubts he had to himself and had set his team to work to produce an adaptation suitable for a London audience. In the meantime he had other concerns. Financially, he was in a tight spot. Although productions like *See See* had been artistically successful— especially for Elsie and her career—they had not been profitable at the box office. Worse, having to pull Elsie out of the show and substitute an understudy meant an immediate drop in revenue. The result as far as Edwardes could see was another 'nitter', as he chose to call those productions that failed to make money.

He'd pulled Elsie out of *See See* because Gertie had been taken ill and had to be replaced in the *Gaiety's* 1906 Christmas show *The New Aladdin*. Lionel Monckton, Gertie's husband, had suggested Elsie as her temporary replacement. Gertie's health scare had concerned everyone but it seemed she didn't have appendicitis after all just a complaint of the stomach specific to women. But it would mean she would be unable to perform for several weeks at the very least. Monckton, who was composing most of the music for the show, felt that Elsie would be able to handle the songs even though they were written for Gertie's more forthright burlesque style. Elsie, herself a little unsure of the songs, had agreed to play the title role of *Laly* in the show in spite of her reservations as to her abilities as a convincing principal boy! However, she was relieved to be released from *See See* and the strain of nightly performances which had resulted in a reoccurrence of her stage fright. In spite of everyone trying to keep him ignorant of Elsie's stage fright, and her missed performances, he was fully aware of the problem and decided not to add pressure on Elsie by making a scene. He admitted to himself that Elsie was the only artist he would accept this kind of problem from simply because she was so unique and so special and audiences were slowly falling in love with her too. He reasoned that if she didn't have such overwhelming self-doubt and anxiety perhaps she would not be so unique and captivating. Placing her in rehearsals for *The New Aladdin* meant she could relax and concentrate on a new role before the show opened in late September.

Edwardes had decided long ago that he knew what his artistes were capable of doing, as opposed to his artistes who only knew what they wanted to do. His greatest challenge in this area was to convince a young American comic actor who had made a name for himself in several London productions that he would be an ideal *Prince Danilo* in *The Merry Widow*. Joseph Coyne, Joe to his friends, was not an actor who would ever spring to mind as a conventional, handsome leading man, but Edwardes had a hunch that he would be ideal. Sometimes he didn't even know himself why he was so convinced about a performer playing a particular role; what he did know is that invariably he was proved right. There was also another rather small matter—Joseph Coyne couldn't sing. In the German original *Prince Danilo* is an operatic tenor and therefore has several songs within the show. It occurred to him that Lehar might not share his enthusiasm for a non-singing *Prince Danilo*, but Edwardes decided he would worry about that later. First he had to convince Coyne to take the part and second he would have to convince Elsie to play the widow. Although she had refused to consider it he knew she was perfect for the part. He had decided not to argue the point with her during their trip to Berlin, reasoning he could work on her once they were back in England. That said, he did decide to consider other actresses for the part as a way of keeping his options open and also to be able to provide a suitable understudy for Elsie when he did convince her to take it. He would worry about Elsie later, Coyne was his initial focus of attention.

He was also under pressure from Boosey and some of his creative staff who all shared the opinion that he was mad to consider Elsie for the role of the widow. So strong was their objection to her possible casting he had even received a letter from Boosey pleading with him to reconsider. They all shared the opinion that Elsie was too young and had insufficient abilities vocally to do full justice to the songs. This had even resulted in a confrontation with Boosey and the rest of the board of directors of the *Gaiety* who had sanctioned the purchasing of the rights of *The Merry Widow* with money from the *Gaiety Theatre's* funds. They intimated that they would prefer to see perhaps Gertie in the lead role and the production staged at the *Gaiety* and not *Daly's*. Edwardes stood his ground and insisted it was either done his way or not at all. When he then informed the board that he wanted Joseph Coyne for the role of *Prince Danilo*, they were dumb struck. To a man they threw their hands in the air in exasperation, shrugged their collective shoulders, and decided that Edwardes had indeed lost his mind. They decided to leave him to his folly, but insisted he find the money to repay the *Gaiety's* accounts for the money used to purchase the rights. Edwardes agreed, deciding to worry where this money was coming from later. He could call in some favours.

Within days he had broached the subject with Coyne, who had just celebrated his fortieth birthday enveloped in his usual gloom. He promptly turned him down flat. Coyne didn't hold back his opinion and was quite direct in his thoughts regarding the story, the characters and what he considered to be a dreadful and depressing title for the show. He couldn't imagine anyone "wanting to see a show about a widow, merry or otherwise" and predicted it would be a disaster where he would be laughed off the stage. Besides which he couldn't sing a note! Coyne was an eccentric and rather dour soul who always saw his glass as half empty. He could often be seen standing on a street corner in Covent Garden having a heated discussion with an unseen companion, or walking along the Strand having similar conversations with unseen friends. On stage he was a master of comedy and his eccentric behaviour had yet to become damaging to his personality or career. Edwardes was determined to have him and decided to play a little dirty. Coyne was under contract to the *Aldwych Theatre* and as Edwardes had his finger in many pies he was able to pull in a few more favours to get what he wanted. Before Coyne knew what had happened his bosses at the *Aldwych* informed him they had "contracted him out" to Edwardes "for the run of *The Merry Widow*". Edwardes had to offer a small percentage of the profits to Coyne's management but considered it well worth it. Coyne was enraged at the entrapment but accepted there was little he could do about it. He rather gloomily resigned himself to playing *Prince Danilo* in *The Merry Widow*; no doubt venting his frustration and the injustice of it all on his real and unseen friends!

Elsie was busy at rehearsals for *The New Aladdin* oblivious to the fact that Edwardes was playing games with her. He hadn't mentioned *The Merry Widow* since they returned from Berlin which baffled her a little as she was convinced he would attempt to persuade her to accept the part. Instead she had heard through whispers and gossip he was looking at other actresses to play the part including her friend Gabrielle Ray! Although Elsie had turned him down when he offered the part, he was unaware, or so she thought, that in fact she would love to play the widow but just didn't think she could manage the singing. The song *Vilja* terrified her because she really believed she did not have the technique to sing such a difficult operatic aria; in general she also felt her voice would be too weak for such a demanding score. Her age also worried her because one almost always associated a widow as being of more mature years and this widow needed to be alluring and considered attractive enough for men to fight over. Try as she might she could not imagine how any man would want to fight over her—widow or not! If she were honest, she was a little hurt that Edwardes had given up on her so readily, but reasoned that perhaps Gabrielle would be a better choice anyway.

Caught up in the demands of rehearsing for *The New Aladdin* she had little time to worry or wonder if she had slipped from Edwardes favour. She was finding the style of the show very difficult because it had so obviously been written with Gertie's inimitable style of performing in mind. Burlesque was definitely not her forte and she was struggling. Monckton reassured her that all would be well but she had her doubts. At one point she became so low with melancholy and fear she considered pleading with Edwardes to release her. However, that little voice in her head kept reassuring her during the darkest and most frustrating moments and she soldiered on. The boys and girls in the cast also jollied her along and this as much as anything kept her spirits up. Since Gertie's illness she had made a point of calling to see her every few days to offer her support and to help facilitate a speedy recovery. Elsie was sincere in this wish for her friend but sometimes felt a little guilty because her wish was more to do with her fears of stepping into Gertie's shoes, shoes that she wanted to give her back as soon as possible! Gertie as ever sensed her insecurity and made sure Elsie received appropriate encouragement—especially from her husband.

Standing high up in the fly gallery during rehearsals for *The New Aladdin* Bert could never get a really good look at Elsie. He had to be careful not to make his interest in her too obvious to those around him. It had taken him months of trying but he had finally been taken on by Edwardes' stage manager and given a permanent position. He would have to be flexible in his working hours and be prepared to work at either the *Gaiety* or *Daly's Theatre*. That was fine by him, it was not like he had any reason to rush home to his lodging room. He had seen Elsie before and wondered what might have been had things worked out differently all those years ago, and if indeed she was his daughter. He had seen her performing at the old *Royal Strand Theatre* and the *Prince of Wales* but he had always been up in the gods—the only seat he could afford—and he hadn't been able to get a good look at her. It wasn't much better up in the flys but at least from here he could see she was a pretty lass. Lottie was still on the scene and acting very grand and imperious—always had airs and graces that one—you'd think she'd never seen poverty and the streets of Salford. That night he'd caught her eye in the theatre and he saw the colour drain from her face when she recognised him. He hadn't wanted a scene, so he just left. He didn't know what he wanted if the truth were known. He'd been captivated since he realised that "Little Elsie" was the bairn born in that squalid room he shared with Lottie in Leeds. He winced at the memory because it always brought back another one: the night he was nearly beaten to death by Billy Cotton. He still suffered aches and pains as a result of that and they got worse as the years slipped by. He wasn't as young as he was and this job was beginning to tell on him, only so many ropes weighted with heavy scenery a man can haul up in his lifetime. Maybe it was time he considered a bit of security for his old age. Maybe Elsie could be useful to him after all. For now he was happy to watch from a distance and consider his options.

The New Aladdin opened at the *Gaiety Theatre* on 30th September 1906 to a fairly positive press. Elsie however felt uncomfortable playing a principal boy and the material was too burlesque for her qualities. She knew it, the press knew it, and so did the audiences. She did her best under difficult circumstances and managed to keep going for the first four weeks until Gertie's welcome return. Elsie had no regrets and because of the difficulties she encountered during this production managed to learn how to control her stage fright. She had been determined not to let anyone down, including Gertie and Edwardes, and something had given her a strength of sorts to ensure that didn't happen. She was the first to admit that she was no replacement for the unique talents of Gertie Millar. Watching her performance from the stalls on her first night was a terrific experience and Elsie could see so clearly how the dialogue and the songs had been tailored to fit Gertie. Everything fell into place and the show had the makings of a success—Elsie felt a sense of pride that she had managed to hold the fort for her friend, especially as she had done so much for her in the past.

Elsie had a pretty good idea what was coming when Edwardes asked her to join him for afternoon tea at *Ellen's* in Leicester Square. She braced herself for a dressing down due to the fact she had been so relieved to relinquish the part of *Laly* in *The New Aladdin* to its rightful owner. Perhaps she should have demonstrated at least a little disappointment at handing the role over to Gertie, but it went against her nature to be insincere. She knew only too well how much faith Edwardes had in her and her abilities and she did try her hardest to live up to them. Sometimes she felt he had perhaps a little too much faith in her. To her astonishment Edwardes staggered her with an announcement that she could never have anticipated. Since he had asked her to consider the role of *Sonia* in *The Merry Widow*, and she had turned it down, he had tried his utmost to find another actress capable of playing the part—all to no avail he informed her. Try as he might, he just couldn't find anyone nearly as suitable as her. He wanted her to reconsider taking on the role of *Sonia* as a personal favour to him. If she agreed he would make sure she had a suitable understudy from the outset, he had Gabrielle Ray in mind, and he would make sure she had all the help and support she needed. Elsie was quick to reiterate her initial reasons for declining the role: she felt she was too young to play Sonia; her physical appearance was slight and, she felt, inappropriate; most importantly the role required an experienced opera singer and she was certain her voice was too thin for the role. Lastly she voiced her fear of *Sonia's* aria *Vilja* in the score: it terrified her. Edwardes reassured her and pleaded with her to trust him and at least try. In the end she gave way and said she would play *Sonia* and do her best. It was the very least she could do under the circumstances—she was genuinely touched at the belief Edwardes had in her and her abilities and she had to admit it gave her confidence. Secretly she was also delighted because she had been attracted to the role and a part of her wanted to accept at the outset but her insecurities had held her back. She was afraid still, but it now presented itself as a challenge to be met head on rather than running away from it.

Lottie shrieked with delight when Elsie returned home and told her the result of her meeting with Edwardes. She had urged Elsie to accept the part of *Sonia* from the outset and had been furious when Elsie told her she had turned it down. Lottie admonished Elsie for being a fool and told her in no uncertain terms she would be lucky to get opportunities like that presenting themselves on a regular basis—if ever! Now she had secured the role Lottie would make it her business to ensure Elsie was not distracted or discouraged by anyone or anything. And of course she would be there to support her daughter in whatever way possible.

Elsie appreciated her mother's enthusiasm but, as ever, she felt her career served more to satisfy her needs than her own. But as long as Lottie was happy, then she too was happy. Life was altogether easier for both of them when her mother was at peace with the world.

Edwardes was feeling rather pleased with himself at the result of the meeting with Elsie. He had been determined to cast her as *Sonia* in spite of all the negative comments as to her abilities and his sanity. Much the same had been the case regarding Joe Coyne, but he too was secured for the role of *Prince Danilo*. He couldn't remember the last time he had had to call in so many favours to get what he wanted—as a result he had Coyne and had raised the money, mainly as a result of luck due to backing some winning horses, to pay back that borrowed to purchase the rights of *The Merry Widow* from the *Gaiety's* account. At least he could now proceed with the production and make it a *Daly's* show. As he sat and reflected on the moment he knew that so much more was riding on this show than anyone imagined.

His cash reserves were still almost non existent and he would have to use every trick in the book to make sure *The Merry Widow* didn't suffer in terms of production values—no expense would be spared on sets, costumes and properties. He knew that *The Merry Widow* could be his last West End production—if it turned out to be a nitter, he would be finished and bankrupt. He shuddered at the thought and swirled the whisky round his glass, then drank it back in one. Instantly revived, his determination and enthusiasm to the fore once more, he began drafting a letter to Lehar asking him to be available for rehearsals early in the new year with an opening date set for June 1907.

Elsie was alarmed at the speed with which the first rehearsal day for *The Merry Widow* was approaching. She felt rested and excited but still terrified at the prospect—more terrified still of meeting the composer Lehar. She had been busy with photographic sittings for the popular post cards and was rather pleased with herself for the new contract Lottie had negotiated on her behalf which had raised her annual income from £100 to £300. This raise a result of increased sales of her image on post cards since *See See* and *The New Aladdin*. Elsie then discovered that most of her friends had been receiving £300 per-year for the last two years at least! With good humour she accepted that she, along with her mother, had little understanding of business matters.

Bert Hodder had heard the gossip about the new show Edwardes was planning for *Daly's* with Elsie as the leading lady. He had been tempted to put himself forward to work on *The Merry Widow* at *Daly's* but decided it might seem odd. He kept his mouth shut and then found himself being asked by the stage manager if he would move to *Daly's* from the *Gaiety* as the Guv'nor needed an experienced man to take charge of the fly gallery as the technical requirements were complicated. That is how he came face to face with Elsie for the first time. He was turning the winch that lowered the huge safety curtain and it was hard work for one man but he managed. As the huge safety curtain finally hit the stage with a clunk, she walked onto the stage from the wing and smiled at him as she passed with Edwardes. It wasn't a smile of recognition, just one of politeness. He managed to climb back up to the fly gallery before Lottie appeared and sat in the wing beneath him. By that time the company and the composer had assembled on the stage and Edwardes made a speech about how delighted he was and that he was sure it was going to be a great success. Bert wasn't that interested, his gaze was fixed on Elsie. She fascinated him.

Privately Edwardes thought *The Merry Widow* was going to struggle because he didn't have the money to spend on it, also because of a run of back luck with his turf accountant—horses he'd backed recently had all limped home last! For the first time he could remember he had instructed that old scenery must be utilised wherever possible; although he still demanded that it be refurbished and made to look new. He had every confidence in Joseph Harker his experienced scenic artist to do his usual magic. Lucille, Lady Duff Gordon, had been contracted to make some of the principal costumes, but most would be hand made by Daly's own wardrobe mistress Mrs. Field. With luck it would all work out and no one in the audience would ever notice the second hand elements. If nothing else he had impeccable taste and an ability to achieve the impossible, or so he reassured himself. His belief in Elsie and Coyne spurred him on. Neither were West End stars in the true sense, but he hoped they would be after the first night. He would never voice these thoughts to those assembled at today's first read through—it was all in the hands of fate. Glancing round at his assembled cast he could see the terror in Elsie's eyes and the dour expression on the face of Coyne. Lehar sat rather nervously with his German librettists and no doubt wondered what travesties had befallen their masterpiece during its English translation. The rest of the cast included Elizabeth Frith, Irene Desmond, Kate Welch, Gabrielle Ray, Fred Kaye, Gordon Cleather, George Graves and WH Berry. The girls from Maxim's were Daisy Irving, Ada Fraser, Dolly Dombey, Amy Webster, Mabel Munro, Gertrude Lester Mabel Russell and Phyllis Le Grand. Edwardes knew them all and had participated in their successful careers—indeed he had given some of them their start and their first role in previous West End productions. He had assembled the best he could and hoped it would be enough. His Stage Director was the faithful Jim Malone and his chosen Musical Director, Harold Vicars, with dance arrangements to be choreographed by Fred Farren. If *The Merry Widow* turned out to be another nitter, it wouldn't be for the want of trying, but it would certainly be his last!

Rehearsals got off to a rather gloomy start with everyone's nerves seeming to jangle the very atmosphere of *Daly's*. Elsie was behaving like a petrified child and Coyne would wander off cursing to some imaginary friend at the frightfulness of it all. He made no bones about the fact he hated the show, hated the story and most of all loathed his part. He was not a singer and could not sing the songs as written by Lehar. He wanted out, Edwardes was equally determined he would stay in. Coyne's dour and negative attitude affected everyone and it took all Edwardes diplomatic skills to keep things at least moving forward. Coyne's mood had made Elsie even more fearful and she again pleaded with him to allow someone else to sing the song *Vilja*. He refused the request by stating again that it was vital to the plot that Sonia sing that particular number. In floods of tears and frustration Elsie at least had George Graves to comfort and support her. Graves had astonished Elsie by telling her he had seen her first ever performance as *Little Elsie* at the *Prince of Wales Theatre* in Salford all those years ago, that he had been a friend of her father and had been instrumental in persuading him to allow her on stage. The fact he had known her father brightened Elsie's mood and reassured her; they formed a firm friendship and supported each other through the trials and tribulations of the rehearsals. Lehar and his associates would mingle and smile whilst not really understanding what was being said. Edwardes thanked God for small mercies and that their English was limited.

Edwardes had known all along that Coyne couldn't sing the part as written by Lehar but had been so convinced that only he could play *Prince Danilo* had decided he could recite the songs instead. Unfortunately he had conveniently put off telling Lehar about this dramatic change and had hoped it would just work itself out. He was sure that when Lehar saw Coyne he would see how good he was going to be as *Prince Danilo* and not worry about the singing. As it had turned out Lehar didn't think much of Coyne and they were uneasy around each other, Edwardes chided himself for being so stupid; now he would have to attend every rehearsal to try and placate the friction between them. To make matters worse Lehar was already upset that he could only have a 28-piece orchestra when he wanted 34. He demanded the latter as it was the only way his score would truly come to life. Edwardes pleaded space in the orchestra pit as the reason for only 28 but it was more to do with cost than anything else. He even arranged for 34 musicians to sit in the pit to demonstrate how cramped it was. For now Lehar was having none of it, it was thirty-four or he went home to Vienna with his score! Off he would storm with his librettists all exiting with perfect military precision out of the theatre and back to their hotel.

Eventually tempers would cool, equilibrium be restored, and everyone would get on with the job at hand. Once the rehearsals had reached a stage where each act could be run through on the stage Edwardes would sit at the back of the stalls to watch the proceedings. It came to a point where Lehar would naturally expect Coyne to sing but Edwardes would shout: "Don't sing it, Joe, just recite it!", explaining to a bemused Lehar that he had a sore throat and needed to save his voice. So often did this occur that it became a standing joke among the cast who could also be heard off saying "don't sing it Joe!" to everyone's amusement but Lehar's. His frustration stemmed from his need for perfection and he wanted to help Coyne with his vocal performance. Coyne was happy to oblige and said nothing in the hope that maybe when Lehar realised he couldn't sing he would be replaced in the role he still loathed with a passion. He could see the tension between Edwardes and Lehar building and expected it would explode at any time.

Elsie had absorbed herself in the experience of rehearsing and found herself genuinely enjoying working opposite Coyne. He could be very glum and miserable but once they were rehearsing scenes his persona changed and he was professional and always word perfect. She couldn't imagine she could be that professional if she hated the part she was playing as much as Coyne professed to hate his. In an odd way the fact he had such an attitude about the role of *Prince Danilo* added to the power of his performance. The character of *Danilo* is no sentimental matinee idol but rather the opposite: he is curt, even rude, to *Sonia* and something of an anti-hero. In the end, of course, his love for *Sonia* is revealed, his earlier boorish behaviour merely a way of protecting himself from possible rejection by her. In Coyne's reluctant hands the character took on a realism that was relatively unusual in musical comedies of the time—certainly none that Elsie could bring to mind. *Sonia* too is a complex and reticent character who hides her true feelings from the world, equally intent on protecting herself from rejection and manipulation. The wealth she has inherited from her late husband makes her powerful but, in a male dominated society, she is aware of her own vulnerability and has no intention of falling for any suitor who may be interested in her purely for her money. The English translation succeeded in bringing to the fore the depth of these characters whilst keeping intact the comedic aspects of the book; the court intrigues amongst the other characters raised the laughs but Edwardes ensured that they were secondary to the romance between *Sonia* and *Danilo*.

As her confidence grew she even began to see the possibility that the aria *Vilja*, which she dreaded so much, would perhaps not be beyond her abilities after all. Lehar was kind and helpful and spent many hours rehearsing with her until they had perfected the musical numbers. It was obvious to Elsie that he was deeply in love with his score and wanted it to be the best it could be. He would always be polite and reassuring in spite of the language barrier between them and eventually they developed their own form of communication which sufficed. He was very German in his bearing and manner and would make her giggle every time he kissed her hand and clicked his heels on meeting or departing. Although she didn't voice her concern to Lehar directly, she had spoken to Edwardes about Coyne's inability to sing a note and wondered whether it was time to share this with Lehar. Edwardes said he would but he never did. She was even starting to worry about what might happen when it all came out.

Edwardes in the end managed to pull off the impossible regarding Coyne's inability to sing the role as written by Lehar. Coyne had done much to smooth the way because as rehearsals had progressed he had mastered the art of reciting the lyrics perfectly in time with the music. As his confidence grew he began to layer his recitations with feelings and emotions. Coyne was also excellent working with Elsie, whom Lehar adored, and she in turn seemed to bring all her best qualities to the role of *Sonia*. The fact she seemed slightly frail and winsome added to the power of her performance, she could be feisty and forthright when the story demanded it and she had mastered those difficult songs with seeming ease. The true power of their performances was being able to believe they were actually in love by the end of the third act—all aided superbly by the lilting waltzes and masterful score by Lehar. Edwardes was beginning to feel that maybe *The Merry Widow* wouldn't be a nitter after all. The dress rehearsal made him think again.

Throughout the weeks of rehearsal he had deliberately misled Lehar about Coyne but as the dress rehearsal was about to start Lehar was insistent that Coyne sing. Edwardes tried to be crafty by asking Lehar if he thought perhaps it would be better if Coyne continued to recite his lyrics because he was doing it so well—why change it now? Lehar was adamant that he had written the role for a tenor to sing. Edwardes had no choice but to tell Lehar the truth. Understandably he was furious but found himself in an impossible situation. He could storm out and take his score and the show would be cancelled or he could accept this man Coyne reciting the lyrics and go ahead. Fortunately for Edwardes he chose the latter course of action. The cast were visibly relieved too because they had all worked so hard. The dress rehearsal went ahead with Coyne reciting the lyrics as he had rehearsed.

Lehar had finally had to accept a reduced orchestra which he was also unhappy about, although most of his fears had been allayed when he heard the sound produced by *Daly's* orchestra. He was conducting for the performances so he worked them hard to create his idea of perfection for his score.

The knockers in the profession had a field day with all the gossip and intrigue they passed around about the terrible rows and problems Edwardes was having with *The Merry Widow*. Many delighted in saying it was his own fault for casting inexperienced artistes like Elsie and

Coyne in leading roles. They had little sympathy for Edwardes, feeling he had brought it all on himself. There were also rumours as to the state of his financial situation, word was circulating that there were unpaid bills to scenic artistes, tradesmen—and even the dance captain still hadn't been paid! All the gossip, malicious and otherwise, had elements of truth to it. There were those who would delight in seeing Edwardes brought down to earth with a thud. As far as Edwardes was concerned, if he was going out, he'd go out with a bang. *The Merry Widow* and its potential success was his last chance.

Elsie's main worry for the dress rehearsal was the hats! On several occasions Gertie had helped Elsie to practice walking whilst balancing these huge creations. At first they seemed to have a mind of their own, tilting this way and that so that Elsie felt she could bear the weight no longer and she and Gertie would roar with laughter at the silliness of it all until eventually she learned to control the recalcitrant hats. Lucille had insisted that they must be large and decorative enough to make an impact even from the gallery, but Elsie feared that they would merely look ridiculous. Gertie, however, declared they were perfect for a shopping trip to Bond Street as they would clear the pavement of other shoppers in a flash! The equally elaborate dresses and heavy costume jewellery added to the crowning glory of a ten-tonne hat had Elsie wondering how she was ever going to move at all, let alone walk gracefully, but after much practice and even more laughter she finally mastered the art and managed to create the illusion of gliding around the stage as if her costume weighed nothing at all. She was still concerned about descending the stairs on set without falling flat on her face, but decided she would face that problem when she came to it.

Gertie watched the dress rehearsal from the back of the stalls and found herself mesmerised by the music and the story as it unfolded; in spite of the predictable technical hitches. She could honestly say she had never seen or heard anything like it. When Elsie made her first entrance down the staircase of the Embassy in full costume and with that enormous hat she took her breath away. She looked incredible and her voice soared through the empty auditorium. Gertie knew then that this show was going to change Elsie's life forever; indeed she also knew that Elsie would probably eclipse her star status in the West End. Gertie decided that *The Merry Widow* had been waiting for Elsie to come along.

Everything she possessed in terms of talent and all her unique qualities and insecurities were serviced by this show—it was Elsie at her best. She was *Sonia*. Coyne was *Prince Danilo*. Gertie found herself so lost in the story she forgot she was watching her friend performing, something she had never experienced before. It also occurred to her that the music was invisibly woven into the story which heightened the power of both. Once you heard those melodies and experienced that story you could never forget them. As she watched *Sonia* and *Danilo* reprise that slow romantic waltz, now as the reunited lovers, she had tears in her eyes. The curtain slowly fell, the spell was broken, and the dress rehearsal was over. For the first time she could remember she was genuinely lost for words. She looked at Edwardes and was astonished to see tears in his eyes.

The following morning Edwardes had a pounding headache. He'd spent a sleepless night going over and over every detail, anticipating everything he thought might go wrong; wondering if Lehar would turn up at all after he'd deceived him over Coyne; would Elsie succumb to stage fright and be unable to go on? It was all too much for him he decided, perhaps he was beginning to feel his age. He had done everything he could to make *The Merry Widow* a success, now it was up to the press and public who would give their verdict after tonight's first night performance. After instructing the front of house manager to make sure the theatre was spotless for that night, he decided to go home and relax and return later that afternoon for the busy night ahead.

Elsie arrived at the theatre early, as was her usual habit on first nights, and spent some time sitting in the empty auditorium. She had surprised even herself during preparations for this show and her instinct told her *The Merry Widow* would be a success for Edwardes. She had heard the rumours regarding his precarious financial position, that he owed money to several of the creative team who had turned a blind eye because they had so much respect for him. She too would happily forego payment of her salary if it would help Edwardes: without his belief in her and his unfailing support she would not be about to perform a leading role in the West End for the first time. She, and others, had much to thank him for. The gossips in the profession could be cruel and vindictive and she had no time for them. Jealousy was such a negative and destructive force, a force that could destroy those with exceptional talent.

Joe Coyne had turned out to also be a revelation to her in spite of his glumness and miserable persona. At first she had found him physically draining to be with as he seemed to suck all the positive energy away from her; as she struggled to feel confident all the time it was the last thing she needed. The longer they worked together the more she liked him and realised his dour and eccentric behaviour was born out of his own insecurities and fears. He was honest enough to say he disliked the show and his character and worried he would be laughed off the stage on opening night, but she knew that wouldn't happen. When they were on that stage they became *Sonia* and *Danilo*—he had made that happen more than her. She felt safe whilst on stage with him, he was such a giving performer and as a result many of her old anxieties had evaporated. As she moved through the pass door to the back stage area to prepare for the show she was determined to enjoy the experience of being *Sonia* in *The Merry Widow*.

The atmosphere was electric with anticipation as the first night audience began to arrive at *Daly's*, filling the bars and auditorium with excited chatter. Lehar was standing nervously by the pass door and wondering what this London audience would make of his widow. He had spent the morning rehearsing over and over with the orchestra to get things just right and they worked hard for him, never once complaining even though it meant they only had a couple of hours break before their call for the evening performance. He had been amazed at the throng of people queuing for the gallery and pit seats, so many more than could ever have been accommodated. His fears about a non-singing *Danilo* had dissolved when he had seen Coyne's performance at the dress rehearsal, but he regretted that Edwardes hadn't been honest with him earlier. However, he bore no grudge because he recognised that Edwardes had put together an outstanding production of his Widow, using all his experience in casting the show and lavishing both money and attention on the details of sets and costumes. Adjusting his white tie and putting on his tailcoat Lehar glanced quickly at himself in the mirror to check he looked his best. He could hear the orchestra tuning up and the excited chatter of the audience. Taking a quick glance into the auditorium he could see the elegantly dressed women with their jewels sparkling; the men in their white tie and tails, some in military uniform providing a bright splash of red here and there. The stage manager asked him to set himself—moving quickly to the orchestra pit entrance under the stage, he stood and waited nervously.

Lottie sat in a stage box with Edwardes and could feel the excitement in the air. The crimson and gold of the auditorium seemed to pulse with anticipation, the deeply polished mahogany skirt which enclosed the orchestra pit reflected a thousand glimmers of light which bounced off the chandeliers. The excited chatter intensified as the orchestra began tuning their instruments. She waved to Gertie Millar and her husband Lionel, Marie Lloyd, Phyllis Dare, Zena Dare, Beatrice Edwardes and Gabrielle Ray, all here to support Elsie. Lottie was willing the house lights to fade in case she fainted with excitement and anticipation. Bert Hodder watched Elsie standing back stage talking to Coyne. They both seemed relaxed. He had been mesmerised watching Elsie during rehearsals and was genuinely excited for her this evening. He had managed to keep out of sight when Lottie had been around. When you are a fly man, you tend to get lost in the shadows so it wasn't too hard. He instructed his crew of five fly men to stand by—they had a busy night ahead.

As the house lights faded there was a ripple of anticipation running through the audience, the gallery first nighters cheered from their place way up in the gods. Those who had left it until the last minute rushed to claim their seats. Lehar entered from the back of the orchestra and stood looking at the audience as a lime light illuminated him. The audience applauded and he turned and held up his baton—after a moment the orchestra began and the curtain slowly began to rise for the first time on the London production of *The Merry Widow*.

By the time the curtain descended at the end of act three the audience was roaring its approval. Elsie and Coyne had to reprise that slow waltz again and again. Curtain call after curtain call was demanded by the audience who had fallen in love with Elsie as the widow and Lehar's magical waltz music. The audience had thundered their approval for them all but the loudest cheers were for Elsie—as she stood in the wings she was unable to believe the cheers and shouts were for her—she thought they must be cheering the sets and costumes. Coyne, ever glum, couldn't understand what all the fuss was about—he'd hated everything about it and retired to the public house opposite the stage door to drown his sorrows. Neither knew it, but their lives would never be the same again.

Mrs Bullough.

"A new play was launched with a new actress, who set the whole town raving over her beauty and a waltz that set the whole world dancing to its fascinating lilt."
LUCILE (LADY DUFF GORDON) ON ELSIE AND *THE MERRY WIDOW* 1907

"*T*he Merry Widow last night consolidated reputations and at the topmost, dizziest peak of this mountain of success stood two people," it's by a young critic called Walter McQueen-Pope, for the *London Evening News*, Lottie said as she continued to read out loud the review to her daughter, "Lily Elsie and Joseph Coyne, almost unknown in London prior to the first night, but now taken to the hearts of the British playgoing public and enshrined there for life—with memories to endure as long as anyone lives who saw them. Their first night was indeed remarkable. The applause went across the foot lights like a prairie fire, accompanied by roars of cheers, warm and glowing with pleasure and affection, such cheers as are seldom heard by players, such cheers, such feeling as a few only encounter once in a lifetime—and the majority never know at all. Such applause is the most intoxicating drink, the headiest stuff of all acclamation and it can only be heard in a theatre."

Lottie put down one newspaper only to pick up another—the *Times*—and began to read out loud: "The men in evening dress cheered and beat their hands together until they were sore; the women quivered and cheered shrilly, and as for the pit and gallery they went quite mad. *Danilo* and *Sonia* had to dance *The Merry Widow* waltz again and again . . ." At this point Elsie silenced her mother, she didn't want to hear anymore.

Elsie was genuinely amazed at the reaction to *The Merry Widow* and her performance in particular. She still could not believe that she deserved such praise. It was also hard to grasp the reality of her newly acquired celebrity status and even Gertie had delighted in telling her she was relieved to be way behind her in the popularity stakes. This was hard to fathom as Elsie had always looked up to Gertie and considered she would be lucky indeed if she could be only half as popular as her friend. But overnight it would seem that the only name uttered by the populace, and the name written about in countless magazines and newspapers, was her own. She had found herself so terrified at being a failure as *Sonia*, as so many had predicted, that she couldn't bring herself to read any of the notices—and still hadn't! She began to find walking along the street or going shopping a great chore because everybody recognised her and wanted to talk about her success. She found these encounters embarrassing at first but then she would become aware of people staring intently at her and feel panic rising up and overwhelming her. The whole situation was beginning to cause her great anxiety and she found herself feeling trapped at home and only leaving the safety of her flat to travel to *Daly's* for the evening performance. Her mother was riding high on her daughter's success and seemed oblivious to Elsie's increasing solitude and unhappiness. Lottie couldn't imagine that with so much success and the whole of London at her feet her daughter could not be enjoying the attention. She had become utterly self absorbed in the quest to find her own fulfilment as the mother of the famous Lily Elsie, and enjoyed being flattered by the sycophantic and less honourable who were more than willing to take advantage of her association with the famous *Daly's* widow. Elsie tried to voice her fears over her health to her mother but she seemed reluctant to acknowledge that anything could possibly be wrong—after all isn't this what they had both worked so hard and sacrificed so much for?

Elsie was also becoming more and more terrified of the messages and flowers she received from men unknown to her. Every night they would wait in their droves at the stage door for her departure. At first she had enjoyed signing picture post cards of herself and chatting to her admirers until one night a man grabbed her arm and insisted she sign his programme. Looking into his eyes, Elsie could see that he was not like the others and she began to panic when he refused to let go of her arm only tightening his hold when she protested. As the fear rose in her the head fly man, who was on his way out of the stage door, suddenly appeared at her side and quickly extricated her from the grip of the stranger. He then escorted her to her carriage where her mother was waiting but, before she could turn to thank him, he vanished into the night. This experience so frightened Elsie that she would sometimes be too afraid to leave the theatre after a performance, fearing an approach from a too-ardent fan. Although she would occasionally still brave the crowds she had begun to panic more and more until Edwardes had to arrange for her to leave discreetly via front of house if she needed to do so. In her calmer moments she recognised how ridiculous it was for her to feel this way; after all, wasn't recognition part and parcel of the desire to succeed on the stage. Now she had the recognition but it had forced her to admit to herself that it was merely the fulfilment of her reluctant desire to succeed for the sake of her mother who, in truth, was undoubtedly enjoying her success far more that she was. As for men, Elsie had no idea what to say to them of how to behave around them: Lottie's belief that men had been the cause of all the unhappiness in her life had also affected her daughter so that men she didn't already know became objects of fear and confusion to her.

Lottie was losing patience with Elsie and tried to encourage her to be a little more forthcoming to some of her admirers. She had been astounded at the gifts and flowers her daughter received from complete strangers. She tried to encourage Elsie to at least acknowledge the more extravagant gifts delivered to her dressing room. Especially the jewellery. She had received strings of pearls and real diamond bracelets all of which she returned with a note of thanks for their kindness but that she couldn't possibly accept. Mostly they would be returned to her accompanied by dozens of roses or lilies with an insistent message that she should keep the gift for all the pleasure she had given as *Sonia*. In the show Elsie wore several items of paste jewellery as the widow. One of these sets amounted to a full diamond necklace with alternate blood red rubies with a very large ruby pendant and matching drop diamond and ruby earrings. One night a velvet box was delivered to the dressing room and Lottie had gasped in disbelief when Elsie eventually opened it. An admirer, who wished to remain anonymous, had had a set made to exactly match the paste set with real diamonds and rubies! Elsie's first instinct was to return such an extravagant gift but realised she was unable to because she didn't know to whom they should be returned. It was unbelievable, flattering and generous but it did make Elsie feel uncomfortable. The obsession attached to the gesture unnerved her because she knew she was not really the person they thought she was.

On the evenings she felt able to cope with leaving by the stage door she had noticed one or two people who stuck in her mind. The first was a young boy of about fourteen years old. He was very polite and always asked her to sign her autograph with eager enthusiasm. Once she had done so he would always say adoringly "Thank you Miss Elsie" and look at her with his big brown expressive eyes. His rapture made her suppress a giggle every time. She eventually asked his name and he replied quietly that it was David. Sometimes during the calls at the end of the performance she would glance up to the gods and see him leaning over the rail applauding enthusiastically—she remembered thinking on more than one occasion he might fall off if he leaned too far over. He was charming and she liked him. The other was a tall, handsome man who always stood very patiently and waited until the initial throng had dispersed. He would then offer to escort her safely to her carriage, then thank her for her performance and bid her goodnight. He introduced himself as Mr Ian Bullough. She would notice him sitting in the orchestra stalls during performances and then he began sending her huge bouquets of lilies. Eventually he asked if she would do him the honour of allowing him to take her and her mother to supper at the Savoy one night after her performance. Elsie liked him and found herself intrigued—she even fancied she would rather have supper with him alone.

Edwardes was back on top form and also solvent once again thanks to the overwhelming success of *The Merry Widow*. Revenue was indeed arriving by the "cart load" every week. It seemed it would run forever—he hoped it might! The *Times* had hailed Elsie as the "brightest new star in the West End" and a "*Sonia* every man will fall in love with instantly" accompanied by "Lehar's magical waltz" score. The *London Pelican Magazine* also ran an article with the headline "*Lily Elsie's Triumph!*" on 8th June 1907 which read:

"As everyone knows by now, *The Merry Widow* is a big success, and Mr. George Edwardes having followed his *Gaiety* triumph with the present piece will now be able to sit down and take a little well earned rest and stack away the coin of the realm as it arrives nightly in cartloads, and verily believe it will do for a long time to come. The surprise of the production has, of course, been Miss Lily Elsie, as *Sonia*, the merry one, whose triumph has been most complete, and who last Saturday night went right up to the top of the comic opera ladder with a jump.

"It might, of course, have been possible for the part to have been played by a greater singer, and a more important all-round performer, but then we should not have had the youthfulness, the dainty charm and grace, the prettiness and the exquisite dancing with which Miss Elsie invests the part. How good the original character is, and was, I do not know, but having only seen Miss Elsie in the part, I share the opinion of most of the first-nighters, who considered it could not have been in better hands, and could not have been better handled, and who said so in the usual way with their hands and voice. The night was a genuine triumph for Miss Elsie, and she well deserved all the calls she received."

Edwardes was delighted with the tone of the press and satisfied that they had all recognised Elsie's success in such a positive and generous spirited way. There was an odd comment which highlighted her youth and inexperience, and also reference to Mittzi Gunther who had played the widow in the original German production, but it was nothing that could lessen the popularity of Elsie or the production. He'd been proved right when he'd expressed his belief to her detractors that "the little girl's got something". Hearing the countesses and duchesses declaring to each other as they arrived for a performance, for all to hear, how they "knew Lily so well" and that "Lily is a dear friend" made him chuckle. Anyone who really knew Elsie as a friend called her Elsie, never Lily! But it was a measure of he sudden popularity among the public.

Elsie had withstood the pressure very well and up to now had not been stricken with her usual stage fright and anxiety. Lehar was also riding high and had proved to have huge popular appeal with the British public and would be equally successful in America when the time came. Edwardes had already contracted him to compose another operetta score just in case any of his competitors attempted to poach him. It was a cut throat business and Edwardes always felt better if he left nothing to chance. Lehar was too valuable a commodity to lose. Never one to rest on his laurels he was busy considering new projects in the knowledge that he had achieved everything he had set out to do in establishing the *Gaiety* and *Daly's* as London's pre-eminent theatres. *Daly's* was also now a venue where all those countesses and duchesses were happy to be seen—although they struggled to get tickets for *The Merry Widow* and as a result he received countless requests for help in this area. Suddenly he was everyone's friend—even the aristocracy since King Edward and Queen Alexandra had graced the royal box for a performance. Riding on the crest of this wave he had made the decision to take over the lease of the *Adelphi Theatre* to expand his West End empire.

Another outcome of Elsie's success, and a very profitable one, was the request to use Elsie's image for commercial products either as herself or costumed as *Sonia*. The range of products was extraordinary and included biscuit tins, face creams, toothpaste, beauty products and numerous couture houses wanted to not only use her image but the rights to reproduce Elsie's gowns and especially the hats she wore in the show as they all reflected contemporary tastes in women's fashions. Edwardes realised it would be even more difficult to walk along the streets of London navigating through a sea of woman wearing their version of a *Merry Widow Hat!* In terms of income it swelled not only Elsie's bank account but also that of *Daly's* and his own, as these lucrative rights were distributed on an amicable percentage agreement between them.

As he had wisely anticipated Elsie's potential bouts of stage fright and exhaustion he had employed Clara Evelyn, instead of Gabrielle Ray who was now playing a role in the production, as her understudy for *The Merry Widow*. Clara was a talented actress and singer and although far from possessing Elsie's particular fragile charms and elegance nonetheless had a spirit all of her own which would serve the production well. Clara was also gracious in as much as she was happy to wait in the wings every night in case she might be required to step at the last moment into Elsie's shoes. Never once did she demonstrate the least impatience with her situation and as a result she and Elsie had become firm friends.

After one performance Elsie had a surprise visitor, Ada Reeve. Elsie had heard of Ada and assumed that she simply wanted to congratulate her, as had many in the profession recently. Ada, however, had quite another reason to visit Elsie's dressing room and on arrival announced to a bewildered Elsie that she was in fact her aunt. Her husband was none other than Wilfred Cotton, the brother of her late father. This was news indeed to Elsie who had never been aware that Billy had a brother—she had never heard him spoken of either by her father or mother. Ada was a robust and jolly woman who had made her name with the wildly successful production *Floradora* in 1899. Elsie liked her immediately and was delighted to receive her congratulations especially when Ada intimated how proud her father would have been had he still been alive. When Ada invited her to have supper with them at Simpsons in the Strand she gladly accepted, her curiosity in these new relatives aroused. Over supper she discovered her new found uncle was a successful actor-manager in London and the provinces—but more delightful to Elsie was his physical resemblance to her father.

Edwardes meanwhile, although happy for her, suggested that perhaps she should demonstrate some caution: her own success may well attract those wanting to benefit from their association with her. A little deflated by his reaction Elsie nevertheless took Edwardes' advice to heart and resolved not to get involved too quickly. It was tho' a source of some comfort to her to have made contact with those she could call 'family' and, even better, to know that there was little likelihood of it upsetting her mother. The issue of her mother's siblings was still a mystery to her and since Lottie had explained her reasons for her bitterness towards them Elsie had decided she would not attempt to seek them out. Fortunately, her mother's only reaction to Ada and Wilfred's sudden appearance in their lives was one of surprise: she too had had no idea that Billy had a brother and she was equally curious as to why he had never mentioned Wilfred nor, indeed, even intimated as to why he should be estranged from his sibling. Wilfred duly explained that he was the younger of the two and had been sent away to be cared for by an aunt when their parents died. The age difference had meant that they had never been close and the fact that their father favoured Wilfred over Billy did not improve their relationship. There was no love lost between the elder son and his father and they quarrelled constantly. As a result Wilfred had lost touch with Billy, their paths only crossing briefly at the *Prince of Wales Theatre* in Salford at the time Elsie made her debut as '*Little Elsie*' all those years ago. Too shy to reveal to Billy who he was at the time, and by the time he'd plucked up the courage to try again he'd heard of Billy's sudden death of a heart attack. The news was particularly saddening to Wilfred as both their parents had suffered and died of the same heart condition. Only some years later, reading an article about Elsie's success in *The Merry Widow*, published in the *Illustrated London News*, had he realised that '*Little Elsie*' and the famous Lily Elsie were one and the same. As soon as he mentioned it to Ada she insisted they get in touch and, as a result, Elsie was pleased to welcome them to her dressing room on many occasions and to get to know more about them.

Leaving the stage door one night Bert Hodder had thought he'd seen a ghost—the ghost of Billy Cotton. He was momentarily stunned when he saw Elsie leaving with the couple and slipped into the shadows quickly so he could get a better look. He did look like Billy but with an overwhelming relief Bert realised it wasn't—the sense of fear which rose up through his chest and made his heart pound precipitated a cold sweat which prickled his body. It was the first time he had realised how the beating he had suffered at the hands of Billy Cotton had unnerved him and sat deeply in his memory waiting to resurface and dominate his senses. As he collected himself he realised how stupid he had been because this man who had a look of Billy was too young to be him and besides he was dead. After some discreet investigation he had discovered it was Cotton's brother, Wilfred. He would be careful just the same because he didn't know how much information had been passed to his brother about his time with Lottie and Elsie.

Hodder had watched Elsie performing from the fly gallery and wondered how he could turn this unique set of events to his advantage. The fact she was now a star and wealthy to boot had increased his desire to somehow benefit from her success, he had been clever enough to keep out of Lottie's way and was quite pleased with himself to have succeeded in that so far. Sometimes it was hard to imagine Lottie as the same person he had known all those years ago. She had reinvented herself so well and was now enjoying life with a class of people she could only have dreamed about once upon a time. She even looked different and certainly had acquired a more matronly appearance. No one would ever guess how she used to behave in the past and it would certainly make her new found society friends flee in horror if they knew even the scantest details of that less than moral existence. Perhaps it was time to have a little reunion with Lottie and discuss some mutually beneficial arrangements? For a price he was prepared to keep his mouth shut. In the meantime he would enjoy causing some ripples in her perfect world.

Elsie looked at the *Times* and his name caught her eye. Mr. Ian Bullough had married a Gaiety chorus girl called Maude Darrell the previous Saturday. She couldn't understand why this news upset her but it did. She had wondered why she hadn't heard from him after he had asked her to dine with him and now she knew why! It seemed ridiculous to think she might be jealous, after all she hardly knew him, in fact she didn't know him at all, but it was ironic because he was the first man she had encountered who she secretly admitted to herself had stirred a need in her and created an interest. She still felt a total disinterest towards men mainly because they frightened her a little, and also because she was just so shy and tongue-tied in their company. She giggled at herself for being ridiculous and put a brave face on her disappointment deciding not to mention this to anyone. The callboy knocked at her dressing room door to announce the half hour which brought her back to reality. She began to apply her makeup for that evening's performance still smiling at her silliness.

Watching that evening's performance from his position on the fly gallery Hodder found himself captivated once again by Elsie and his mind was a whirl of contradictions about what he should do. Having decided to approach Lottie the next day he found himself doubting himself and wondered what right he had to inflict upset into Elsie's life. He liked the girl and admired her talent and ability; his association with Lottie was no fault of hers. If she was his daughter, what kind of a father was he to even think of trying to profit from her hard earned success? Sometimes he hated himself—that he had such a thought about his own character surprised him. He watched as Elsie stood stage centre to sing Vilja, which he had to admit was his favourite, when he saw a slight movement out of the corner of his eye. The fly rope which held a heavy, battened front cloth began to move on its cleat. The heavy batten which weighted and held the cloth taught was right above Elsie as she sang—if it fell it would kill her. Hodder leapt through the air and gripped the ropes above the cleat and knew he was being foolish, there was no way his weight would prevent the cloth from plunging down on top of her. With a whoosh he hurtled upwards still gripping the rope with both hands and knew if he didn't let go his hands would be mangled in the pulleys. If he held firm his flesh would jam the pulley wheels and stop the curtain crashing down, if he let go Elsie would be seriously injured or die. He decided to hold on and clenched his teeth. It all happened in slow motion and even though the pain was excruciating he didn't make a sound and held on fast. The other fly men had by this time been alerted and were taking some of the strain but there was nothing they could do but watch Bert hang there high up in the fly tower. On stage Elsie was oblivious to the drama above her, she had felt a slight breeze but that was all and it wasn't until the end of her song when the lights faded to a blackout she knew something was wrong. The house tabs closed and Edwardes whisked her off stage and to her dressing room.

When he knew Elsie was safe Hodder let out a blood curdling scream which sent shivers through everyone back stage. As the other fly men attempted to pull the rope down it released him from the pulleys but he had no fingers left to grip with and plunged to the stage with a thud. His last thought was that he had saved Elsie's life and for that he was pleased.

Edwardes was informed that Hodder had died instantly. Determined the show must continue he gave instructions that Elsie must not be informed of his death until after the performance and under no circumstances was she to be told how close she came to being injured herself. He was afraid this would unnerve her and cause her anxiety.

He was grateful to Hodder for what he had done but sad it had cost him his life. Lottie had rushed to the stage to see what was going on, she saw the fly man fall and hit the stage, and from her vantage point in the shadow of the wing she instantly recognised Bert Hodder. She watched with horror as they carried his lifeless body away on a stretcher. After a moment she collected herself together and returned to Elsie's dressing room.

After an unscheduled break the orchestra started up again under Lehar's baton and the curtain rose for the performance to continue. The audience were unaware of the events that had occurred back stage and had assumed a technical problem as they had seen an edge of a curtain fall beneath the proscenium opening whilst Elsie was singing. Edwardes suffered some hostile looks that evening from his back stage staff and some of the performers but his instinct was to complete the performance so as not to upset Elsie. Later, as kindly as he could, he told her what had happened and comforted her as best he could. He agreed to allow her a few days of rest and informed her understudy, Clara, that she would be going on as *Sonia*.

Lottie was horrified and visibly upset over Hodder's death. She was equally distressed at the thought he had been there lurking in the shadows of their lives all along. What could have been his intention she wondered? Why had he not made himself known to her? The fact he had saved Elsie from injury or worse was the kind of selfless act she could never imagine someone like Hodder being capable of. They had once experienced a brief but unhappy period together and she had at first found him charming and agreeable company and fleetingly enjoyed the love they shared. Was Elsie his daughter? Had that courageous last act of bravery she thought him incapable of been brought about because he believed she was? Now it didn't matter. Elsie was distraught at the death of a brave fly man and had no thought he could have been anything other than that in her life. Lottie decided that is how it must always remain but had sought guidance and support from Edwardes over the matter after confiding in him. He had forbade her to reveal anything to Elsie lest it upset her delicate state of mind. It would serve no purpose now Hodder was dead.

Elsie continued to play *Sonia* but her appearances became more and more infrequent and she began to enjoy the experience less and less. The press were unsympathetic and articles sneeringly describing her as "a part time actress" and criticising her voice as "mediocre" became more frequent. The truth was she was mentally and physically exhausted and try as she might she found the demands of the role unbearable and as a result her stage fright and anxiety attacks became more frequent. Those close to her knew her constitution was not robust and she easily tired and vocally the strain the role had put on her voice was intolerable. She had never had a powerful trained voice and the result of a long run had resulted in terrible bouts of laryngitis leaving her for days without even being able to speak let alone sing. After nearly a year Edwardes eventually relented and replaced her, allowing her understudy Clara to take over the role on a permanent basis. Fortunately this did not diminish the publics' love affair with *The Merry Widow* and it still played to full houses.

After her release Elsie decided to take a well earned break from the demands of the stage and restore her health. Accompanied by her mother she travelled to the South of France and enjoyed the sunshine and rest cures on offer in Biarritz, staying at the Majestic Hotel. Having time to reflect on her success she realised sadly she had not enjoyed it as much as she should have done. It never ceased to amaze her how others in the profession seemed to genuinely celebrate their successes and never seemed to over criticise their own abilities as she criticised her own. She had been silly to torture herself so and allow herself to slip into a gloomy world of her own where all she could focus on were the things she believed were lacking in her abilities: at these times the whole world seemed devoid of colour and was instead washed in tones of black and grey. Perhaps she needed to care less about her own opinion and listen more to that of others, and certainly that of the public who saw no wrong in anything she did.

Gertie had sympathised with her and, although she had not been particularly surprised at the strength of her popularity, she had been disturbed at the obsessive nature that Elsie's success had garnered among the public. She had never seen people so intrusive in their behaviour towards any artiste as they had been with Elsie; even whilst walking in the street during the day she would be followed and mobbed by excited little crowds. Gertie said even she would find this unnerving so could understand why Elsie felt so threatened and robbed of any privacy. Even in Biarritz there were scores of people who recognised her and would speak to her as if they knew her, but thankfully it wasn't as intense as in London. It had even crossed Elsie's mind that she might retire from the stage in the hope this would put an end to it and she could slip back into a world of anonymity. However her mother was less than enthusiastic at this course of action, suggesting that once she had restored herself she must carry on and not waste her rise to stardom.

Elsie often thought about Ian Bullough tho' she didn't really know why. She had met him briefly on several occasions but since she had read about his marriage she had not seen anything of him at all—even across the footlights. There was something that fascinated her about him and he was certainly one of the few men she had ever met who hadn't left her lost for words or blushing to the point of embarrassment when he spoke to her. She would find herself day dreaming about what might have been and wondering if she had done something wrong for him to disappear so abruptly! Most girls of her age looked forward to the prospect of marriage and a family, and Elsie decided it did seem rather appealing as it would allow her to escape the limelight and be normal again. What her mother would make of her thoughts didn't bear thinking about. She would declare her to be quite mad, no doubt, and remind her she was the envy of many young girls who would do anything to be in her position.

Edwardes had agreed with Elsie that she could have recuperation breaks in-between engagements from now on. He knew this was the only way to manage Elsie as she needed time to restore her strength otherwise she would become exhausted again. He had much to be grateful to her for because had *The Merry Widow* not enjoyed financial success he would not still be in business. With that in mind he engaged Elsie to play *Alice Condor* in *The Dollar Princess* which opened at *Daly's Theatre* in September 1909 and ran for over a year—Elsie as ever missed numerous performances. Her co-star was again Joseph Coyne who for all his doom and gloom had not missed a performance of *The Merry Widow* and now had similar negative feelings about this new show and his part. Elsie found his off stage persona a little depressing and exhausting but on stage he was a delight to work with: at times she felt he was two people so extreme was the difference in his character. Rehearsals had been strained and Coyne difficult to the point where Edwardes had given him a dressing down, whereupon his attitude improved slightly. As a result the first night of *The Dollar Princess*, 25th September, 1909, had resulted in Coyne receiving several negative comments which infuriated him but seemed to make him take stock and pull himself together. Elsie worried that his two distinct personalities were possibly a result of either his drinking or perhaps some kind of illness—his eccentricities and his conversations with people no one else could see were unnerving to say the least! However the negative press had startled him and she noticed he kept a cutting from the *Playgoer & Society Illustrated* magazine, stuck to the wall in the prompt corner, which reported on the production again several weeks into the run:

"*The Dollar Princess* is out for business. She is going to show *The Merry Widow* what can be done in the matter of long runs. And it looks as though the public is going to help her all it can. To the average playgoer there is something very attractive in watching the antics of the vulgar when surrounded by the refinement of art which he can neither understand nor appreciate. The satire is of such a nature that its keenness loses none of its edge on a second visit. One can see this very jolly little piece several times without feeling bored. Miss Lily Elsie, as Alice, shows even an improvement on her performance . . . the inimitable Mr. Joseph Coyne has put a lot more into his part than was possible on the first night. We were inclined to feel disappointment on that occasion, but our opinion has changed. He is great! His American accent is a thing to listen to. It surrounds him with the atmosphere of life across the herring-pond." Much to Elsie's dismay the reviewer finished this piece with a reference to her missed performances thus: "During Miss Elsie's absence London had the opportunity of seeing Miss Clara Evelyn in the part, and those who missed the opportunity must avoid doing so on a future occasion . . ." Elsie accepted the comment with good grace and was pleased for her understudy Clara.

Elsie was then instructed by Edwardes in January 1911 to cover the part of *Franzi* for Gertie Millar in *A Waltz Dream* at the *Hick's Theatre*, in order for Gertie to take a well-earned break. He then cast her as the star in Lehar's *The Count of Luxembourg* due to open at *Daly's Theatre* on 20th May 1911.

Elsie had enjoyed *The Dollar Princess* and covering for Gertie in *A Waltz Dream* but she was the first to see they were just trifles and pale imitations of Lehar's *The Merry Widow* in terms of substance and popularity; although they were financially lucrative for Edwardes. The new Lehar operetta was a different story and she was excited to be starting rehearsals for *The Count of Luxembourg*. Lehar had been desperate for her to accept the star role in his new operetta and she had been flattered, as always, by his sincerity and charm. Basil Hood, Edwardes chief book writer in residence at *Daly's*, who had written the book for the London production of *The Merry Widow*, was also keen to persuade her to accept the role. She was a conundrum even to herself at times and gladly admitted she would happily never set foot on a stage again, only to find she would miss the excitement and thrill of it all once she had restored her health after a break. Edwardes as always was kind and patient with her.

Whilst playing in *A Waltz Dream* she imagined she was dreaming herself one night when across the footlights she saw Ian Bullough in the stalls. She was convinced she had caught his eye and sure she noticed a flicker of a smile race across his face. It wasn't until she got back to her dressing room she knew she was right, for there was a huge arrangement of lilies with a card signed by him asking her if he could take her to supper that night. She was a little nervous and unsure but uncharacteristically she shooed her mother out of the way and agreed to go. Lottie was not pleased and reminded her he was after all a married man and she should at least have a chaperone with her, which Elsie thought ridiculous, and said so, because she was twenty five years of age and quite capable of taking care of herself. Besides, what on earth could happen over supper at the Savoy?

Bullough had been captivated by Elsie the moment he saw her for the first time in *The Merry Widow* and had found himself behaving like a smitten school boy by standing at the *Daly's Theatre* stage door hoping to catch a glimpse of her up close. That he had succeeded in doing this and had had the chance to speak to her had excited him.

But he realised his behaviour was less than chivalrous because he was at the time engaged to Maude Darrell and as a result had decided not act upon his invitation to take Elsie and her mother to dinner. He had never forgotten her. His marriage to Maude had been happy and he did truly love her, but tragedy was to strike them as she became ill with a disease of the blood which could not be treated in any way. Within a matter of weeks of first starting to feel tired and unwell Maude was reduced to skin and bone and literally wasted away before his eyes. It was heartbreaking but death was a welcome release for poor Maude. She died on the 15th October 1910 and he was shattered both mentally and physically. In his grief he found himself wondering why fate had not only been so cruel to Maude but also decreed he should be a lonely widower? Then he remembered the *Merry Widow* he had seen at *Daly's* in 1907 who was now appearing in *A Waltz Dream* in 1911. He was drawn to the *Hick's Theatre* and had caught his breath and smiled when their eyes met and he knew she remembered him, it was also the moment he knew there was something between them.

Bullough's family had prospered in the North West of England and had amassed great wealth in the cotton mill industry. They employed thousands of workers and owned numerous mills in Lancashire. Ian Bullough's uncle was the head of the family and owned a Scottish castle, a house in Eaton Square and a villa in the South of France. Ian enjoyed a military career in the Coldstream Guards, was heir to the Bullough fortune, and independently wealthy due to his father, Sir John Bullough, who died when he was aged just five. Elsie would be enchanted by him and found herself enjoying a romance for the first time in her life. Lottie had her concerns and worried Elsie was too naïve where men were concerned, but even she found herself charmed by Bullough. The greatest irony for Lottie was the fact that Bullough and his family owned the Lancashire cotton mills in which she and her mother had toiled for a pittance all those years ago. Edwardes knew that Elsie would become Mrs Bullough, it was just a matter of time. He also knew he would lose her as a result.

Joseph Coyne, Lily Elsie's leading man, as *Prince Danilo* in
The Merry Widow at *Daly's Theatre*, London, 1907.
(DSC)

Publicity photograph of *Lily Elsie* in *The Blue Train* at the *Prince of Wales Theatre*, London, 1927.
(Courtesy of Rob Sedman)

Publicity photograph of actor and singer *Bertram Wallis* at the time he starred with *Lily Elsie* in *The Count of Luxembourg* at *Daly's Theatre*, London, 1911.
(DSC)

Ian Bullough and *Elsie* celebrate at Drury Lane Farm after the Gloucester Hunt 1912. Elsie's mother *Charlotte* is first left.

Lisa Hodder (Elsie's cousin/niece) with *Elsie* and her friend *Winifred Graham-Hodgson* at Biarritz 1938.

Rare photograph of reclusive *Lily Elsie* in retirement. Printed in the *Sphere Magazine* at the last reunion of the '*Gaiety girls*' in London, 1949.
(Courtesy of Matthew Lloyd)

Lily Elsie and *Ivor Novello* in a publicity photograph for
The Truth Game, the *Globe Theatre*
(now the *Gielgud Theatre*), 1928, *Daly's Theatre*, London, 1929.
(Courtesy of Rob Sedman)

Lily Elsie as *Angele Didier* and Bertram Wallis as *Count Rene* in *The Count of Luxembourg, Daly's Theatre*, 1911.

(DSC)

David Slattery-Christy and *Mrs Sonia Berry*, 2009

Lily Elsie as *Franzi* in *A Waltz Dream* at the *Hicks Theatre* (now *Gielgud Theatre*), 1908. *Elsie* stood in for *Gertie Millar* whilst she recovered from an illness.

(DSC)

Lily Elsie as *Sonia* and *Joseph Coyne* as *Prince Danilo* in The Merry Widow at Daly's Theatre, London, 1907.

(DSC)

Lily Elsie as *Alice* and Joseph Coyne as *Harry Condor* in *The Dollar Princess, Daly's Theatre*, London, 1909.

(DSC)

Lily Elsie in *The Merry Widow* hat, 1907.
(DSC)

Lily Elsie as Franzi and *Robert Michaelis* as *Lieut Niki* in *A Waltz Dream*, *Hicks Theatre* (now *Gielgud Theatre*), London, 1908.
(DSC)

Lily Elsie as Pamela in the production of the same name, London, 1917.

(DSC)

Lily Elsie as Angele Didier and Huntley Wright as Grand Duke Rutzinov in The Count of Luxembourg, Daly's Theatre, London, 1911.
(DSC)

Lily Elsie with *Ivor Novello* (right) and American actor *Clifton Webb* (left) - snapshot from one of Bobby Andrews' albums, August 1932.
(Courtesy of John Culme's Footlight Notes Collection)

Lily Elsie (Mrs Bullough) court dress 1913.

The Last Edwardian Waltz

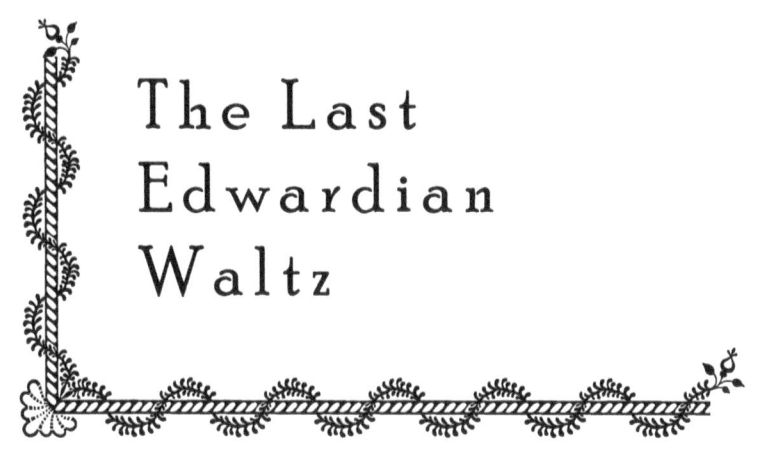

"An electric current ran through me at the sight of smiling postcards of my favourite Lily Elsie—and gave me a terrible desire for ownership which only a collector knows"

CECIL BEATON

*T*he *Count of Luxembourg* would be staged during a time of great change for England. King Edward VII died suddenly in 1910 and plunged the whole country into mourning. Black and grey enveloped London and seemed to dampen everyone's spirits. George V succeeded his father as King Emperor supported by his wife the new Queen Mary. Queen Alexandra became the Dowager Queen Mother and overnight was transformed into a sad, lonely figure. Life went on in spite of official mourning and business also continued in the theatre. Edwardes was determined to press ahead with plans as they were and not alter anything because, as he declared to anyone who questioned otherwise, it is what the old King would have wanted!

Gertie and Joseph Coyne were starring together in *The Quaker Girl*, another of Edwardes successful musical comedies at the *Adelphi*

Theatre which opened during the autumn of 1910 and was set to run for many months. This created a problem for Edwardes in as much as it meant Coyne would not be available to play opposite Elsie in Lehar's new operetta *The Count Of Luxembourg*. An opening date had been scheduled for May, 1911, so Edwardes decided he must look elsewhere for a leading man. Basil Hood, the librettist was secretly pleased because he felt that Coyne was all wrong for the part of *Count Rene of Luxembourg*. Coyne was a tremendous actor and, in spite of his eccentricities, a very charismatic man, but he could never play the dashing, romantic hero that Hood had created for the English version of the production. Lehar had written to him expressing his hopes for the future of his operettas. He also expressed his sadness that the phrase 'nonsensical as an operetta' had passed into the English language.

"I searched for the reason, and found that it lay at bottom in the many improbabilities and stupidities of the plot. The characters on the stage were agreeable and pretty, but they lacked heart and soul. I formed the resolve (with The Merry Widow) to create real people, and to depict them in such colours that they might actually live among us. They had to experience love and suffering as we do. Naturally I had to express this deeper intimacy in the music. I had, without realising it, to employ operatic means whenever the plot demanded it."

Lehar was desperate to lift the art form above its reputation as "something to be diverted by and then forgotten". His hope was to build on the developments achieved with the London production of *The Count Of Luxembourg*.

Hood had seen the original German production of Lehar's *Der Graf von Luxembourg* during its premiere at the *Theatre an der Wien* in Vienna and, after his work adapting *The Merry Widow* for London, could see the potential of the story and again the strength of Lehar's score. However he realised that it would have to be rewritten considerably to work for an English audience.

The story involved the plight of a *Grand Duke* who is infatuated by *Angele Didier* but cannot marry her because she has no title. He approaches his friend, the womanising and handsome *Count Rene*, who is also penniless, and offers him half a million francs to marry *Angele* (but he must not see her face nor have any contact with her) and then divorce her three months later. *Angele* would assume the title of a Countess on marriage and thus be eligible to marry him once divorced. During the arranged wedding ceremony the *Count* and *Angele* are separated by a silk screen and unable to see one another: she passes her left hand through a hole in the screen for him to place the ring on her finger. Later they meet accidentally and fall in love—not realising they are husband and wife they assume their romance is hopeless. All is resolved and they have a happy ending, accompanied by Lehar's lilting music and waltzes. Hood, excited by the project, justified his work on the libretto for the English adaptation in a letter to Lehar:

"There are not, I think, thirty lines of dialogue in the English adaptation which are actually translated from the German; the action of the play has been constructed in two acts, instead of the original three; while the entire part of *Brissard*, to be played by W H Berry, has been invented and introduced, and, as a consequence, new situations and scenes have arisen which do not exist in the original play. Three or four minor characters also have been created to help the construction of the new effects, such as the opening of Act I, and the dialogue scene towards the end of Act II, where *Angele* and the *Count* each discovers the identity of the other, through the jealous interference of *Monsieur de Tresac*. This particular episode was in the original treated musically, with a full stage, being the subject of the Finale of Act II; and in doing away with the third act it became necessary, of course, to sacrifice this Finale and to approach and develop the dramatic moments of the recognition by different methods, in spoken dialogue."

Elsie was excited about the role of *Angele* and was anxious to start rehearsals with Bertram Wallis, her new leading man. Wallis was a tall and handsome romantic matinee idol, a very good actor, having trained in the classics, and he also possessed, much to Lehar's relief, a powerful lyric tenor voice. Unlike *The Merry Widow's Danilo*, the *Count of Luxembourg's Count* needed to be able to sing, and Lehar would not be disappointed with Wallis. Hood had championed Wallis for the part since he had seen him at the *Prince of Wales Theatre* in a musical *The King Of Kadonia* by Paul Rubens. His first appearance in a musical made him unique in that he was not only a fine actor, he was also a fine singer. Edwardes couldn't disagree and Wallis was signed up for the part.

Due to the adaptation Hood had achieved on *The Merry Widow*, Lehar and his German librettist were happy to let him do as he wished, knowing the end result would be first class and that Lehar's score would be perfectly complemented by Hood's skill and vision.

The Count Of Luxembourg opened at Daly's Theatre on 8th May 1911 and much to everyone's delight was an instant hit with the public and the critics. The first night was unusual in that King George V, Queen Mary and Queen Alexandra all attended which Edwardes, Lehar and all the cast considered a huge honour. Lehar was particularly delighted that the royal party invited him to their receiving room after the performance and spoke to him in German. Edwardes was a little bewildered as he spoke no German and as a result, much to Elsie's amusement, spent the whole time nodding and smiling in what he thought were appropriate places.

Elsie was enjoying the experience of this production much more than any she had previously embarked upon—but perhaps she thought this about every production, because by the time she started a new project the old one had been forgotten. For whatever reason, her mood was light and there was little evidence of the anxiety attacks and bouts of stage fright. Wallis was enjoyable to work with and seemed to make even the most difficult tasks in the performance easy for her. The final act required they waltz together, but waltz slowly whilst on a staircase! When it was first suggested Elsie could see the potential magic in the situation but the practical aspects of such a feat seemed impossible. However, Wallis had insisted they at least try and after many hours of rehearsal time spent on one task they had managed to pull it off. Once achieved they polished the technique until it appeared effortless and flawless to the audience. Its magic was enhanced because Wallis was such a powerful and charismatic actor and Elsie found herself swept away in the make-believe romance of it all, as did the audiences. Ian Bullough was also swept away by the moment, but wondered if he might have a rival for Elsie's affections in Bertram Wallis!

The press notices were all fairly good and the *London Herald* declared: "*The Count Of Luxembourg* . . . could not mark a step in the progress of Lehar's art; it could not be another *Merry Widow*; but, written with fine carelessness, and suffused with the memories of Lehar's own brief days of bohemian striving and shifts to keep alive, it sang its light-hearted way to the hearts of his public . . . it was received with tumultuous applause. Its waltz seemed for the moment to eclipse even the *Merry Widow* waltz." It went on to describe Elsie as "enchanting and in sweet voice" and Wallis as a fine specimen of romantic manhood who "women will fall in love with nightly" declaring their slow waltz on the staircase as beautifully mastered and will "guarantee not a dry eye in the house for many a night to come".

After the success of the first night, Bullough wasted no time and asked Elsie to marry him. After discussing his proposal with her mother and Edwardes, who both gave their blessing to the marriage, she accepted. Elsie had never felt happier than she did at this time and it seemed all her anxieties and demons had left her at peace for good—or so she hoped. Bullough was delighted and relieved and was amused to find himself the envy of every man in London when the gossip began to circulate about their impending wedding.

Elsie had little time to herself what with performing in *The Count of Luxembourg* as well as rehearsing the role of *Ellena* for a Gala performance of Sheridan's *The Critic*, which they would perform at *His Majesty's Theatre* on 27th June, to celebrate the Coronation of King George V. It was hard work for just a single performance but hugely enjoyable and as the King and Queen Mary had requested her presence in the production she felt very honoured. It seemed as if everybody was making demands upon her time and energy and seemed to forget she had a wedding to think about.

Elsie was brought down to earth with a bump by the change in attitude of the press who had picked up on the rumours that she was not only intending to marry but also to retire from the stage. Much to her surprise she found the press seemed to resent this fact as if she had somehow betrayed them and the public by deserting them for the sake of a "comfortable and privileged" marriage. Some sections of the press also started to be hostile in their editorial coverage of Elsie by demanding to know if she was "retiring from the stage" and why didn't she "go as soon as possible", even some accused her of manufacturing the rumours to "gain publicity" for *The Count Of Luxembourg* to ensure its success—and her own! Elsie was outraged by these terse comments and privately very upset indeed. She had always been the last person to court publicity and had always done her utmost to shy away from it. Inevitably she became exhausted and upset and began to miss performances as a result. Hiding herself away in the flat she would refuse to go out because she felt scared and intimidated by what she perceived to be the hostile looks some people would give her. Bullough and her mother tried to reassure her but to no avail. The press then picked up on her supposed betrothal to Bullough and decided that was perhaps also a sham. The articles in the papers asked "Is she going to retire and marry or not?" and hurtful comments stated how "she was a mediocre talent" and how her voice "was now weak and ineffectual". This printed hysteria was brought to a head by an article in *The London Watchdog* with a headline declaring "Too Much Lily Elsie!" it went on to say:

"London has hardly simmered down after its great excitement. For weeks its jaded appetite has fed on such headlines as: Miss Lily Elsie's Hats!, Miss Lily Elsie's Trousseau!, Miss Lily Elsie's Wedding Dress?, Will Miss Lily Elsie Leave The Stage?, Miss Lily Elsie To Retire!, Miss Lily Elsie Not To Retire!, Miss Lily Elsie's Wedding Day Fixed! . . .

"For months London has hung on every gracious reported word of its popular favourite—licked up the crumbs of her smallest confidences—gone wild over the question of whether she would or would not retire, and above all, wondered WHEN IT WOULD BE? Who is Lily Elsie? She is a young musical comedy actress with a pretty face, a pretty voice and a mediocre talent. But she wears her clothes smartly, is amiable in disposition, and has an attractive personality on the stage . . . and has captured the great London public, and makes it dance to any tune she likes and draws it after her wherever she goes. It is a strange, mad world, my masters!"

Edwardes could see why Elsie was so upset by the negative comments in the press but considered it to be part and parcel of success. His advice to ignore it and carry on with a smile had not gone down too well with Elsie, her mother, or indeed Bullough, but there was little else he could do or say. Besides, from his point of view any publicity was good publicity and as a result the public were booking tickets in their droves to see Elsie in *The Count Of Luxembourg*. Elsie had suffered bouts of anxiety again which had caused her to miss performances but by now he accepted it as part of the deal when Elsie was the star. Elsie with stage fright on occasion was preferable to no Elsie at all. She hadn't mentioned it yet but Edwardes knew that as soon as Elsie married Bullough he would lose her—so it seemed prudent to make financial hay whilst the sun still shone. He knew Bullough's type, he had seen many of his female performers married off to others like him, and knew he would not allow her to continue working on the stage once the ring was on her finger. Elsie would have a role to fill within his family and the expectations of the upper echelons of society into which she was marrying. It saddened him greatly to lose Elsie, but he knew there was nothing he could do about it. Besides, he was happy for her and hoped she might find some peace and contentment. Her anxiety attacks had become more frequent and he had seen first hand the agonies she went through when overwhelmed with stage fright. Maybe her health would improve if she retired from the stage—at least she would be going whilst at the height of her success.

Amidst all this rather frustrating business, and whilst still performing nightly in *The Count Of Luxembourg*, Elsie received a letter from a firm of City solicitors by the name of Wills, Forsyth & Anderson, who asked that she contact their offices at her earliest convenience as they had an urgent matter to discuss with her. It unnerved her and she contacted Edwardes before she told anyone else. She had never received a letter from a solicitor before and she wondered what on earth it could mean. Edwardes reassured her it did not mean she was in any kind of trouble and offered to accompany her, which she gratefully accepted. In the meantime he advised her to tell no one—not even her mother and Bullough.

On arrival at the solicitor's offices in Monmouth Court, they were ushered by an efficient secretary into a cosy office with a small coal fire burning cheerfully. The flames reflected off the cherry wood panelling creating a warm and cosy atmosphere and then a tray of tea was brought in. Edwardes sensed Elsie's nerves and gave her a smile and a wink. After a few moments a rather stern looking gentleman entered and introduced himself as Mr Anderson informing them he was the senior partner. He went on to inform Elsie she was a beneficiary in the last will and testament of their late client Lord Broughton. Elsie was speechless, but after a few moments to compose herself and arrange her thoughts she explained that she knew of no such person and had not met anyone by that name. Mr Anderson smiled at her kindly and explained that his client had stated in his will that Elsie had brought him so much happiness whilst performing in *The Merry Widow* that he had briefly been able to forget his sadness at the loss of his late wife and his subsequent loneliness thereafter. Furthermore, she had reminded him so much of his daughter who had died when quite young leaving him childless. Mr Anderson asked Elsie if she recalled being sent a gift of a ruby and diamond necklace with matching earrings? They had been from her benefactor too. The amount Lord Broughton had left to Elsie was in excess of £250,000. Elsie couldn't take it in and looked at Edwardes for reassurance she wasn't going mad. They thanked Mr Anderson and Elsie promised to let him have details of her banking arrangements so he could arrange for the transfer of funds. In the carriage travelling back along the Strand, Edwardes laughed at Elsie's shock but told her to look at the positive aspects of her good fortune. From this point she was financially independent and would be for the rest of her life. He advised her to tell her future husband and her mother but to keep it to themselves. If it became common knowledge, the gossips would have a field day.

Lottie listened and smiled appropriately while Elsie told her and Bullough of her remarkable good fortune. The name Lord Broughton rang a bell with Lottie but she couldn't remember why as hard as she tried. Elsie told her she had set up a trust for her to provide her with an income so she would be independent once Ian and herself were married. Lottie was grateful and relieved that she could afford to remain in the flat they had shared on Portland Place. Lottie noticed that Ian was not in the least interested or concerned at Elsie's new found wealth—she imagined that even the sum Elsie had been left would be tiny in comparison to his own personal wealth.

Elsie had discussed her release from *The Count Of Luxembourg* with Edwardes and had agreed a date in early October, which would allow her some time to prepare for her wedding in November. They had also discussed the future and Elsie had told him she would be retiring from the stage because Ian wanted to start a family. She hoped he would understand. They had come such a long way together and their meeting was tinged with sadness, and probably for the first time Elsie embraced him and gently kissed him on the cheek. How could he not feel emotional but he did his best to hide it which made Elsie smile.

Edwardes decided that the stage was losing Lily Elsie, but he would always have her friendship. Elsie then asked Edwardes if he would do her the honour of giving her away at the wedding. He had, she told him, always been like a father to her and as her own father had died, it would mean a lot to her if he would consider it. Edwardes caught his breath, smiled at her, then turned to look out of his office window across Leicester Square because he knew his eyes were full of tears and he didn't want Elsie to see. Elsie sensed this and told him brightly that she would take that as a yes, but had to go because Lottie was expecting her. When she had gone Edwardes poured himself a large whisky, put a few more lumps of coal on his fire, then relaxed in his chair and savoured the moment.

It didn't take the gossips long to catch on to the fact that Elsie had been left a considerably large sum of money by a Lord of the realm. How this news had leaked out was a mystery to Edwardes, but he supposed Elsie had mentioned it in confidence to Gertie, who could never keep a secret even if her life depended on it, who had innocently told one of her friends in confidence, and so it went. What concerned Edwardes was the malicious rumour that had started to circulate back stage among the profession that Elsie was the illegitimate daughter of this Lord, which is why he had left her his fortune—which with the inevitable Chinese whispers now stood at a million pounds! If the press were to pick up on this story it would be a disaster for Elsie and he decided, if necessary, to call in a few favours among the proprietor's of Fleet Street to make sure this didn't happen. Lottie had been to see him and expressed her concern, and even more intriguing was her tearful declaration that she might have briefly known the Lord in question many years before. Whilst touring with Nelly Power, she had been acquainted with a young noble gentleman whilst in Bristol and they had become close for a week or two. She couldn't be sure it was the same man, but the name did ring a bell for her. Edwardes was not one to judge or be surprised by much but Lottie never ceased to amaze him. He told her not to concern herself any longer and that he would see to it that no public scandal would ensue as a result of this tittle-tattle.

Elsie was so busy and caught up in plans for her wedding she was oblivious to everything around her—even the gossip hadn't reached her.

As she prepared for her final performance in *The Count of Luxembourg* she wondered if she would miss performing and all her friends in the theatre world. At least she would no longer have to endure the anxiety and sickness she suffered as a result of stage fright. She did have a tinge of regret but her future was with Ian, and it would not be acceptable for her to consider continuing her career even if she wanted to—which she didn't. Elsie decided she couldn't wait to be anonymous again and able to live a normal life as a wife and mother. She wondered what it would be like.

Edwardes would never forget the 7th November, 1911. It was the day he escorted Elsie down the aisle of All Saints Church, Ennismore Gardens, London. She looked so fragile and ethereal in the gown Lucille had designed for her, and Ian Bullough seemed a tall and powerful young man by comparison. As he glanced round at the smiling faces of the congregation as they made their way to the altar, he recognised so many from his world: stars like Gertie, Coyne, Wallis, the Dare sisters, Gabrielle Ray and even Marie Lloyd as well as many of those who worked back stage. And of course Elsie's mother, Lottie, with all her secrets hidden behind a façade of respectability, and Elsie's dearest friend, and bridesmaid, Gertrude Glynn. He hoped this marriage would bring Elsie some contentment and happiness—and would prove to be the cure for the anxiety she suffered on so many occasions. He was sad to be losing his brightest star but, he reasoned silently to himself, there were other stars in the making out there. Elsie for all her problems had meant more to him than any of his protégé's and had managed to be unique in that she was like a daughter to him, more than she would ever know. She knew so little of life outside the make-believe of the theatre, her whole life had been entwined with the stage, so he hoped the routines of a normal life would never dampen her enthusiasm for it. Bullough seemed a kind and gentle man and had a genuine love and affection for Elsie, he hoped he would be patient with his new wife and allow her a period of readjustment to find her place comfortably in his world. For the first time in her life she would truly have someone who would take care of her—as she had taken that responsibility for her and her mother from too young an age—her fragility needed a protective shield he hoped Bullough would provide. As he sat and watched Elsie and Bullough take their vows he couldn't help feeling sad that his waltz dream, a dream he had so closely developed to aid Elsie's career, was perhaps coming to an end? Lehar would continue composing and he would continue to produce operettas in London theatres, but he couldn't imagine that anyone would be capable of taking her place.

As for Elsie she was excited to be embarking on this new life. A life where she hoped her marriage would bring her some peace and contentment. Ian had given her a beautiful Cartier clock as a gift to mark the occasion of their wedding. Elsie knew she would treasure it always, especially as it demonstrated such devotion on the part of her new husband. Ian had taken her to see the partially refurbished flat he had taken a lease on for their London home at Stanhope Place, Hyde Park, and also the country house he had purchased at Red Marley, Gloucestershire, which they had named Drury Lane Farm. Being a wife and hostess for her husband was going to prove a challenge, as she had to develop so many new skills to ensure she was worthy of the role.

Comeback & The 1920s

"How the stalls shouted and 'the gods' roared when they welcomed back their old favourite, Lily Elsie..."
THE TATLER

Walking through the familiar stage door of *Daly's Theatre* Elsie couldn't quite believe that it was 1929 and so many years had passed since the first time she had entered the theatre. There were so many memories attached to the place it was almost heartbreaking. But it seemed somehow fitting to be here today of all days. She decided to arrive early as she had called at her solicitor's office to sign her divorce papers. In a couple of months Ian would be free—ironic because the first time she had seen him was standing outside the stage door of *Daly's* during the run of *The Merry Widow*. The play she was appearing in tonight was called *The Truth Game*, which also seemed appropriate.

Initially their marriage had been amiable but there had been problems from the very start. He found it hard to cope with her moods and melancholy which seemed to get worse as time went on. She had also failed to give him what he really wanted, children. Having suffered a miscarriage it became evident she would be unable to bear children for, as her doctor informed her, the miscarriage had caused the onset of her menopause, more than likely due to her blood disorder. The physical side of their marriage, about which she had been naïve in the extreme, she found unpleasant and difficult. Intimacy of that kind frightened her and proved to be unbearable. She had tried because she did love Ian, but it became impossible. He never voiced his disappointment but it hung in the air between them and seemed to mock her making her feel inadequate. His disappointment made him turn to drink on occasion, driving a wedge further between them. Once the war broke out in 1914 they virtually led separate lives as he became more involved with his military obligations. He wanted an heir and she could understand that, it is why, once her mother had passed away in 1922, she finally agreed to discuss an amicable divorce. Ian had to arrange a convoluted farce at an hotel with some woman he had paid to be photographed with in order for Elsie to file for the divorce on the grounds of his adultery. How sordid their marriage should have to end with such deceit to satisfy the divorce laws. Her mother would have been so ashamed and Elsie was glad she was not here to witness it.

Elsie thought of how heartbroken her mother would have been to know that her marriage would end in divorce, and how she would have found the shame of it all so degrading and unbearable. For all her faults her mother had been a constant in her life, one that would be irreplaceable. It was sad she had to die at such a young age but Elsie was glad that she hadn't suffered any more than was necessary and that her final days had been peaceful enough. Nevertheless it had left a void in her life she doubted anything else would ever fill. On occasion she regretted not having at least tried to forge some kind of relationship with her relatives, and her mother's sister in particular, but it was too late now. She had done what she thought was right at the time.

Moving through the door to the wings she hesitated and instead of walking out onto the stage she went through the pass door and into the auditorium. Glancing round at the gilded plasterwork, the chandeliers and the deeply polished mahogany skirt of the orchestra pit, she felt as if she had stepped back in time. It was fitting she would be making her last appearance in this theatre, the theatre she had performed in so many times since her debut in *The Merry Widow* had made her a star. Sitting in a stalls seat a few rows back she took a deep breath and as she did so the memory of George Edwardes overwhelmed her and brought a tear to her eye. His world had fallen apart when war was declared, fallen apart literally. His great misfortune was to find himself in Germany that August day in 1914, as ever looking for the next operetta he could transform into a London hit, when the police arrived at his hotel and arrested him as an enemy alien. After all he had done to establish German operettas in the English speaking world, they could treat him so terribly. For several weeks he endured the privations of a German prison, then suffered a stroke which weakened him further. But the good offices of his friends in both England and Germany, including Lehar, finally managed to prevail and he was repatriated in the late spring of 1915. It was too late, his spirit was broken, his dreams shattered, and he died of heart failure in October of that year. Elsie felt then, and still did, that he died of a broken heart exacerbated by the death of his son d'Arcy on the fields of Flanders. It was saddest of all for his wife and remaining children, but his loss denied the theatre of one of its most successful producers.

Elsie had spent the war appearing in charity concerts on behalf of hospitals and the war effort—arranged by her friend Mrs. Asquith. She smiled as she remembered the afternoon in 1915 when Mrs Asquith had invited her for tea and to introduce her to composer Ivor Novello, who had a hit with his song *Keep The Home Fires Burning* that year. He had tried to play some music he had composed in her honour, *The Argentine Widow*, and every time he started to play the piano the band would strike up in Horse Guards and drown him out—then Mrs. Asquith started waltzing round the furniture until they were both in fits of giggles. Little did she know then that she would be appearing in Novello's play *The Truth Game* and starring opposite him.

She had appeared briefly in 1915 in the play *Mavourneen* at *His Majesty's Theatre*, to the displeasure of her husband, then decided to make a serious attempt to revive her career towards the end of the 1917, borne out of frustration and loneliness. When she was approached to appear in a West End production *Pamela,* a comedy with music, she eagerly agreed. It had been fairly successful but it brought home to her the deterioration in her singing voice, in spite of favourable reviews, and from that she decided she could no longer sustain a long run, having to appear in eight performances a week if she was required to sing. By this time Ian was indifferent to what she did or didn't do, and she was certainly unable to discuss such things with him. He was too busy with the army, the war and no doubt his mistress. He had always been discreet and she could honestly say she had only suspected it to be the case as their own married life was a shambles but she never knew for sure.

By 1927 she had left Drury Lane Farm in Gloucestershire and moved into the Stanhope Place, Hyde Park flat—from which Ian had moved out of and signed over the lease to her. Trahearne, the parlour maid, Mrs. Thomas the cook, and her personal maid, Evelyn, all remained with her along with the chauffer, Scott. Elsie couldn't imagine life without them to look after her.

Spending several months in the South of France at the *Majestic Hotel* in Biarritz had fortified her and lessened the increasing panic and anxiety attacks she suffered when in public. Her old demons were still there and increasing their hold and intensity on her nerves. She had many days where the world seemed to appear to her in shades of grey, devoid of any joy or colour. It struck her that these attacks continued and progressed in spite of her retiring from the theatre when she had always thought these bouts were brought on by the stress of live performances, but now she quickly realised her affliction would prevail whether or not she chose to perform. It unnerved her because she felt less and less in control of herself when enveloped in these dark moods.

The offer of a part in the musical comedy *The Blue Train* was a way to take her mind off the machinations surrounding the divorce and also to lessen her increasing sense of loneliness. She was sure if she put herself among other like-minded people and had a purpose she would be able to restore her equilibrium and strength. *The Blue Train* had been rewarding, and her role as *Eileen Mayne* fun, the play, a musical comedy, opened at the *King's Theatre* in Southsea in March 1927. It proved to be so successful it transferred to the *Prince of Wales Theatre* in the West End in May 1927. King George V and Queen Mary came to a performance and congratulated her on a successful comeback. Trouble was, Elsie decided, she wasn't sure she wanted to come back at all! She felt like a dinosaur in many ways and the world of theatre she knew and loved so well had already been consigned to history. Before the war people behaved differently, there was a deference and respect shown to managers and producers like Edwardes, and courtesy to performers. It was a more graceful and mannered environment, certainly more so than the fast-paced and cut-throat attitudes prevalent in the 1920s.

She walked back to the pass door and slipped back stage. Walking into the wings she smiled at the memory of the child she had been hiding in the safety of the shadows. Walking to stage centre the ghosts of past audiences seemed alive in her mind and, unlike the black and white images of the films, they were vibrant with colour and life. She gazed up at the gods and could see as clear as day that charming teenage boy applauding and leaning over the rail cheering her, remembering how her heart missed a little beat, as it did in 1907, when she was sure he would fall off as a result of his enthusiasm. It struck her how strange life and fate can be. She would never have guessed that young boy would one day share this very stage with her having earned his own fame as Ivor Novello. It brought to mind the song by Nelly Power *The Boy I Love Is Up In The Gallery* and how Marie Lloyd had sung it to great acclaim after Nelly died. Marie was also gone. There would never be another like either of them and it was so sad they should both die so young.

Even *The Truth Game* had experienced its problems and she had witnessed how badly some people had behaved towards Novello in the early stages. As much as she felt like running away to avoid the stress on her nerves she genuinely liked Novello and wanted him to have his dream come true: the chance to act on stage with herself as his leading lady. Elsie laughed to herself and realised that she was also lucky to be acting with Novello as her leading man! Most of the female population would envy her proximity to their hearts' desire.

In spite of her letters imploring Novello to secure the *Theatre Royal, Haymarket* for the London opening he had been unable to do so because of a prior booking. As a result they were to open at *Globe Theatre*, Shaftesbury Avenue, for the first London run of *The Truth Game*. Tonight would be the start of the second London season for the play.

At the start Novello had encountered problems. With the cast assembled—including Constance Collier and Viola Tree, and the director Sir Gerald Du Maurier—rehearsals for *The Truth Game* began. To say the production did not have a good beginning is an understatement. Novello found himself embattled and frustrated from day one. Du Maurier never arrived for the start of rehearsals, so Novello and the rest of the cast carried on and utilised the time until he did appear. Frantic telephone calls were made by Novello trying to contact Du Maurier, then out of the blue he received a call from Noel Coward informing him that Constance Collier had decided to pull out of the production. Novello arranged for Ellis Jeffries to take over and then as quickly she decided she didn't want the part after all, and promptly left the theatre. Novello was understandably aghast at what was happening around him. Du Maurier then arrived and announced he didn't think the play was any good and advised Novello to cancel the production. On questioning his reasons, it transpired that Du Maurier hadn't even bothered to read the play. Novello pointed out to him he should perhaps actually read the play before making such a negative assessment. Du Maurier answered patronisingly: "My dear boy, you won't even get to the end of the second act."

Furious but undeterred Novello battled on and declared he would recast and find another director. Graham Brown duly arrived at the theatre and after watching the first act declared: "What are you worrying about, this is charming." He subsequently took on the job. The pre-production period was fast turning into fodder for a more intriguing play than *The Truth Game* with which it was preparation for. The whole situation was farcical and extremely frustrating for Novello. But it does demonstrate his tenacity and resolve to never take "no" for an answer when faced with adversity. A trait he had inherited from his mother, no doubt. Constance Collier was his friend, or so he had thought, and she chose to tell him of her decision to withdraw through Coward, which baffled and hurt Novello.

Behind the scenes there was much gossip and tactical manoeuvring going on that Novello was unaware of. Many of his friends believed his idea to write a play in his own right and present it in the West End was simply beyond his abilities. They were pessimistic almost to a man and woman. Constance Collier, colluding with Coward, decided to pull out of the production in the hope Novello would cancel it completely. They feared certain disaster and were supposedly protecting their friend. Ellis Jeffries picked up on the negative gossip and suddenly saw herself involved in a flop which would not only humiliate her but damage her career. The psychology of theatre artistes was hard at play and the first thing it attacks is their insecurities. Du Maurier was also aware of the gossip and decided they were probably right and he should try and bring an end to it. As much as all those concerned seemed to be concerned primarily for their friend, it must have been a huge blow to Novello. He had committed himself to a great deal of money and would stand to lose everything—something he could ill afford to do. It must have also occurred to him that not many of his friends had much faith in his abilities, even after everything he had achieved. A lesser person would have retreated wounded and bitter, but not Novello.

It spurred him on, prodded and supported by Bobbie Andrews and Edward Marsh, making him even more determined he would produce the play. Marsh was at Chartwell, Churchill's country home, keeping abreast of the unfolding drama and fearing "the venture would collapse" offered reassurance where he could. "My only comfort was when I thought of making a list of pictures I could sell," Marsh wrote, "to help if you were forced into cutting your loss." There would be no cutting of losses. Novello had engaged another director and cast Lillian Braithwaite to replace Jeffries. Rehearsals went ahead and all began to come together, albeit slowly. Working against the odds, as they had lost nearly two weeks of valuable rehearsal time due to the fracas, it began to take shape and the first night seemed ever closer.

The plot was simple, revolving around the themes of sex and money. Elsie played a wealthy widow, Rosine Browne, who finds herself involved with a charming adventurer, Max Clement, played by Novello but impoverished. Rosine eventually falls in love with Max only to discover he is a distant relative. If she marries him it would mean he would inherit her fortune. She then switched her affections to Sir George Kelvin, and they announce their engagement. After further intrigues and pleading it all ends happily for Max and Rosine. Also included in the cast were Viola Tree, Mabel Sealby, Glen Byam Shaw and Frederick Volpe. Novello once again decided not to credit himself as author of the play, this time his pseudonym was H.E.S. Davidson. Unsurprisingly after all the problems that had ensued, he felt insecure in using his own name.

From the first night, October 5th, 1928, *The Truth Game* was an immediate success. The critics were favourable in their comments and Novello had succeeded with all the odds stacked against him.

"Lily Elsie and Ivor Novello are the most picturesque pair that feminine playgoers could wish to see," declared *Theatre World*, "and as women form the greater part of any given audience, their complete satisfaction with the entertainment is practically guaranteed in advance."

Punch in their review did offer some praise for Novello's ability to create interesting characters and effective dialogue but suggested he could possibly refrain from swamping everything with sentimental baggage!

The Times in their review were more down to earth in their appraisal. "The Third Act was all the more inane than it need have been," they opined, "and it is pleasanter to remember the earlier acts which are full of good humoured nonsense and the ingenious decorations of impudent dialogue". There are compliments to be found in the pompous tones of the reviewer who declared Novello to be in "high spirits" and Elsie to have a "charming grip on the not very subtle intricacies" of her character. In summing up it was decided "the play is shallow and scattered in its conclusion, but the trimmings are often very good fun."

The Truth Game ran for six months at the *Globe Theatre*, then embarked on a national tour, where they played at Manchester's *Queen's Theatre*, which had given her an opportunity to say goodbye to Manchester, only to return for another West End season at *Daly's Theatre*. So life and art had come full circle for Elsie with this production. She had already decided it would be her last London appearance and perhaps fate had ensured she left from the same theatre where she had started; where *The Merry Widow* had made her a star in a forgotten Edwardian England. This time her departure and retirement would be done quietly and with dignity, certainly not through the press shouting it from the roof tops. She had told no one of her intention as yet. She would enjoy the time she had left at Daly's but tell Novello she did not want to travel to New York with him for the planned production on Broadway.

Looking at her watch she decided it was time to prepare for this evening's performance. Crossing the stage she walked to her dressing room, decorated for her at Novello's insistence, to be met by a huge arrangement of sweet smelling lilies. Smiling at his thoughtfulness she considered herself lucky and was glad their paths had crossed.

Gertie watched Elsie's performance and was pleased this success had come her way. Novello was in his element when they were together on stage, and they looked marvellous together; and Elsie had lost none of her talent for comic dialogue, delivery and timing. She really was a very good actress and could easily create a whole new career for herself in straight plays. She still looked so youthful and slim! Gertie readjusted her ample self in her seat, convinced they were making them smaller these days, and joined in the applause as enthusiastically as all those around her. Unlike Elsie, Gertie didn't have a choice but retirement, after the war she knew her career was well and truly over. She had become akin to a precious object of the past to be admired as old fashioned and past its prime. Not that she minded, better that than people despise you, or worse, ignore you. No, she quite liked the reverence with which some of the young held her as this icon of Edwardian theatre, asking her to regale them with stories and witticisms about her past glories and youth.

She was sad that Elsie was about to be divorced but she had advised her to brush herself down and get on with life. Gertie knew full well how life can smack you in the face! Her husband, Lionel, had died suddenly and left her distraught because she couldn't imagine not having him with her after all those years of marriage. Her grief nearly destroyed her until one day she realised she had to either live or die. She had chosen to live as she was convinced that Lionel would have given her a real dressing down if she'd passed over to him too quickly. Laughing to herself at the thought, she could imagine dear Lionel thinking he had a bit of peace for a while—and along comes Gertie marching into heaven before her time all horns blaring and symbols crashing! There was nothing else for it—she decided to get married again as she couldn't possibly live on her own. She needed company and to know someone else on the planet cared about her. She hadn't been short of offers, which pleased her, so she went for the top of the heap. Well, she'd played enough make-believe countesses in her time, so she might as well be a real one for a change! Marrying William, the second Earl of Dudley she was now addressed by all but her friends as Lady Dudley: and she'd had no cause to regret the marriage as she had long been friends with William who had always flirted with her since before the war.

Elsie found the final six weeks of *The Truth Game* rushed by at such a pace that before she knew it the final performance was upon her. Novello was impatient to finish the run because he wanted to depart for New York where the play would have a Broadway season. His disappointment was obvious when she informed his she didn't wish to go with him, but with his usual grace he accepted her decision without question or umbrage. She had enjoyed the experience and glad she had seized the opportunity to work with Novello. In his manner he reminded her of Edwardes in that he was kind and considerate but did not allow anyone to dampen his determination and enthusiasm even when faced with dissent. Had Edwardes listened to his dissenters she would never have played *Sonia* in *The Merry Widow* and had Novello listened to his *The Truth Game* would never have been performed. Both had stuck to their instinct and forged ahead in spite of everything—and were proved to be right to follow that instinct. Through it all they remained perfect gentlemen and held no grudge against those who fought against them. Elsie thought it was a shame they could not have known each other, they would have worked so well together, and the irony was that Novello found his fame in 1915 at the same time Edwardes's came to an end with his untimely and tragic death. She smiled to herself and thought it was fitting these two talented men had prevailed at the beginning and end of her career. She could not have hoped for anything better.

The final blow to her self esteem had come several months after *The Truth Game* closed. Her divorce from Ian had become final and she was no longer Lady Bullough. The title had been brief and as a result of Ian becoming Sir Ian Bullough and, although she had never used the title, and cared less about it, the letter from the solicitors informing her the decree nisi had been granted had caused her deep feelings of sadness none the less. Gertie had taken her to lunch at the Savoy Grill for one of their regular meetings in an attempt to cheer her up. It had been Gertie who had tactfully informed her that Ian was remarried. Although she realised that Ian was now free, the speed with which he decided to remarry hurt her. It seemed as if she had been discarded. To make matters worse, Ian's new wife provided him with two healthy sons, the first just months after their marriage. It became too much for her to bear any longer.

Elsie was aware her health was the subject of gossip and rumour and that many felt her mental health was questionable. She had always been so successful in her career and had been blessed in ways she felt grateful for, but the one thing she truly desired had been denied her. Had she been able to bear Ian children perhaps their marriage would have survived and she would not have become the subject of gossip. With the final humiliation of divorce she felt as if her life was over and there was nothing left to live on for. In spite of Gertie's efforts, Elsie determined she would surrender herself to the shadows again. If she could find any contentment anywhere, it would be there. She had no desire to see her every move, or her perceived decline, picked apart by an ever intrusive newspaper industry. If she was to lose everything else, she would not lose her dignity.

Elsie decided she should count her blessings because she had some steadfast friends, especially Gertie, Ivor and dear Cecil—the latter always making her giggle because he was determined to photograph her at any opportunity! She had also her friendship with Sonia, the daughter of her friend Winifred, with whom she helped with charity work and helped organise Bazaars at the Hyde Park Hotel. She had also made the acquaintance, and formed a friendship with her cousin Elise, whom she called Lisa, and had enjoyed getting to know her. It was strange because she had never experienced having close relatives and although Lisa was from the Hodder side of the family, she decided to let it take its course and see what happened. She had invited Lisa to take a couple of holidays with her to Biarritz and they seemed to get along quite well.

Another important matter she determined to look into further was talk of a new treatment that may be capable of helping with her depressions and dark moods. Her doctor had told her about this new electric shock therapy, developed in Germany, that a clinic in North Wales would shortly be offering. It was a residential clinic and discreet. She would have to commit to stay for between two and three weeks at a time. It was also very expensive. Elsie was determined to explore this new treatment, whatever the cost. If it could make her feel well again it would be worth it.

The Last Act: Room 34

"Lily Elsie, the one and only Merry Widow. It is unnecessary to say more."
GEORGE EDWARDES

She looked so tiny and fragile, this elderly lady in room 34, lying there motionless and unaware of his compassionate gaze. As he flicked through her medical notes again he couldn't help wondering what she could be dreaming about—her hand would move as if to make a gesture it was incapable of, her lips mumbled something inaudible. He found himself hoping it was a nice dream for her—she had suffered enough waking nightmares. He had struggled to retain a dispassionate doctor-patient relationship, but had been seduced by this frail old woman and intrigued by the life she had led in that other world that existed even before the first war of 1914-18. In 1907 she had been a young woman and star of the West End stage! At the age of 25 he found it hard to imagine what that world could have been like, although his grandmother had told him many stories of her own youth and had even shown him some faded post cards of this woman as she was in her prime. Lily Elsie was a link to his grandmother's past when she had attended Elsie's first nights at Daly's Theatre in Leicester Square and only later discovered it had been demolished to make way for a new Warner Cinema in the late 1930s.

The old lady sighed again and he wished he too could have been at her first night.

Sitting in the comfortable armchair by the window he studied the photographs in silver frames which adorned every surface. All faces from her past, all of whom meant something to her, he supposed. Where were they now? His eye was then drawn by the ticking of the beautiful carriage clock as it ushered away time, its whispering movement seeming to underline the fact that time waits for no one. Sister Maria had called him at home to tell him that they feared she had deteriorated during the day. He asked if he could come to sit with her and now he was here because he wanted to make sure that she would not be alone when the time came. He placed a few lumps of coal onto the fire to keep the chill from the air: December had turned into a cold month and it was nearly Christmas.

He had been shocked when he read her medical notes. According to the many entries her mental health had deteriorated to such a frightening level that they had performed a frontal lobotomy on this poor woman. That anyone could sanction something so brutal in the name of medicine enraged him and he was glad that this barbaric practice had now been discredited. The theory had been that by drilling through the skull and removing nerve fibres from the frontal lobe of the brain the paranoias, manic depression and other neurotic symptoms could be controlled. The thought of such a procedure being carried out on an already fragile woman angered him immeasurably. He had been attracted to the profession because he cared for people and wanted to heal them or at least attempt to alleviate their suffering, but his idealism had been dealt many blows and he now realised that the medical profession had its darker side too.

Looking across at Elsie he noted that her breathing had become heavier, rasping in her chest, but she looked peaceful enough. Once he thought she had whispered a name but he couldn't be sure. No wonder, he mused, she had become reclusive and locked herself away from the world as the lobotomy changed her personality beyond all recognition. Sister Maria had told him that she was once visited by her niece and a friend quite regularly, but Elsie had become so irascible that she would scream at them to leave her alone—it seems she had gone to live with her niece Lisa, and her friend, Binkie Moss, at their house at Eades Place, Palehouse Common, Sussex. As much as this arrangement appeared to work for a time it eventually proved a disaster. It resulted in a serious breakdown of their relationship—at her worst Elsie would throw whatever objects came to hand at her unfortunate niece, who was understandably reduced to helpless tears. At other times she would simply sit and stare blankly into space for hours on end, not even acknowledging her visitor's presence. The tragedy of this was that she no longer had control over he behaviour: her brain had been irretrievably damaged by her 'treatment' and she was no longer aware of what she was doing. He empathised with those close to her for they had no idea why she behaved as she did—no matter how much you cared for someone there is a breaking point. In the end they walk away from the loved one that has become a stranger. There were one or two other friends who visited, according to Sister Maria, but always on Elsie's terms. Cecil Beaton often telephoned and occasionally caught her in the right moment and would take her for a drive and lunch somewhere. Zena and Phylis Dare would telephone and send best wishes but found it too distressing to visit because of her illness.

St Andrews Hospital was a comfortable place for those who could afford it. The nuns of the religious order were dedicated and efficient and carried out their duty to care for the sick and dying with grace and serenity. Elsie at least had the comfort and dignity in her last days denied to those unable to afford such attentions. As a doctor he knew there was rarely dignity in death whether rich or poor. He was suddenly startled by the carriage clock chiming midnight, which coincided with Sister Maria coming through the door with a mug of hot cocoa for him. She smiled as he took it and thanked her, then just as quickly she had gone and the door clicked shut.

Elsie couldn't understand why she didn't recognise the faces coming into her mind. She knew she should know who they were but try as she might she couldn't put a name to them. Was she dreaming or was she awake? She wasn't even sure of that anymore. She could hear the clock chiming and it seemed to take an age until it finally fell silent again to be replaced by the distant tick, tock, tick, tock . . .

Sometimes she would dream about the past and always *The Merry Widow* and *Daly's Theatre*. So vivid were those dreams she could almost hear the strains of the *Merry Widow* waltz; see dear Joseph Coyne smiling at her as they waltzed almost reluctantly as Lehar conducted the orchestra. Glancing into the wings she would see a smiling George Edwardes and behind him her father—and always the young boy up in the gallery leaning over the rail cheering and clapping so enthusiastically she worried he'd fall off! Sometimes she would wake from that dream terribly upset, upset because she hadn't taken the trouble to enjoy the special moments in her life.

How she wished she could remember them all. Sometimes she would see faces and no recognition was there, or she would dream she was rushing to each of them and speaking but they couldn't see or hear her. Those dreams would frighten her and she would wake in a cold sweat, afraid to go back to sleep. Lying there she was aware of her own breathing but could also sense that someone else was in the room. He was humming a tune, a tune she recognised but couldn't put a name to.

Fortified by the cocoa he closed Elsie's medical notes and became aware of her whispering a name. He had to listen really carefully but he was sure she had said the name Joseph or George. Her breathing was getting heavier by the minute and he feared that pneumonia was setting in. He smiled as he realised he was humming a tune his grandmother had played for him whilst relaying one of her stories about the past—she mentioned names of famous people he'd never heard of—he laughed at her frustration and his own ignorance. He remembered some of the words:

Do you remember Gertie Millar?
No, you wouldn't I'm afraid . . .
Some gone, but not forgotten
There was Phyllis Dare,
And Zena Dare,
Lily Elsie as The Widow . . .

He knew it had something to do with 'vitality' and it was a song that remembered all the stars of Edwardian England and Elsie was mentioned. His grandmother was pleased he was looking out for her. She'd confided that his grandfather had courted her, and won her undivided attention, by getting tickets for them to see Elsie in *The Merry Widow* in 1907.

Of course, It's Gertie! Elsie was trying to put a name to the face she could see in her mind's eye and she heard her name and there it was. Her sudden sense of elation was quickly replaced with sadness as she remembered that Gertie had died in 1952. Try as she might she couldn't think how many years had passed since then . . . she was too tired to think any more . . . but the sound of his voice, the man in the room, was it Ian? She called his name.

It was so definite it made him jump. First she had called out "Gertie?" and then she had called out again "Ian?" He crossed to the bed and held her hand as Sister Maria came in; alerted by her shouting. Elsie was still unconscious and her breathing heavy with an ominous rattle in her chest. Sister Maria wiped Elsie's brow and straightened the bedclothes. Once satisfied she was comfortable she smiled at him and left. He stood there holding Elsie's small, cold hand and just for an instant thought her eyes flickered open and looked at him, then just as quickly closed as a little smile appeared across her lips. It was fleeting and reassuring, but he wasn't sure why.

Elsie had enjoyed her life away from the limelight, glad to be anonymous again. She had found being reclusive had its positive sides and she had never any need to worry about money. She had been well taken care of in that area. Her life had been her garden and her friends, at least those who were still alive, and she had managed to control her fears and anxiety in the early years. Ian's death in 1936 had come as a great shock to her: in spite of everything a part of her would always love Ian Bullough. He had been too young to die. The outbreak of war in 1939 had distressed her and her health deteriorated rapidly from that point onward. She had tried to contribute to the war effort but her health gave out in the end she rented a house in Windsor Park and then made another move to a rented house in Bournemouth for the duration. Once the war was over she returned to London and had undergone medical treatment and operations in the hope it would help her illness. Eventually, after Gertie and other close friends died, she arranged to live in Sussex with her cousin and then in the late 1950s moved to Saint Andrew's, Dollis Hill.

He sat in the armchair again, knowing there wasn't long to go. He glanced at the carriage clock and the time was just after 3am. Her breathing was heavy now accompanied by a gurgling rattle—at intervals she would seem to hold her breath—then just as suddenly start breathing again. There was little he could do except make sure she was comfortable. Looking across at her face he couldn't help thinking she looked quite lovely and it was hard to believe she was 76 years old, she had an elegance about her even under these circumstances. He found himself wishing he could have known her when she was young and vital and full of life.

Elsie could hear someone calling her and then she could see a figure in front of her but all blurred and she just couldn't think, couldn't remember, who was this? It was then she recognised her mother. Elsie was elated to see her mother and tried to call out but no words seemed to come. Reaching out to her, Elsie called her name and suddenly Lottie was there and took her hand.

He filled out the death certificate stating the cause of death as bronchopneumonia and signed and dated the certificate for the 16th December 1962. At the very end Sister Maria had also been in the room. Elsie held her hand out and opened her eyes, and whispered a name he couldn't make out, as if she could see someone at the foot of her bed. Then she was gone. It unnerved him but Sister Maria told him it was quite common for people to see a loved one who'd passed on when they died. He would take her word for it. Ever efficient, Sister Maria opened the window, covered Elsie's face with the sheet, then witnessed the death certificate with her signature. He was glad he'd been here with her and couldn't help thinking that Lily Elsie's life, for all her success and celebrity, had in the end proved to be anything but merry!

Tempus Fugit Semper Amici

(Time flies but love remains)

"When she was well she was such fun. I have many happy childhood memories of her . . ."

SONIA BERRY

Elsie's death was the start of yet more intrigue and disappointment for some and unexpected elation and surprise for others. The mental health problems that had plagued her all her life, against which she had fought so hard, made it difficult for her to form stable relationships that could survive the starkness of daily reality. Her staff from her time living at Stanhope Place, Hyde Park, through the 1920s and 1930s, who subsequently followed her to several rented houses during the war, included Trehearne, the parlour maid, the cook Mrs Thomas, and her personal maid, Evelyn, and lastly her chauffer, Scott. All would remain loyal and steadfast and never speak about her even after her death. But they were her paid employees and as a result Elsie was in control of their relationships.

Her relationship with her supposed niece, Elise Hodder, otherwise known as Lisa, was fraught and troubled and remained always difficult. There were exceptions to this and, aside from Gertie Millar and Ivor Novello, two other people stand out. Cecil Beaton, who photographed

Elsie on numerous occasions, fulfilling his boyhood ambition, who was a firm friend and companion up to her death in 1962. Her other long-term friend, Winifred Graham-Hodgson, whom she met in the early 1920s, was also loyal and supportive of Elsie and her illness. Her daughter, Sonia, would also bring much joy and affection into Elsie's life—in many ways the daughter she never had.

Elsie's death brought bitter disappointment for her niece Lisa, and her friend Binkie Moss, which would result in a continuation of the catastrophic breakdown of their relationship that started when Elsie agreed to live with them at Binkie's house, Eades Place, Palehouse Common, Sussex, during the late 1950s. It would seem that Lisa was actually Elsie's cousin and not her niece—although confusion still hovers over that fact. Lisa, it appears, was from the Hodder side of Elsie's life and the memories of her mother's treatment at the hands of Bert Hodder were still vivid in her mind. This was a huge foreboding shadow hanging over their relationship, a disastrous and destructive element for someone like Elsie who suffered such debilitating depressions and paranoia. Elsie never considered Bert Hodder as her father, always maintaining Billy Cotton held that position in her life. That said, it was never proved and paternity tests just didn't exist in those times. It is also worth bearing in mind that the shadow and stigma of illegitimacy, a stigma we find hard to comprehend in the 21st century, created real fear in case it should become public knowledge. Careers and reputations had been destroyed—and for someone like Elsie the ever-present threat of social exclusion and ridicule was never far away. This may also explain why Elsie never felt completely relaxed in her relationship with Lisa, and it was either "on" or "off" depending on Elsie's mood at any given time, but also in case anyone questioned familial ties too deeply. That aside from her justifiable distrust of the Hodder side of the family. It may also account for why there is confusion as to whether Lisa was her niece, as Elsie liked to refer to her, or her cousin as she is referred to at other times. Reviewing the physical likeness as evidence, which amounts to a single surviving photograph taken on the beach at Biarritz in 1938, does show a remarkable likeness between Elsie and Lisa. So perhaps Bert Hodder was her father after all? It would seem possible that this, when added to the clumsy attempt to control her life when she moved into Eades Place, and the subsequent pressure perhaps to allow them to take over the management of her finances, proved too much for Elsie. She is accused of behaving very badly whilst living there by abusing them in a verbal and physical way. Letters written by Binkie, herself a psychiatric nurse, to friends at the time, now held in the Cecil Beaton archive at Cambridge University, make desperately sad reading because it shows that by May 1957 the situation had become intolerable for all concerned. Binkie writes to a friend:

"No, it is not true that Elsie has gone away—she is here—but very difficult—& as is usual with mental people has a violent dislike of everyone who has been closest to her. She will not see Lisa at all as she has invented some imaginary grievance against her—& she is consistently as unpleasant to me as she can possibly be—while behaving as though my house belonged to her. It really is an awful problem. I cannot go on with my career because it is now necessary to do a year living in Hospital & it is impossible to get anyone to live with Elsie, as she is so difficult. I was ordered to have a month's holiday away from here last autumn and it was really such a performance trying to get a cook to stay—she [Elsie] is rude to them and treats them like dirt, & they give notice . . ."

One has to bear in mind that Elsie had also undergone a lobotomy by the 1950s, which had disastrous consequences in terms of her mental health, and also how it drastically changed her personality. It was not uncommon for patients who had undergone this horrendous procedure to become violent and abusive. The procedure, at the time seen as a possible cure for those with various mental health issues, involved drilling a hole into the skull at the frontal lobe, or though a hole created at the side of the eye socket, and scraping away nerve fibres of the frontal lobe of the brain. One thing was certain, life at Eades Place was not getting any better; another letter by Binkie to a friend in June 1957 shows how fast things were deteriorating:

"I should love to see you, but Elsie is very difficult about seeing anyone. Anyway, do let me know when you are down here, but better leave it a bit as she is in bed with an attack of acute bronchitis and temperature of 102 at the moment, so am sure will not feel like seeing anyone for some time."

Reading these letters one cannot but feel sorry for all those involved in this sad situation. It would appear that Elsie really did suffer a drastic change of personality as a result of the lobotomy, and her treatment of Lisa could be linked to all those irrational fears and doubts about her own legitimacy, or the even perhaps the sincerity of the relationship. Binkie's letters, to her credit, do at times have a softer, more compassionate tone:

"The hardest part about all this is that it is so difficult to retain a feeling of affection for someone who is consistently unpleasant to one. I am anything but a saint and I don't want to have to do it, but there is no one else to do anything or anywhere for her to go. Lisa cannot come here because Elsie has invented some grievance against her, and she really had to leave as Elsie attacked her quite savagely on two or three occasions. Of course, Elsie has always been a person who concocted grievances, and there was usually a feud going on with somebody ever since I have known her, but the leucotomy [lobotomy] seems to have fixed and magnified this characteristic."

Binkie then goes on to express her opinion as to why Elsie ended up as she did. I understand it as perhaps an attempt to analyse her illness and therefore try and rationalise it for her own sake and because deep down she did still hold Elsie in some affectionate regard in spite of her terrible behaviour; although this is the one and only time where any reference is made to Elsie being "a person who concocted grievances." It is more likely to be a reference to her treatment of Lisa, which is why it is such a bitter subject for Binkie to discuss.

"How sad it is that she could have had so pleasant a life, but I do not believe things would ever have come to this pass if she had never become such a success and had had to work for her living. Her charm was her undoing, and she had too immature a personality to be able to take it. She has retained the self-centred greedy outlook of a small child, and as long as she exercised her charm, nobody really was quite aware of it, or forgave it anyway. Poor Elsie, it is so sad, and it must be terrible for her because she lacks insight and is incapable of ever beginning to see what is really wrong."

With respect, that final description of Elsie could be applicable to many famous and wealthy actresses of her time. Sadly for Elsie the lobotomy had certainly diminished the natural charm she had always taken for granted. Those with the kind of wealth and financial security Elsie enjoyed didn't have to face the real world unless they chose to do so, and they did behave like spoilt indulged children because that is how everyone in life had treated them. With regard to Binkie and Lisa, there are always two sides to every story and it does seem that whatever had happened to sour their relationship with Elsie was enduring. It was a matter of weeks after this last letter was written that Elsie arranged to move from Eades Place to Saint Andrews Convent, Dollis Hill where she would remain for the rest of her life. Interesting that she would pay for accommodations to end her days in a convent as she became very religious in her early life, in part perhaps due to the breakdown of her marriage, and became more obsessed and comforted by religion again in the last years of her life.

To their credit Binkie and Lisa, although Lisa was aware that Elsie had provided for her in her will, did attempt to visit Elsie at Dollis Hill but it always ended violently as Elsie would throw the nearest object to hand at Lisa and scream abuse at her. In the end they kept in touch with the sisters regarding her welfare but stopped going to see Elsie in person—one can only imagine how distressing and traumatic these scenes were for all concerned. The bitterness is palpable in Binkie's letters but there is still an edge of pity for Elsie, which springs from her professional understanding of Elsie's mental health problems. Elsie's death would not be the end of the unhappiness. The reading of Elsie's will would prove to be devastating for them.

Some months after the first edition of this book was published I received a letter that made my heart sing. For so long I had tried to uncover the details of Elsie's life through research alone but had never managed to find any living link to shine a light on the personal details of her life. I viewed Elsie's like a fascinating antique jigsaw puzzle with some of the pieces missing. Early on when I was planning the form her biography would take, I decided to create her story in more of a novel form than a formal biography as I felt it would make her accessible to a wider audience—the hope was her story and achievements could be enjoyed even if the reader had never heard of Lily Elsie and The Merry Widow and the glittering theatre world of Edwardian London. Her life fascinating enough to stand alone as a story. The letter in question, that shone a light on her from a personal angle, was from Sonia Berry:

"I have been reading your biography of Lily Elsie with great interest and pleasure, especially because as a child in the 1920s up to her death in 1962, she played quite a large part in my life. My mother, Winifred Graham-Hodgson met her in the mid 1920s, when they were both helping at a Charity Bazaar at the Hyde Park Hotel and they became close friends.

"I have quite a few snapshots of her on family holidays with us, and I remember her flat near Marble Arch well, where she was looked after by the faithful Trehearne and Mrs. Thomas, and by her personal maid Evelyn. After she moved to Dollis Hill, she still came to see my mother and spent Christmas with us one year at Stanhope Gate. When she was well she was such fun, and I have many happy childhood memories of her."

There are some charming pictures of Sonia's 6th Birthday Party in 1930 taken at a rented house called Dulvers where the family and Elsie all stayed for the summer holiday at Thurlestone, Devon. The happiness of the occasion is clear to see on Elsie's face and she obviously derived much joy from her relationship with Sonia.

Sonia has been kind enough to share her memories of Elsie with me and has brought Elsie even more vividly to life with these small personal details and stories. She has also allowed me to reproduce in this new edition a few rare informal photographs of Elsie on those family holidays. She also explained why she thought Elsie and her mother's friendship had endured whilst others had not. There were times when Elsie would withdraw and not make any kind of contact, even by letter. During such times, her mother just allowed Elsie to withdraw and never attempted to contact her, or ask for explanations, or put Elsie under any pressure. When the time was right, Elsie always came back and contacted her again. During the 1930s, when Elsie would travel to clinics, to undergo the new electric shock treatments, these periods would coincide with her withdrawal from friends. The silence could last for weeks and even sometimes for months. Elsie explains her hopes and frustrations with her illness in a letter to Cecil Beaton in July of 1941:

"I am going away next week for about a month to try & get patched up again at a clinic in North Wales as I've been feeling pretty awful again for months. Oh! To be well continually. I am not looking forward to this visit but I shall be so thankful if they help me as they have before . . ."

Sonia's mother was aware of Elsie's plight and remained a firm, supportive but undemanding friend. However, there was an unexpected revelation in Sonia's letter:

"After her death my mother learned, to her amazement, that Elsie had left her everything in her will, with the exception of a few bequests to other friends. So we still use and love so many of her beautiful possessions . . ."

When I eventually met Sonia in her home near Bath she explained further that Binkie and Lisa were upset that Elsie had changed her will, as apparently Lisa, or so they claimed, had been the main beneficiary in an earlier version. As a result of this they attempted to contest the will through solicitors but to no avail. Sonia's mother duly received everything as Elsie had wished. No doubt it was a terribly bitter blow for Lisa and Binkie but with the volatile course their relationship with Elsie had developed along they couldn't have been that surprised.

During my time with Sonia we discussed Elsie's marriage to Ian Bullough and how sad it was they remained childless, and how hard it must have been for Elsie to agree to divorce so he could marry again and have an heir. I had always felt that Ian was never a bad husband, in spite of his alcoholism, and that for all the problems they both brought to their marriage the love Elsie had for him was enduring. Indeed she had been devastated in the mid 1930s when he died suddenly at so young an age. Sonia agreed with me. It then transpired that Sonia still possessed the beautiful Cartier jewelled and enamelled carriage clock that Ian had given Elsie as a gift on their wedding day in 1911. The clock featured on the Antiques Roadshow from Bath in January 2010 and Geoffrey Munn explained that it contained a secret coded message in Latin, 'tempus fugit semper amici', which translates as 'time flies but love remains'. The design of the clock is all about eternal unfailing devotion and the triumph of love. Elsie cherished this gift, it was always close by and was on her mantelpiece whispering away time until the day she died.

For Elsie the tragedy of her marriage was her difficulty with intimacy. This is not uncommon for those suffering with mental health problems; some find it totally impossible and unbearable. It was also not unusual among young women in the early part of the 20th Century, especially those from working class and poor backgrounds, who had been undernourished as children, as Elsie had, to find it created fertility problems later in life. Had Elsie been able to carry full term and they had enjoyed children as part of their marriage, one suspects it would have been more enduring.

Cecil Beaton's relationship with Elsie was one of adoration, similar in many ways to that of Ivor Novello's. Both had admired Elsie from afar as young boys, either in The Merry Widow or adorning all those picture post cards, and she became an icon of style and beauty to both. Elsie recalls her first introduction to Beaton around 1915, when he was 11 years old, in a letter she wrote to him where, as a footnote, she states:

"I clearly remember my first meeting with you & your mother at the Carlton [Hotel]—so long ago!"

No doubt Beaton as a young schoolboy would have been tongue-tied and in awe of meeting his glamorous idol. The first letter Elsie wrote to him regarding a sitting [to be photographed] is dated 11th June 1930, form her London address at Stanhope Place:

"Dear Mr. Beaton,

I am sorry I haven't replied to your letters of 23rd May before this but I have been away too from London a lot lately and have got in such a muddle with my letters. I quite thought I wrote to you ages ago in reply to your precious letter proposing a date in May to pose for a sitting. Didn't I?"

At this time Elsie was performing with Novello in the Truth Game, which had originally opened at London's Globe Theatre [now the Gielgud Theatre] in 1929, then gone on tour, only to be booked for another London run. Elsie was about to give the final performances of her career in The Truth Game opposite Novello on the stage of Daly's Theatre, the very theatre where she had become a star so many years earlier. She was also dealing with her painful divorce from Ian Bullough at this time. Her being in a muddle with her letters can, under the circumstances be forgiven. She goes on to say:

"I will try very hard to give you a sitting the week after Ascot—but I am not sure as I may have to go away again that week. I glowed [with pride to be asked] to be in your book & do so hope you won't have to leave me out."

Although they are relatively few in number, the first dated 1930 and the last dated just weeks prior to Elsie's death in 1962, her relationship with Beaton brings out the girlish and coquettish side of Elsie, a side that is miles away from the formal posed reflection we have of her as a result of all those picture post cards. That Beaton adored her and spoilt her is without doubt, but one can sense that they flirted with each other, full of warmth and charm and are a world away from the less flattering recollections of Elsie others choose to recall. This natural warmth and trust, as with Sonia's mother, seems to have endured the lobotomy, which unsurprisingly had changed Elsie's personality so much.

By the mid 1930s Elsie, writing from a friend's house in Finchampstead, Berkshire, is still having problems organising suitable dates with Beaton. This again is a time when much was happening in Elsie's life as Ian Bullough had died suddenly leaving Elsie devastated:

"My Dear Mr. Beaton,

I wish I could come on the 24th but alas I cannot. It is ever so nice of you to have thought of me & [Ian's family] at this time. Thank you & [sic] I do hope we shall meet when I come back to London later on but you always seem to be in America.

Again many thanks and regrets."

Elsie underlined the "regrets" heavily and twice. Regret that she could not organise a date convenient for them both and perhaps also a reflection of her own regrets at the sudden death of her ex husband. She also chides Beaton playfully for always being "in America" to perhaps express her sadness at not seeing him as much as she would like.

By 1941 Elsie was living in a rented house in Windsor Forest, Berkshire. It was one of several places she lived during the war as she also spent some time in Bournemouth. Her mental health had deteriorated after Ian Bullough's death and the onset of war and everything it brought added to her distress and her health suffered as a result. That said she was still protective of her image. In July 1941 she wrote to Beaton a telling letter, by now addressing him more informally as:

"My Dear Cecil,

Ever so many thanks for sending me the four photographs, it is really most [kind] of you. If you would like to publish them of course you may. Perhaps you could just slice off a bit of hips of the one standing by the wall as I look enormous. I hope you won't publish the group, I'm sitting so badly (sound like a hen!) & my figure looks a bundle . . . My favourite one is the half sitting position, full face, [thank you for] making my old face look sweet . . ."

In spite of everything Elsie is still determined to make sure her image, or at least those published to the world, are up to her exacting standards. She continues the letter by stating she is again going for treatment [electric shock therapy] to the clinic in North Wales. She sadly states she is "not looking forward to this visit" but again hopes they will "help me as they have before." Elsie is fully aware of the effects her illness has on her and her relationships. It also demonstrates how determinedly she fought her depressions and paranoia with everything at her disposal. She closes this letter to Beaton thus:

"If it is successful I shall look you up as soon as I [return] & shall look forward to it immensely . . . again thank you so much for sending me the photographs. As I've known you since you were a little boy I can surely send you my love."

She signed this letter with just her name "Elsie" which she underlined twice to perhaps punctuate the affection and trust she placed in Beaton and also to demonstrate how much she appreciated him as a friend and confidante.

In the late 1940s Elsie's illness worsened to the point where she was feeling ill more than she felt well. It could be because the electric shock therapy she had been treated with for so many years was becoming less effective in terms of how long she would feel any positive benefits. This coincided with the belief, in certain areas of the medical profession, that the surgical procedure known as a lobotomy could really help those like Elsie who were plagued with mental health problems. As Elsie had always been willing to try any treatments available in the hope they would cure her, and the fact she had the financial ability to pay for the expensive treatments, she would have been more than willing to undergo such a procedure in the hope it would alleviate her of her symptoms permanently. One cannot help admiring Elsie's courage and determination, and the fact she never stopped looking for a cure no matter what horrendous treatments she willingly subjected herself to.

By the early 1950s Elsie had undergone the lobotomy and, as has been documented by Binkie and Lisa, did indeed change her behaviour quite radically towards some. It was also a period of great sadness for Elsie as two of her greatest friends, Ivor Novello and Gertie Millar, passed away. It is most probable that this would have had a very negative impact on Elsie in terms of her depressions, depressions which sadly the lobotomy had done nothing to help. If anything they seemed to increase. It was also a period when Elsie was not protected and looked after by her faithful staff who had been loyally at her side since the pre war days at Stanhope Place. It created fertile ground for Lisa and Binkie to perhaps make their move and suggest that Elsie lived at the house at Eades Place, Palehouse Common, Sussex. Sonia also told me that it was during this time that there had been talk of Elsie coming to live with her mother, Winifred, but it never came to pass.

By the late 1950s Elsie had made the move from Sussex, where the situation had become impossible for all of those concerned with, one suspects, the assistance of Cecil Beaton, to St Andrews Convent, Dollis Hill, London. Here Elsie was able to take control of her life again. On the rare occasion her niece visited she would be uncharacteristically abusive and violent towards her. In the end she stopped visiting altogether.

Elsie still kept her friendship with Beaton. From Dollis Hill she wrote to him in December 1961:

"My Dear Cecil,

You are much too kind to me in sending me such lovely carnations & cyclamens this Christmas. I had a nice long letter from Beau [friend] this morning, she made me laugh because I had asked how the children were, meaning her grandchildren, she replied: 'Don't ask me about children, when I say children they are all aged 45, 47 & 50 years old!!!' I thought my heavens, if that is the age of her grandchildren what on earth is my age! I tried to work it out but I got over the shock when I suddenly [crossed out word] [crossed out word] realized she meant her own children. I can't spell as you can see, I start off quite well at first & then!!!"

It is nice to see that Elsie had lost none of her humour and that she enjoyed exercising her girlish charm in letters to Beaton. She continued the letter and made reference to his costume creations in the hit West End show—a show which starred her old friend Zena Dare as Mrs. Higgins at the Theatre Royal, Drury Lane:

"Again thank you Cecil very, very deeply for your most kind and good thoughts of me. As soon as I am well enough I am going to see My Fair Lady & I shall say to myself: Oh! I know the man who made all those exquisite creations. With love & prosperous New Year—I am sure you won't have the patience to read through this puzzle"

It seems that Beaton took it upon himself to make sure Elsie felt loved and cared for. A letter dated June 1962 reads thus:

"My Dear Cecil,

What beautiful flowers you have sent me again, thank you from the depths of my heart. I would love to see you & love for a drive with you next week. Could you ring up one morning about 10.30am & I will try my hardest to come, there are several things to be done to [my will], which I will not bore you with. But when you see me don't have a shock because I have put on weight—I really have ['really' and 'have' both underlined] so be prepared. I have a longing [underlined three times] for sweets which of course is fatal! Bless you for your goodness to me & with love."

Elsie was in the final months of her life. She seems to make a reference to her will in this letter and her exasperation over it. Perhaps this is the point she changed her will and left most of her estate to

Winifred Graham-Hodgson after disinheriting her niece/cousin Lisa [Elise] Hodder. Her relationship with Beaton was as jolly as ever and her concern at having put weight on because of a love for sweets is almost childlike; but also shows how her image is still important to her. The final letter to Beaton, in which she appears to tease him for taking pictures of her, Elsie wrote just a week later on 8th June 1962:

"My Dear Cecil,

What a lovely day you gave me on Wednesday & as for taking my face on your camera I was really thrilled—just imagine you taking a picture of me, well! I almost cannot believe it!!! I am writing in bed, almost in the dark after our afternoon out, so forgive a hurried scrawl. Can you possibly let me know the name of the place where we had tea & the name of where it was? Thank you very much if you will & again thanks ever so for Wednesday.

With love to you from Elsie"

After Elsie's death Cecil Beaton received letters from those who had known and worked with Elsie and their memories were always positive and demonstrated real warmth and affection. It leads me to believe the animosity that existed between Elsie and her niece/cousin Lisa [Elise Hodder] and her friend, Binkie Moss, was the exception rather than the rule. Cecily Webster, who worked with Elsie, recalled the time of The Merry Widow in 1907:
"I first met her in a dressing room at Daly's which she shared with a friend who had a small singing part in the [Little] Michus—she had only recently come to town to try her luck & except for the picture postcard craze, was hardly known. She subsequently left Daly's to play the lead in See See, a charming little Chinese musical comedy, with excellent music. I think it must have been then that George Edwardes realised her possibilities (she was under his management there too). During that time, I had been accepted for the chorus at Daly's, having gone to one of the weekly auditions just for fun—I remember very well, while the very small chorus of us were being taught the music on the empty stage,

that Elsie came in quietly to listen (she did everything quietly). I asked her why she was there and she told me that Edwardes had asked her to read the part of The Merry Widow. Edwardes did not want a big star for the part for he was hard up after the comparative failure of the previous show, & he had nothing to follow it up. It is one of the mysteries of Edwardes' judgement that he underestimated the beauty of the little opera [The Merry Widow], still more underestimated the beauty of the Widow herself. However he did everything possible for her, he sent her to a voice trainer who did a lot of work for him, I forget her name—she took Elsie in hand, did marvels with her sweet voice—she drilled her in every line of music, and as we all know, produced a miracle."

Another colleague, Rebecca West, from those Edwardian days remembered Elsie for her beauty after an article about her by Cecil Beaton in The Daily Telegraph:

"Thank you so much for waking the beauty of Lily Elsie and her lovely pensive amiability, how beautiful Lily Elsie and Ivor Novello were together, like two fawns in a Sultan's Garden, they should have eaten flowers . . . How kindly you convey the continuing likeability of her in old age."

Elsie's funeral service was held at London's Golders Green Cemetery just before Christmas 1962. She was cremated according to her wishes and her ashes scattered in the garden of remembrance, where so many of her true friends had gone before her.

Recalling the coded message of love and eternal devotion embedded in the Cartier carriage clock Ian Bullough gave Elsie on the occasion of their wedding held true for Elsie, and one suspects for Ian Bullough too. It is also true that time did indeed fly for Elsie, as it does for us all, but love also remained in the way she is still appreciated through her image in the many picture post cards that are a window to the past that fascinate people still; even those who do not know who they are admiring or what she achieved in that other world. Lily Elsie was indeed the last and possibly the brightest Edwardian star of them all.

… Reference Section

Short Biographies:

Robert Andrews
Constance Collier
Noel Coward
Joseph Coyne
Sir George Dance
Phyllis Dare
Zena Dare
George Edwardes
Harry Greenbank
Mizzi Gunther
Owen Hall
Basil Hood
Franz Lehar
Victor Leon
Marie Lloyd
W. McQueen-Pope
Lionel Monckton
Sir Gerald du Maurier
Gertie Millar (Lady Dudley)
Sir Edward Marsh
Owen Nares
Frederic Norton
Ivor Novello
Nelly Power
Gabrielle Ray
Ada Reeve
Adrian Ross
Leo Stein
Leslie Stewart
Bertram Wallis

Brief History of Theatres

Prince of Wales Theatre (Music Hall), Salford.
Regent Theatre (Music Hall), Salford.
Queen's Theatre (Music Hall), Manchester.
Palace Theatre (Music Hall), Manchester.
City Varieties Music Hall, Leeds.
Royal Strand Theatre, London. (Demolished)
Gaiety Theatre, London (Demolished)
Daly's Theatre, London. (Demolished)
Waldorf Theatre, London.(*formerly the Witney, then the Strand, now the Novello*)
Aldwych Theatre, London.
Olympic Theatre, London. (Demolished)
Opera Comique Theatre, London, (Demolished)
Old Globe Theatre, London. (Demolished)

Play Pictorial: References 1902-1929
Further Reading.
Newspaper & Magazine Articles: 1886-1950

Production Details:
The Silver Slipper (1901)
A Chinese Honeymoon (1903)
Lady Madcap (1904)
The Little Michus (1905)
See See (1906)
The New Aladdin (1906)
The Merry Widow (1907)

A Waltz Dream (1908)
The Dollar Princess (1909)
The Count Of Luxembourg (1911)
Mavourneen (1915)
Pamela (1917)
The Blue Train (1927)
The Truth Game (1928-9)

Lily Elsie encountered and worked with many famous people during her life and career, and it seemed appropriate to create a short biography for most of those I have mentioned in this book as part of her story.

BIOGRAPHIES

Robert Andrews (Actor)
1895-1976

Robert Tobias Andrews was born in London and first appeared on the stage as a child in the same company as two other child actors Noel Coward and Gertrude Lawrence. At the outbreak of WWI Andrews was enlisted and served in the *Royal Flying Corps* and was befriended by Churchill's secretary Edward Marsh. Marsh subsequently introduced him in 1916 to Ivor Novello, the composer of the hit song '*Keep The Home Fires Burning*', whilst attending a play titled *Under Cover* at London's *Strand Theatre* (now the *Novello Theatre*). Andrews and Novello became friends and lovers and lived in the flat on top of the *Strand Theatre* until

Novello's death in 1951. After the war Andrews returned to the stage and was responsible for Novello's casting in the play *Debareu* at the *Ambassadors Theatre* (1921) in which he had also been cast. Andrews would appear in many of Novello's plays and musicals including: *Party* (1932), *Proscenium* (1933), *Glamorous Night* (1935), *Careless Rapture* (1936), *Crest Of The Wave* (1937), *The Dancing Years* (1939), *Perchance To Dream* (1945) and *King's Rhapsody* (1949). When Novello died suddenly in 1951 Andrews, whose career relied heavily on his association with Novello, found himself cut adrift and eventually faded into obscurity. He was known as a great wit and also largely responsible for managing Novello's successful career. He survived his lover by twenty five years, and died at his home in Maidenhead, Berkshire, in 1976 aged 81.

Frank Curzon (Producer/Theatre Manager)
1869-1927
Frank Curzon was an English actor who became an important theatre manager and producer, and the lessee of several of London's West End theatres including the *Royal Strand Theatre*, *Royal Avenue Theatre* (now the *Playhouse Theatre*), *Criterion Theatre*, *Comedy Theatre*, *Prince of Wales Theatre*, *Wyndham's Theatre* and the *Playhouse Theatre*. He married actress and singer *Isabel Jay* in 1910, the star in many of his productions. Some of Curzon's biggest successes as a producer, along with the financial backing of *George Edwardes*, included *Monsieur Beaucaire* (1902), *A Chinese Honeymoon* (1903), *The White Chrysanthemum* (1905), *Sergeant Blue* (1905), *The Girl Behind The Counter* (1906), *See See* (1906), *Miss Hook of Holland* (1907), *King of Cadonia* (1908) and *The Balkan Princess*, co-written by Curzon, in 1910. Many of Curzon's shows were spectacular with exotic sets, elaborate costumes and beautiful chorus girls. He wanted to put Lily Elsie under contract when she appeared in *A Chinese Honeymoon* but George Edwardes signed her first, behind his back, which infuriated him. One of Curzon's few mistakes was to turn down the opportunity to produce *The Maid of the Mountains* (1917) which became a huge success and which, ironically, saved Edwardes' estate from bankruptsy after his untimely death in 1915.

Constance Collier (Actress)
1878-1955

Born Laura Constance Hardie in Windsor, Berkshire. A child actress she went on the join George Edwardes' Gaiety Girls at the age of 15 in 1893 at London's famous *Gaiety Theatre*. She was a tall and striking woman with a big personality and great determination. By 1906 she played *Cleopatra* opposite Sir Herbert Tree's *Anthony* in a major revival of the play at *His Majesty's Theatre* thereby establishing herself as a popular actress. In 1908 she starred opposite Tree again in *The Mystery of Edwin Drood* and then toured the America and made several appearances on Broadway. During the 1920s she established a close friendship with Ivor Novello and co wrote his first hit play *The Rat* (1924) and appeared with him in *The Firebrand* (1926). She fell out of favour with Novello briefly over his play *The Truth Game* (1928) due to her attempts, aided by Noel Coward, to dissuade him from producing it as they considered it awful and would damage Novello's career. Novello went ahead and *The Truth Game* was a huge success for Novello and his leading lady Lily Elsie, and the play was also successful on Broadway. She appeared in Hollywood films such as *Stage Door* (1937), *Kitty* (1945), *Rope* (1948) and *Whirlpool* (1949). During the making of Stage Door she became friends with Katherine Hepburn, a friendship which lasted for the rest of her life. Collier also has a star on the Hollywood walk of fame. She died aged 77 at her home in England in 1955.

Noel Coward (Actor/Playwright/Composer)
1899-1973

Born in Teddington, Middlesex, England to a middle-class family he was the second of a family of three sons. A student at the *Italia Conti Academy* (stage school), Coward's first professional engagement was in January 1911 in the children's play *The Goldfish*. After this appearance he was much sought after for child roles by professional theatre companies. He featured in several productions with Sir Charles Hawtrey, a Victorian actor and comedian, whom Coward came to idolise and subsequently worked for until he was twenty years old. It was from Hawtrey that Coward was to learn comic acting techniques and the art of writing plays. Coward was drafted briefly during WWI but discharged due to ill health. He appeared in D.W. Griffith's film

Hearts of the World in 1918 in an uncredited role. Coward then found his real voice and began writing plays that he and his friends could appear in—and also writing for comedy revue shows—his first full length play *I'll Leave It To You* was staged in 1920 when he was aged 20. The play was thought to be lost until a typescript was found in the archive of the Lord Chamberlain's Office in 2007—at the time Coward would have had to submit the script to receive a licence to perform it. He went on to enjoy a moderate success with *The Young Idea* in 1923—at the time he aspired to be as famous as his friend Ivor Novello—and his next play would grant his wish. *The Vortex* (1924) which contains references to both drug abuse and homosexuality caused a sensation on both sides of the Atlantic (Novello would star as Nikki in the silent film version) and established his international celebrity. Coward followed this with *Hay Fever* (1925), *Fallen Angels* (1925) and *Easy Virtue* (1926). In 1927 he presented his new play *Sirrocco* at *Daly's Theatre* in London, which starred Novello, to unprecedented scenes of disapproval—Coward attempted to make a speech only to be booed and jeered off the stage. It closed the same night and was a disaster. Much of Coward's best work came in the late 1920s and early 1930s. His full length operetta *Bitter Sweet* (1929) and his satire on WWI *Cavalcade* (1931) and the enormously successful *Private Lives* (1930) in which he starred with his childhood friend Gertrude Lawrence. *Design for Living* came in 1932 in which he starred with Alfred Lunt and Lynn Fontanne to great acclaim. He continued to compose songs which became very popular and are still played today including: *I'll See You Again, Mad Dogs and Englishmen, The Stately Homes Of England* and *Don't Put Your Daughter On The Stage*. His popularity dwindled in the post WWII era but he continued performing in London and Las Vegas in a cabaret style show and also appeared in cameo roles in various films including *The Italian Job*. He noted in his diary on 16th December, 1962, that "Lily Elsie is dead, terribly sad." Although they had never worked together he admired her terribly and they were friends. Coward's final stage work was a trilogy of plays set in an hotel penthouse suite, with him taking the lead roles in all three, under the collective title of *Suite in Three Keys* (1966)—the play had excellent reviews and did good box office business in England. Coward intended to take the plays to *New York* but was unable to travel due to illness—his memory was failing him and he struggled to remember his lines. By this time he was suffering from severe arthritis and memory loss and he decided to retire from the theatre. He was knighted in 1970, and died at his home in Jamaica in March of 1973 aged 73.

Joseph Coyne (Actor)
1869-1941

Joseph Coyne was born in New York and making a name for himself in small touring productions as a comic actor, he eventually appeared on Broadway in several productions including *The Girl In The Barracks* (1899), *Star & Garter* (1900), *The Night Of The Fourth* (1901), *The Toreador* (1902), eventually breaking into musical comedy in *The Social Whirl* (1906) and *My Lady's Maid* (1906) among others. On arrival in England under contract to London's *Aldwych Theatre* management he was contracted against his will by George Edwardes to play Danillo in Lehar's operetta *The Merry Widow* (1907) opposite Lily Elsie. Coyne hated the show and the character he played, he couldn't sing and Edwardes insisted he recite the tenor's lyrics, which infuriated Lehar, but in spite of this he was a big hit in the production and stayed with the show for its run of nearly two years. He then appeared in *The Dollar Princess* (1909), again with Lily Elsie, and *The Quaker Girl* (1910) in which he starred alongside Gertie Millar. He made fewer appearances and after WW1 he faded into obscurity. Always an eccentric character, he could often he seen having heated discussions with an invisible companion on street corners in Covent Garden. His mental health deteriorated and his delusions became more severe. He died in 1941 at the age of 72 still voicing his dislike of his role in *The Merry Widow*.

George Dance, Sir (Lyricist/Librettist/Producer)
1857-1932

George Dance was an English lyricist and librettist in the 1890s and an important theatrical manager in the early part of the 20th Century. His father was Isaac Dance a humble pipe maker. His son Eric, who died in WWII was responsible for building the *Oxford Playhouse*. Dance was educated at the *National School*, Nottingham and early in his life became a prolific songwriter. Some of his most famous songs were for the music halls performed by Vesta Tilley including *Girls Are The Ruin*

Of Men and *Come Where Me Booze Is Cheaper* and *His Lordhsip Winked At Me*. During the 1890s Dance turned to writing libretti for operettas and musical comedy at the *Savoy Theatre* among others, which included *The Nautch Girl* (1891), *The Rajah Of Chutneypore* (1891), *Lord Tom Noddy* (1896), *The Girl From Paris* (1897), *The Gay Grisette* (1898), *The Ladies Paradise* (1899) and *A Chinese Honeymoon* (1898-1903) in which Lily Elsie would make her mark after taking over the role of *Princess Soo Soo* from Beatrice Edwardes in 1903. *A Chinese Honeymoon* was also the first musical comedy to run for more than one thousand performances. His fortune made with this show, Dance became one of the most successful theatrical managers in the United Kingdom having as many as 24 companies on tour at the same time. He was financially behind the scenes in many West End productions prior to WWI. Dance was knighted in 1923 in recognition of his services to theatre: which included his gift of £30,000 to enable the reconstruction of the *Old Vic Theatre* as a permanent home for the *Royal Shakespeare Company*. He died at his home in London aged 75.

Phyllis Dare (Actress/Singer)
1890-1975

Phyllis Constance Haddie Dones was the second daughter of Arthur Dones. She was three and a half years younger than her sister Zena. They became famous as the 'Dare Sisters' when contracted to appear in pantomime together in *Babes In The Wood* (1899). At the time Phyllis was just nine years old. A few months later she played Little Christina in a touring play and the following Christmas the title role of *Red Riding Hood* (1900) in a Manchester pantomime. She then went on to play in Haddon Chambers production of *The Wilderness* and for the Christmas season Seymour Hicks cast her as Mab in his production of *Bluebell In Fairyland* (1901). The following Christmas she played Sesame in The Forty Thieves (1902). Just after her fifteenth birthday she took over the part of Angele in Hicks' long-running hit *The Catch Of The Season* (1905) the part previously played by her sister Zena. She left this production to star in the pantomime *Cinderella* (1906) in Newcastle. She then created the part of Eileen Cavanagh in what would be her first long-running West End musical *The Arcadians* (1909) at the *Palace Theatre*. She delighted audiences with her girlish charm, natural singing voice and delicate movements. *The Arcadians* was presented by George Edwardes and she went on to appear in his other productions including *The Girl In The Train* (1910), *Peggy* (1911), *The Sunshine Girl* (1912). She continued to work in revue and musical comedy after WWI when in the 1930s she appeared in several of Ivor Novello's musicals—most famous for her appearance in *King's Rhapsody* (1949) at London's *Palace Theatre*, along with her sister Zena—the first time they had appeared together since the pantomime in 1899. *King's Rhapsody* ran for two years and, after Novello had died during the run, she decided to retire from the stage. She spent her retirement years in Brighton and died there aged 85. She never married.

Zena Dare (Actress/Singer)
1887-1975

Florence Hariette Zena Dones appeared in her first stage engagement with her younger sister Phyllis in the 1899 pantomime *Babes In The Wood* at the *Coronet Theatre*, London. They changed their surname and became ever after known as the 'Dare Sisters'. At the age of fourteen she went on tour with Seymour Hicks playing Daisy in the musical comedy *An English Daisy* (1902). Frank Curzon then signed her to play Aurora in *Sergent Blue* (1904). In September of 1904 Curzon released her from her contract because Hicks needed an urgent replacement for his pregnant wife, Ellaline Terriss, who had been playing the lead in *The Catch Of The Season*, a retelling of the *Cinderella* story. Zena was a great success but, mid-December, she had to surrender the part to her sister Phyllis because she was already contracted to appear at Bristol in the pantomime *The Sleeping Beauty*. George Edwardes then signed her to play in his productions including *Lady Madcap* (1905), *The Little Cherub* (1905) and *The Girl on Stage* (1906). In 1906 she returned to Seymour Hicks company and appeared in productions at the new *Aldwych Theatre* including *The beauty of Bath* (1906), *The Gay Gordons* (1907). She came to the attention of Ivor Novello after WWI and subsequently became firm friends during the 1920s. As a result he asked her to appear in several of his plays and musicals including *Proscenium* (1933), *Murder In Mayfair* (1934), *Careless Rapture* (1936). She also appeared in John Perry's production of *Spring Meeting* (1937 with Margaret Rutherford directed by John Gielgud. She continued o work throughout WWII including Novello's *Full House* (1940) and in his post war musical *Perchance To Dream* (1945) which led to Zena and her sister Phyllis being cast in Novello's musical *King's Rhapsody* at London's *Palace Theatre* which opened in 1949. After Novello's death she appeared in several plays including Coward's *Nude With Violin* (1954) and later she was cast as Mrs Higgins in the musical *My Fair Lady* with Rex Harrison and Julie Andrews in 1958. It ran for over five years and was seen by almost four and a half million people. Zena was the only one of the principal characters to stay for the complete run. When the show closed she decided to retire. She died a few weeks after her sister at the age of 88 in 1975.

George Edwardes (Producer/Theatre Manager) 1855-1915

Theatre manager and producer credited as the father of musical comedy in England. He started his career at the *Savoy Theatre* where he managed and produced some of the most successful *Gilbert & Sullivan* comic operas. In 1885 be became joint manager of the *Gaiety Theatre* producing burlesques like *Little Jack Sheppard* in which the *Gaiety* had specialised. By 1886 Edwardes had sole control of the *Gaiety* and developed his own ideas for the theatre's future. Shows included *Dorothy* (1886), *Faust-up-to-date* (1888) and *Carmen-up-to-date* (1890). He believed that topical, light comedies were the way forward and had the potential to be hugely successful and he employed Lionel Monckman and Owen Hall as composer and librettist respectively for his *Gaiety* shows. This collaboration resulted in many successful productions including: *The Shop Girl* (1894), *The Circus Girl* (1896), *A Runaway Girl* (1898), *The Orchid* (1903), *The Girls of Gottenberg* (1907), *Our Miss Gibbs* (1909), *The Sunshine Girl* (1912) and *After The Girl* (1914). The heroines were independent young women who often earned their own living. The stories had a similar plot—a chorus girl breaks into high society or a shop girl makes a good marriage. One reviewer declared that Edwardes musicals were always "light, bright and enjoyable". The *Gaiety* also produced musicals about boys—*The Messenger Boy* (1900), *The Toreador* (1901), *Two Naughty Boys* (1906) and *The New Aladdin* (1906). In 1895 Edwardes took control of *Daly's Theatre* where he developed the musical comedy style further with productions like *An Artistes Model*,

The Geisha, A Greek Slave, The Merry Widow (1907) and *The Dollar Princess* (1909)

As his success grew he needed another theatre and added the *Adelphi Theatre* to his stable where he produced *The Earl And The Girl* (1903), *The Quaker Girl* (1910), *The Dancing Mistress* (1912), *The Girl From Utah* (1913) and *Tina* (1915).

At the outbreak of WWI Edwardes had the misfortune to be in Germany looking for suitable operettas. He was imprisoned as an enemy alien and spent several months in prison. Eventually repatriated to England in the summer of 1915, his ordeal broke his spirit and his health and he died suddenly of heart failure on 4th October 1915 at the age of 60—leaving his estate in considerable debt. His business partner Robert Evett produced several more hits under his name and management, the most notable being *The Maid of the Mountains* (1917), which saved his estate.

Harry Greenbank (lyricist)
1865-1899

Henry Harveston Greenbank was born in London and started his career at the *Savoy Theatre* where he came to the attention of George Edwardes. Once Edwardes had taken control of London's *Gaiety Theatre* he appointed Greenbank as lyricist along with music director Sidney Jones and dramatist Owen Hall to create the hit musical comedy *A Gaiety Girl* (1893). After the worldwide success of that piece, the three stayed together and subsequently formed the backbone of the team which produced the famous series of very successful series of *Daly's Theatre* musicals, including *An Artiste's Model* (1895), *The Geisha* (1896), *A Greek Slave* (1898), and *San Toy* (1899). At the same time, *Greenbank* also provided lyrics for two of the most successful of the lighter shows produced by Edwardes at the *Gaiety Theatre: The Circus Girl* (1896) and *A Runaway Girl* (1898). He also ventured twice as librettist-lyricist, once with an original musical, *Monte Carlo*, and once with an adaptation of *Lecocq's La Petite Mademoiselle* as *The Scarlet Feather*. He also contributed additional lyrics for *The Bric à Brac Will* (1895) and, posthumously, a song for the London production of *A Chinese Honeymoon* (1901) in which Lily Elsie first made a name for herself on the West End stage, but which he never saw. Greenbank was often in ill health, and during the production of *A Greek Slave*, he moved with his wife and son to England's southern coast in an attempt to regain some strength. He died there while writing lyrics for *San Toy*, and the piece was completed by Adrian Ross, who, with Greenbank, was largely responsible for establishing the post of lyricist (as opposed to librettist, or co-writer) in the modern musical theatre. He died in Boscombe at the age of only 33.

Mizzi Gunther (German Soprano)
1879-1961
Mizzi Gunther was born in Varnsdorf, Bohemia, which is now part of the Czech Republic, in February 1879. She became famous as a Bohemian-Viennese operetta soprano making her debut in 1897 in Hermannstadt, Romania, eventually becoming a star of the genre in Vienna's *Theater an der Wien* as *O Mimosa San* in the *Geisha* in 1901. An English translation/version of this operetta was also successful the score was arranged and new songs added by Sidney Jones to a libretto by Owen Hall, with lyrics by Harry Greenbank. Additional songs were written by Lionel Monckton and James Philip, although Mizzi Gunther was not the star in London. She went on to create the title role in Franz Lehar's *Die lustige Witwe (The Merry Widow)* at its debut performances at the *Theatre an der Wien*, Vienna,1905, but she was not invited to perform the role in the English translation of the operetta at London's at *Daly's Theatre* by George Edwardes because he had decided he wanted Lily Elsie to originate the role in the West End production. Edwardes considered Mizzi too old, and as she was rather rotund, with a huge soprano voice, too overpowering. Mizzi did however travel to London to see Lily Elsie in the role and was full of praise and delighted at her success. Mizzi would also take the lead role in Vienna in Leo Fall's *Die Dollarprinzessin* in 1907, only to find that Lily Elsie was cast as the star again in the 1909 English translation/production of *The Dollar Princess*. After WWI, like so many of her contemporaries, she found the operetta musical form had fallen out of fashion and she faded into obscurity. She died in Vienna aged 82 in 1961.

Owen Hall (Librettist)
1853-1907

Born James Davis in Dublin he grew up to have a chequered careers in law, politics and journalism. He was an inveterate gambler and wrote his first musical script on a dare from a friend, London producer George Edwardes (with whom he shared his love of horses). The result was *A Gaiety Girl* (1893), the first in a series of international hits that would enrich both men—with Davis using the pseudonym Owen Hall for all his stage credits. The success of *An Artist's Model* (1895), *The Geisha* (1896) and *The Greek Slave* (1898) could hardly prepare anyone for the popularity of *Florodora* (1899), which was a sensation in the UK, US and Europe. Hall also penned libretti for *The Silver Slipper* (1901) in which Lily Elsie made her West End debut, *The Girl From Kay's* (1902) and several less memorable shows. Despite his success, gambling left him nearly bankrupt when he died at age 54 in 1907.

Basil Hood (Librettist)
1864-1917

Basil Charles Hood was born in Yorkshire and was the youngest son of Sir Charles Hood. Educated at Wellington and Sandhurst he joined the army at 19, rising to the rank of Captain in the *Prince of Wales'* own regiment. In his early twenties he began writing for the theatre and soon came to the attention of George Edwardes of London's *Gaiety Theatre* where he worked on musical comedies including *Cinder-Ellen Up-to-Late* (1894), *The Hansom Cabbie* (1895), *The French Maid* (1896) and *Dandy Dan The Lifeguardsman* (1897). He gave up the army to concentrate on his theatre career and worked almost exclusively for George Edwardes at either *The Gaiety* or *Daly's Theatre* writing for musical comedies including: *The Belle of Mayfair* (1906), *Les Merveilleuses* (1906). His English translations for German operettas would include: *The Merry Widow* (which made Lily Elsie a star) (1907), *The Dollar Princess* (1908), *A waltz Dream* (1908), *The Count of Luxembourg* (1911) and *Gypsy Love* (1912). At the outbreak of WWI he took a job in the War Office for the duration, recognising that his services were needed to aid the war effort. He died in his chambers at St James Street in 1918 aged 53. His early death was a mystery but official explanation stated he died from "overwork" and not having "the desire to eat".

Franz Lehar (German composer)
1870-1948

Franz Lehar was born in Komarno (then Austro-Hungary, now Slovakia) as the eldest son of a bandmaster in the Austro-Hungarian army. He studied violin and composition at the Prague Conservatory but was advised by Antonin Dvorak to focus on composing music. After graduation in 1899 he joined his father's band in Vienna as assistant bandmaster. In 1902 he became conductor at the historic Vienna *Theater an der Wien*, where his first opera *Wiener Frauen* was performed in November that year. He is most famous for his operettas—the most successful of which is *The Merry Widow* (*die lustige Witwe*), but he also wrote sonatas, symphonic poems, marches and a number of waltzes. Individual songs from his famous operettas have become standards, notably *Vilja* from *The Merry Widow* and *You Are My Hearts Desire* (*Dein ist mein ganzes Herz*) from *Land of Smiles*. By 1935 he had formed his own publishing house to allow him more control over the sale and performance rights of his works. He died in 1948 in Bad Ischl, near Salzburg, at the age of 78.

Victor Leon (German librettist)
1858-1940

Viktor Hirschfeld was born in Vienna in 1858 and became a prolific writer of libretti for operetta productions in Germany, creating over seventy five Viennese operettas including: *Der Doppelganger* (1886), *Der Operball* (1898), *Wiener Blut* (1899), and composer *Franz Lehar's Der Rastelbinder* (1902). His most frequent collaborator was Leo Stein with whom he created the book and lyrics for *Die Lustige Witwe* (The Merry Widow) presented at the *Theater an der Wien* in Vienna in 1905. He was invited by *Daly's Theatre* impresario George Edwardes, who had seen the production at the *Theater an der Wien* in Vienna, to collaborate in the English translation of *The Merry Widow* for its London debut in 1907. However Edwardes, as was his custom, was just offering a courtesy to keep Lehar happy and had no intention Leon would influence the translation. Edwardes had his own team of librettist and lyricists—very little of the dialogue and lyrics were a direct translation of the original, because Edwardes knew it wouldn't work for English audiences. In spite of this he continued to work and collaborated with Lehar again on his operetta *Das Land des Lachelns* in 1930, which also had a London production at the Theatre Royal, Drury Lane. He died at his home in Vienna in 1940 aged 82.

Marie Lloyd (Music Hall Artiste/Singer)
1870-1922

Matilda Wood was born in Hoxton, London, her early interest in the music hall was fostered by her father who worked part-time in the nearby *Royal Eagle Tavern*. Lloyd formed her sisters into a singing group called *The Fairy Bells Minstrels*, singing temperance songs in local missions and church halls, costumed by their mother Matilda Mary Caroline Wood. In her teens she adopted the stage name Marie Lloyd and quickly became very popular in the east-end halls. Progressing to the more lavish and popular West End halls she began to sing *The Boy I Love Is Up In The Gallery* with great success, the problem was this song belonged to Nelly Power, then Queen of the halls, and a dispute broke out. Due to Power's sudden death in 1887 aged just 34, it allowed Lloyd to continue using the song—one of the songs she is now best remembered for. Lloyd's siblings also performed fairly successfully in the halls including Daisy, Rose, Grace and Alice. All but Daisy used the name Lloyd in honour of their more famous sister. Lloyd's songs, although perfectly harmless by modern standards, began to gain a reputation for being 'racy' and filled with double entendre largely thanks to the manner in which she sang them ("She'd never had her ticket punched before!"), adding winks and gestures and creating a conspiratorial relationship with her audience. As a result of complaints from women's vigilante groups she had to perform her songs in front of morality inspectors—which she did, but 'straight' to show their supposed innocence. She also received disapproval from the royal family who, when it became public knowledge she was having an affair with a famous jockey who'd won the Derby, asked that she withdraw from the *Royal Variety Performance*. Seething at the hypocrisy she booked the *Alhambra Theatre*, Leicester Square, with her own money, on the same night as the *Royal Variety*. It was packed to the gods and she performed her new song *My Old Man Said Follow The Van* for the first time—and delighted in the fact it became the most popular song everywhere as a result. During WWI she worked tirelessly to help recruitment for the army and would sing songs with lyrics like "I didn't like you much before you joined the army, John, but I do like you, cockie, now you've got your khaki on". She also performed many free concerts for the returning wounded. In October 1922 she was appearing in Edmonton, London, During the last song in her act *I'm One Of The Ruins That Cromwell Knocked About A Bit* she staggered about on the stage. The audience laughed delightedly when she fell, thinking it was all part of the act. However, she was desperately ill, and died three days later, aged 52.

W. McQueen-Pope (Journalist/Theatre Historian) 1888-1960

Walter McQueen-Pope was known as 'Popie' to his friends and colleagues in the theatre world. He started writing articles and reviews for theatrical productions around the time of Lily Elsie's rise to stardom in Lehar's *The Merry Widow* (1907) at London's *Daly's Theatre*—indeed he vividly recalls these times in the books he would write later in his life. Fleet Street he enjoyed, but inevitably he crossed over to the theatre and started working as a press officer for theatrical managers. Eventually he would become the main press representative for Ivor Novello from the 1930s up until Novello's death in 1951. It was Popie who sensitively manoeuvred Novello through the turbulent waters which resulted in Novello's prison sentence during WWII, for petrol rationing offences, and his subsequent swift return to perform his role in *The Dancing Years (1939-1944)* once released. Popie's actions certainly helped Novello's career to survive this disastrous event. After WWII, Popie began to write books on theatre history, based on his own experiences in the profession, which included *Carriages at Eleven, Theatre Royal (Drury Lane), An Indiscreet Guide to the Theatre, Haymarket: Theatre of Perfection, Twenty Shillings in the Pound, Gaiety: Theatre of Enchantment, The Melodies Linger On, Ladies First, Ghosts & Greasepaint, Shirtfronts and Sables, Fortune's Favourite* (with D.L. Murray), *Back Numbers, Pillars of Drury Lane* and *Ivor: The Story of an Achievement*. Many of these books were produced in the late 1940s and 1950s. He recorded for posterity a remarkable wealth of facts and information which is invaluable to theatre historians. His style may be seen as sentimental, if not sycophantic, but he was a man of his time, and he truly revered the places and personalities he remembered so vividly. He died at his home in London in 1960 aged 72.

Lionel Monckton (Composer/Lyricist)
1861-1924

Lionel John Alexander Monckton was a writer and composer of musical comedy. He was Britain's most popular musical theatre composer in the years preceding WWI. Born in London the son of a town clerk, Sir John Monckton, and his mother Lady Julia an actress. He was educated at Charterhouse School and Oxford University, where he composed music for amateur productions. He initially joined the legal profession but also worked as a part—time music and theatre critic for the *Pall Mall Gazette* and the *Daily Telegraph*. At the age of 29, in 1891, he finally managed to have a song accepted for a professional musical show co-written with lyricist Basil Hood. Monckton soon became a regular composer (and sometime lyricist) of songs for musical comedies performed at London's *Gaiety Theatre* under the management of George Edwardes including *Claude Du-Val* (1894), *The Shop Girl* (1894), *The Circus Girl* (1896) and *A Runaway Girl* (1898). In 1902 he married Gertie Millar, one of the most successful actresses of the period, who starred in Edwardes' *Gaiety Theatre* shows. These '*Girl*' musicals were followed by a number of '*Boy*' musicals at the *Gaiety* including *The Messenger Boy* (1900) and *The Toreador* (1901), the latter being the last production at the old *Gaiety Theatre* prior to its demolition in 1903 (replaced by the new *Gaiety Theatre* on the same site which opened also in 1903). Monckton's songs were very popular and continued to be performed until as late as the 1960s. After WWI Monckton contributed to some revues but had little enthusiasm for this and other new forms of musical entertainment. Unwilling to adapt his style of writing to the newly popular dance rhythms and 'noisy numbers', *Monckton* stopped composing altogether. He died at his home in London aged 62.

Gerald du Maurier, Sir (Actor/Manager)
1873-1934

Gerald Herbert Busson du Maurier was born in Hampstead, London and attended Harrow School. Due to his father's friend John Hare, manager of the *Garrick Theatre*, London, he secured small parts in plays various. At the start of the new century he played in two of J.M Barrie's plays: as *Ernest* in *The Admirable Crichton* (1902) and *Captain Hook* in *Peter Pan* (1904) receiving critical and popular acclaim in both roles which established his reputation. He went on the manage *Wyndham's Theatre* with co producer-manager Frank Curzon (1910-1925), where he appeared in and directed many plays, then moved to the *St James's Theatre*. Knighted in 1922 and in later years continued to act in films, most notably with Michael Balcon. His daughter Daphne du Maurier became a famous novelist (*Rebecca*) and produced a biography of her father *Gerald: A Portrait* which was released in the same year as his death. He died of cancer in 1934, at his home in London, at the age of 61.

Gertie Millar, Lady Dudley (Actress/Singer)
1879-1952
Gertie Millar was born in Bradford, North Yorkshire, she performed as a child in pantomime progressing as a singer and dancer in the music halls. She moved to London and made a name for herself appearing in variety shows. She was then taken under the wing of George Edwardes who placed her in his musical comedy shows at the *Gaiety Theatre*, as a result she became the most famous of the "Gaiety girls". Productions included: *The Toreador* (1901), *A Country Girl* (1902), *The Orchid* (1903) progressing to leading roles in *The Spring Chicken* (1905), *The New Aladdin* (1906) and *A Waltz Dream* (1908). Her biggest successes included *Our Miss Gibbs* (1909), *The Quaker Girl* (1910), *Gipsy Love* (1912) and a major revival of *The Country Girl* (1913). The outbreak of WW1, and the death of George Edwardes, initiated a change in the public's taste and her star diminished. Her husband, composer Lionel Monckton, died in 1924 and she remarried William Humble Ward the second Earl of Dudley, elevating her to a title and thereafter she was known as Lady Dudley. She died in Chiddingford, England, in 1952 aged 73.

Edward Marsh, Sir (Patron of the arts)
1872-1953
Born in Cambridge Marsh became a classical scholar and translator, forming the *Georgian Poets Society*, in addition to his Civil Service career

where he became Winston Churchill's private secretary. He was also descended from Spencer Percival, the only British Prime Minister to be assassinated, from which he received a share of a trust set up by the Prince Regent at the time of Percival's death. Marsh referred to this as his "murder money" and used it to help artists he considered worthy of his personal patronage. They included Rupert Brooke, Siegfried Sassoon and Ivor Novello. Brooke's death shattered him and he kept a camp bed Brooke used whilst staying with him and would refer to it adoringly as "Rupert's bed" to his guests, whilst Novello received his support on many occasions to save him from financial disasters whilst producing his plays in the West End. He also acted as editor in chief for the many books Churchill produced whilst out of office. Marsh produced his own biography in 1939 titled *A Number of People*, a memoir of his life and times containing memories of those writers and politicians with whom he had associated. He died at his flat in London aged 81 still shattered by Brooke's death years before, and Novello's sudden death in 1951.

Owen Nares (Actor)
1888-1943
Owen Ramsay Nares had a long stage and film career and, for most of the 1920s, was one of Britain's favourite matinee idols and silent film star. Besides his acting career he was the author of *Myself and Some Others* published in 1925. Educated at Reading School, Nares was encouraged by his mother to become an actor, and in 1908 he received his training from actress Rosins Filippi. The following year, he was playing bit parts in West End productions at the *St James' Theatre*. Over the next few years, as his reputation grew, he performed with many of the leading actors of the time including Sir Beerbohm Tree, Constance Collier and Marion Terry. In 1914 Nares appeared in *Dandy Donovan*, the first of twenty five silent films he would make, his leading ladies included Gladys Cooper, Fay Compton, Madge Titheridge and Ruby Miller. In 1915 he played Thomas Armstrong in Edward Sheldon's play *Romance* at the *Lyric Theatre*, and in 1917 he starred with Lily Elsie in the musical comedy *Pamela* at the *Palace Theatre*. With the advent of the 'talkies' his considerable stage experience meant he was initially in demand for the new medium and starred in four films, however in the end he proved to be too old to play handsome leading roles. Nares

married actress Marie Pollini in the spring of 1910 and had two sons, David and Geoffrey. During a tour through Wales in 1943 he visited Brecon and *The Shoulder of Mutton* public house (now *The Sarah Siddon* public house named after the famous actress). Whilst in the very room in which Sarah Siddons had been born Nares had a heart attack and died. He was just 55 years old.

Frederic Norton (Composer)
1869-1946
Frederic Norton born Gordon Frederic Norton on 11 October 1869 in Broughton-in-Salford, England. Died on 15 December 1946 in Holford, England. British composer, most associated with the record breaking *Chu Chin Chow*, which opened in 1916.
A trained singer, *Norton* studied opera and appeared on stage in variety theatre. Some of these acts included the delivery of monologues. These monologues led Norton to compose songs, many of them humorous. Songs published included 1908's *Rosemary* with words by *Graham Robertson*, and *Maid of the Morning, When a Pullet is Plump* and *The Elephant and the Portmanteau*. In turn, these songs resulted in Norton composing music for stage shows, starting with *The Water Maidens* (1901). In 1911, Norton provided additional music for a production of *Orpheus In The Underworld* at *His Majesty's Theatre*, which was based on the *Offenbach* opera of the same name. He contributed to the musical comedy *Pamela* (1917), which marked one of Lily Elsie's last West End appearances. Norton was never again to achieve the same degree of success that he earned with *Chu Chin Chow*.

Ivor Novello (Actor/Playwright/Composer)
1893-1951
David Ivor Davies was born in Cardiff in 1893. He attended *Magdalen College Choir School*, Oxford, and subsequently became Head Chorister. He then moved to London and began composing popular songs changing his name to Ivor Novello (Novello was his mother's maiden name). At the outbreak of WWI in 1914 he was found to have a heart murmur and was initially exempt from military service. It was during this time he composed his first international hit '*Keep The Home Fires Burning*' in collaboration with his lyricist Lena Gilbert Ford in 1915.

After a medical he was given the all clear and, after the intervention of his friend Edward Marsh, Churchill's secretary, was enlisted into the *Royal Flying Corps*. After crashing three aircraft he was moved to a desk job at the War Office for the duration. Marsh introduced him to fellow airman Robert (Bobbie) Andrews in 1916 when they attended a play titled *Under Cover* at the *Strand Theatre*: they subsequently became lovers and life-long partners. By 1920 he had established himself as a film actor and made many silent films including *The Call Of The Blood* (1920), *Carnival* (1921), *The White Rose* (1923), *Bonnie Prince Charlie* (1923), *The Vortex* (1928) and most notably two films with Alfred Hitchcock *The Lodger* (1926) and *Downhill* (1927). After an unsuccessful attempt to break into Hollywood, he returned to London and made a few 'talkies', although he had great comedic talents he shrewdly saw his future in films was limited and his final film was *Autumn Crocus* (1934). However, his handsome and striking profile established him as the "English Valentino" and he used this appeal in films to carve out a career in theatre as an actor appearing in plays including *Debareu* (1921), *Spanish Lovers* (1922), *Enter Kiki* (1923), *The Firebrand* (1926), *Lilliom* (1926) and *Coward's Sirroco* (1927). He also wrote his own plays which had successful West End productions including *The Rat* (1924), *Downhill (1926)*, which he wrote in collaboration with Constance Collier, *The Truth Game* (1928/9 in which he starred with *Lily Elsie*), *I Lived With You* (1932), *Party* (1932), *Fresh Fields* (1933) and *Proscenium* (1933). He is perhaps best remembered today as the composer and deviser of glamorous musicals initially at the *Theatre Royal, Drury Lane*, influenced by Lehar's operettas from the early part of the century, with co stars Mary Ellis, Dorothy Dickson, Vanessa Lee, Elisabeth Welch, Olive Gilbert and sisters Phyllis and Zena Dare, which included *Glamorous Night* (1935), *Careless Rapture* (1936), *Crest Of The Wave* (1937), *The Dancing Years* (1939-1944), *Arc De Triomph* (1943), *Perchance To Dream* (1945), *Kings Rhapsody* (1949) and *Gay's The Word* (1951). His lyricist for all his musicals was Christopher Hassall apart from *Gay's The Word* which had lyrics by Alan Melville. *Gay's The Word* was written especially for comedienne Ciceley Courtnidge and Novello attended the first night in February 1951 just two weeks before his sudden and unexpected death from coronary thrombosis. He died in his bedroom in 'the flat' he lived in on top of the *Strand Theatre*,

Aldwych, London, after performing in *King's Rhapsody* at the *Palace Theatre*. He was only 58 years old. In 2006 the *Strand Theatre* reopened after extensive restoration by owners *Delfont Mackintosh Theatres* who renamed it the *Novello Theatre* in recognition of his contribution to the West End musical theatre genre.

Nelly Power (Music Hall Singer/Actress)
1853-1887

Nelly Power was a famous dancer, comic and singer in the music halls who was popular around the United Kingdom for singing the song *The Boy I Love Is Up In The Gallery*, among others, which was specially written for her. This song caused her to have a dispute with a young performer called *Marie Lloyd* who started using the song without permission. Power also played travesty roles throughout her short career in addition to performing in pantomimes—and character parts in the ballets at the *Canterbury Music Hall*. She was a special favourite for audiences at the *Canterbury* as she had made her debut there when a teenager with the song *Up In A Balloon, Boys*. At the time of her death she was performing at the *Trocadero Music Hall* and still in dispute with Marie Lloyd over *The Boy I Love*—many would say that Power's rendition of this song was far superior to Lloyd's. After Power's death Lloyd made the song her own and is still associated with it nearly a hundred years after her own death. Power had a 'blood disorder' which caused her early death, which could have been either leukaemia or diabetes. Married for fifteen years to Israel Gideon Barnett, she died suddenly at her home in London aged just 34.

Gabrielle Ray (Actress/Dancer/Singer)
1883-1973

Born Gabrielle Elizabeth Clifford Cook in Stockport, Cheshire, she first appeared on the stage at the age of ten. By sixteen her dancing skills brought her to the attention of managements and she was employed by the *Ben Greet Players* who toured low budget productions to mainly working class audiences. By the start of the 20th century her career progressed and she found herself performing in the West End. Gaining attention as a beautiful young ingénue, her photograph was much sought after by leading publications who described her as "the most beautiful woman in the United Kingdom". productions included *The Toreador* (1902), *The Girl from Kays* (1903). Next she played in the hit *Orchid* (1904) increasing her fame by singing "*The Pink Pyjama Girl*". She was then contracted by George Edwardes and appeared in several of his most successful shows most notably *The Merry Widow (1907)* in which she played *Frou Frou*: Ray's dance number in this show, complete with high kicks, all performed on a table at Maxim's held high by four men was a show stopper. She went on to appear in *The Dollar Princess* (1909) and *Peggy* (1911) at which time she announced her retirement from the stage to marry the wealthy Eric Loder in 1912. The marriage didn't last (they divorced in 1914) at which time she attempted to make a comeback but in vain. She fought depression and alcohol abuse and by 1936 was committed to a mental hospital where she remained until her death forty years later at the age of ninety.

Ada Reeve (Music Hall Artiste)
1874-1966

Born in London to a family of actors, she made her first appearance on the stage at the age of four in the pantomime *Red Riding Hood* in 1878 at the *Pavillion Theatre*, Whitechapel. A series of pantomimes and dramatic roles followed, before she began working as a music hall performer in her teens. She enjoyed a hit with the risqué song *She Was A Clergyman's Daughter* sung with knowing winks and gestures. She also starred in George Edwardes big hit *The Shop Girl* (1894) at the old *Gaiety Theatre* opposite Seymour Hicks. During the run she found herself pregnant and was replaced by Hick's wife Ellaline Terriss. She went on to appear in *All Aboard* (1895), *The Girl From Paris* (1896) among others. Her biggest hit was the musical comedy *Florodora* (1899) at the *Lyric Theatre* in the West End where she created the role of Lady Holyrood. She was then cast in the hit show *San Toy* (1901) playing Dudley, but eventually taking over the lead role from Marie Tempest. Reeve married Wilfred Cotton in 1902—he was the uncle of Lily Elsie and thus she became her aunt. She continued to work in music hall, variety and musical comedy and toured the world appearing in productions various and returned to England to star in musical *Black Velvet* (1940). After WWII she began appearing in supporting roles in films. At the age of 80 she retired from the stage but made two more films, the last of which was at the age of 83 in *A Passionate Stranger* in 1957. She died in 1966 at the age of 92.

Adrian Ross (Lyricist/Librettist)
1859-1933
Arthur Reed Ropes, better known by his professional name Adrian Ross, was a King's College, Cambridge, history graduate who had won the Chancellor's Medal for verse, and was subsequently a fellow and lecturer at Cambridge, Ross made his first attempt at stage writing with the libretto and lyrics for a burlesque, *Faddimir*. *Faddimir* got itself a showing at a showcase matinee and won sufficient praise for its author and his fellow Cambridge man, Frank Osmond Carr, who had composed the music, to be commissioned to write a burlesque for George Edwardes. Edwardes did, however, take the precaution of pairing his new writer with the experienced comedian John Shine on his first outing. *Joan of Arc* was a big success, and Ross and Carr were promptly put to work this time unaided on another, slightly different kind of piece for Edwardes. *In Town*, with its cocky tale of backstage and society doings, broke away from the burlesque pattern and helped set the up-to-date style for the famous series of *Gaiety* musicals which followed. For these early works, Ross worked on both libretto and lyrics but, as from his next piece, *Morocco Bound*, he limited himself almost entirely to writing lyrics, and his few subsequent ventures into original book-writing were the less successful side of a remarkable career. During the great days of the *Gaiety Theatre*, Ross contributed many lyrics to virtually all of that theatre's shows from *The Shop Girl* onwards, sharing in all the greatest international hits of Edwardes' *Gaiety Theatre* era of musical comedy. Edwardes also put him to writing additional numbers for the shows at *Daly's Theatre* and, after small contributions to *An Artist's Model* and *The Geisha*, he became a fixed part of the *Daly's* team from *A Greek Slave* onwards, a function increased on the premature death of *Daly's Theatre's* lyricist-in-chief, Harry Greenbank. He remained in the Guvnor's service through the whole *Daly's Theatre* era of British musicals and, when Edwardes switched to importing continental shows, he took over adapting the lyrics of those shows into English. His first assignment was *Die lustige Witwe*, and his songwords to *The Merry Widow* (*Vilja* etc) became the standard English version

of that piece, performed throughout the world for many decades and rarely equalled by subsequent adaptors. Amongst the other Continental musicals which Ross anglicized were *The Girl on the Train, The Marriage Market, The Dollar Princess* and *The Count of Luxemburg*, all of which had a wide and enduring success in their English versions. He died in London in 1933 aged 74.

Leo Stein (German Librettist)
1861-1921

Leo Rosenstein was born in Lemberg, Austria in 1861 and went on to become one of the most famous of the German operetta librettists writing some of Vienna's most loved operettas including *Weiner Blut* (1899), *Das Susse Madel* (1902), *Vera Violetta* (1907) and *Die Csardasfurstin* (1911). His most famous contribution was made whilst working with Victor Leon creating the book and lyrics for composer Franz Lehar's *Die Lustige Witwe* (The Merry Widow) in 1905. He was invited by *Daly's Theatre* impresario George Edwardes, who had seen the production at the *Theater an der Wien* in Vienna, to collaborate in the English translation of *The Merry Widow* for its London debut in 1907. However Edwardes, as was his custom, was just offering a courtesy to keep Lehar happy and had no intention Stein would influence the translation. Edwardes had his own team of librettist and lyricists—very little of the dialogue and lyrics were a direct translation of the original, because Edwardes knew it wouldn't work for English audiences. In spite of this disappointment Stein was delighted at the world wide success of *The Merry Widow* and the benefits to his reputation as a result. After WWI the operetta had fallen out of fashion because of the changing times, but he continued to work on projects until his death in 1921 aged 60. Stein remained active until shortly before his death.

Leslie Stuart (Composer/Lyricist)
1863-1928

Thomas Augustine Barret was born in Southport, Lancashire, but was known professionally as Leslie Stuart. While working as an organist at *Salford Cathedral* he began composing music hall songs and his first hit *Lily Of Laguna* was written for Eugene Stratton. He enjoyed classical music and had aspirations in that direction but found composing, and writing lyrics for pantomime more lucrative. Coming to the attention of George Edwardes he was commissioned to compose music for *The Shop Girl* (1894) at the *Gaiety Theatre* and from there also worked at *Daly's Theatre* for *Edwardes* on shows including *An Artistes Model* (1895), *The Circus Girl* (1896), *A Day In Paris* (1897, *The Ballet Girl* (1897) and *The Yashmak* (1897). Stuart's greatest success as composer-lyricist was *Floradora* (1899) with book by Owen Nares and this was followed by *The Silver Slipper* (in which Lily Elsie made her West End debut at the *Lyric Theatre*, 1901). The success of these led George Edwardes to hope that Stuart would be able to replace the Caryll and Monckton writing partnership on their departure from the *Gaiety Theatre*. Stuart's next show, *Captain Kidd* (1909), however, was not for the *Gaiety*, and it was a flop. *Peggy* (1911) was produced at the *Gaiety* and although it achieved reasonable success and he wrote another show, *The Slim Princess* (1911), for Broadway at the same time, he did not produce any major new hits during this period. In 1911, due to changing fashions in musical theatre, and mounting debts, he was made bankrupt. A 1940 biographical film entitled *You Will Remember*, directed by Jack Raymond, starred Robert Morley in the Leslie Stuart role and Emlyn Williams. The screen writers were Lydia Hayward, Sewell Stokes and Christopher D. Morley. Stuart was evasive about his true age. Various different years of birth have been given, and no official birth record is known to exist. However, his 1871 and 1881 census entries seem to establish that he was born in 1863. He died in London aged 65.

Bertram Wallis (Actor/Singer)
1874-1952
Born in London Bertram Wallis was a renowned actor and singer in British plays and musical comedies. He studied voice at the Royal Academy of Music and his first professional engagements were as an actor in Shakespeare productions of *As You Like It* (1896) and *Much Ado About Nothing* (1898). Wallis was a tall, handsome man and perfect as a matinee idol—with that rare talent of being able to sing beautifully and also act superbly. He went on to make a name for himself appearing in musical comedy productions on Broadway, including *A Madcap Princess* (1904), *Miss Hook of Holland* (1907) and returning to England he established his career by appearing in *King of Cadonia* (1908) at the

Prince of Wales Theatre in the West End and then in George Edwardes' productions at *Daly's Theatre*, including *The Balkan Princess* (1910), *The Count of Luxembourg* (1911) with Lily Elsie, *The Happy Day* (1916) and the hit revue *Zig Zag!* (1917) among others. Between the war he made several films: *The Cost of a Kiss* (1917), *Victory and Peace* (1918), *The Wandering Jew* (1933), *A Dream Love* (1938), *Chips* (1938), *A People Eternal* (1939) and *Shipbuilders* (1944). After WWII he retired from the stage and died aged 78 in 1952 at his home in Kent.

THEATRES

The history of the theatres mentioned in Elsie's story need some clarification for those unaware of the changes of name in some cases, and because many have long since been demolished. Manchester and Salford's theatres associated with Elsie started life as music halls and as times changed were eventually converted to cinemas in the early part of the 20th Century only to be demolished either before or after WWII. London's old theatreland which had grown up in the shadow of Drury Lane was almost wiped out at the turn of the 20th century in the reconstruction of the area between Wellington Street, Strand and the beginning of Fleet Street. The whole maze of slums, stretching up towards Drury Lane on one side, and Lincoln's Inn on the other, was demolished, and the new streets Aldwych and Kingsway constructed. This vast operation began in the last years of the nineteenth century and was not finally completed until after WWI. Five theatres were demolished during the early stages of the work: the *Olympic Theatre* in Wych Street and the *Opera Comique* in the Strand were closed in 1899, the *Globe Theatre* in Newcastle Street shut its doors in 1902. This was followed by the closure of the old *Gaiety Theatre* in the Strand. The *Royal Strand Theatre* had also been demolished to make way for the new Aldwych Underground Station built on the site the theatre occupied. The new *Gaiety Theatre* straddled the new Aldwych and the Strand opening in 1903. On the large oblong site in Aldwych, between Catherine Street and Drury Lane with Tavistock Street in the rear, two theatres were built with identical facades and an hotel, the *Waldorf*, constructed between them. These are now known as the *Aldwych Theatre* and the *Novello Theatre (*formerly the *Strand Theatre)*.

Provincial Theatres:

The Prince of Wales Theatre, Liverpool Road, Salford, was built in 1882 as a music hall. It was a very popular venue and certainly the one Lily Elsie's father and mother worked at for a period; and where Elsie made her first appearance as 'Little Elsie'. By 1905 the popularity of the music halls was in decline and the theatre began showing early films—probably of the Mitchell & Kenyon type where local people were filmed during festivals and whilst leaving work—until 1915 when it abandoned live performances and became a cinema and occasional ballroom. It was at this time its name changed to the **Prince's Theatre**. In 1929 the theatre underwent a major refurbishment to create a luxurious cinema and was fitted with new seating and an organ. By 1944 it had closed completely and was used as a storage warehouse for office supplies and as a result the fabric of the building deteriorated. It was boarded up and derelict for several years—eventually demolished in 1973.

The Regent Theatre, Cross Lane, Salford, was designed and built in 1885 by Frank Matcham. Initially it was a music hall, again 'Little Elsie' would have performed here, but did show early Mitchell & Kenyon type films as early as 1901 alongside the live entertainment on offer. By this time it was also known as the **Regent Opera House**. A change of ownership in 1919 resulted in another change of name to **The Palace Theatre** and housed a live theatre and a cinema. In 1929 **The Palace Theatre** became two cinemas—the **Salford Palace Theatre** and the **Palace Cinema**—and abandoned live performances altogether. They were the first cinemas in Salford to present the new 'talking pictures'. After the 1939-45 war the **Salford Palace Theatre** reverted to live performances but it was not successful and became a cinema again within months. The building was gutted by fire in 1952 and the auditoriums completely destroyed. It lay derelict until 1963 when the council purchased it and demolished what remained. Where the **Regent Theatre** stood is today a large roundabout and the entrance to the M602 motorway.

Queen's Theatre, Manchester, was also known as the **London Music Hall**, was converted into a theatre from an hotel in 1862. It underwent considerable reconstruction circa 1870 but was eventually demolished. On or near the site occupied by the **Queen's Theatre** now stands the **Palace Theatre** which opened in 1891 as the **Manchester Palace of Varieties**. The theatre was redecorated by renowned theatre architect Frank Matcham in 1896 and further alterations were made in 1913 to the auditorium. The façade was remodelled in 1953. Having survived a period of uncertainty during the 1970s, the **Palace Theatre** is still in use as a popular number one touring venue for West End shows. Elsie would have appeared at the **Palace Theatre** as 'Little Elsie' and also as Lily Elsie in pantomime, a production of *The* Merry Widow (1908) and her final appearance in Ivor Novello's play **The Truth Game** (1929).

Thornton's Music Hall, Leeds, is still in existence and is now known as the **City Varieties Music Hall**. The City Varieties is regarded as the jewel in the crown of popular live entertainment for music hall enthusiasts. Other halls from the same era still exist but is recognised by the Guinness Book of Records as being the longest continuous running music hall in Great Britain today. This wonderfully intimate music hall is listed as a grade II* historic building of extreme rarity. It is also in a relatively untouched condition retaining many of its original features, for example, the roof construction has all its truss members still bearing the carpenters mark.

The City Varieties can trace its origins as a music hall back to 1865 when it was known as **Thornton's Fashionable Lounge**. It is known to millions throughout the world as the home of BBC Television's *Good Old Days*, shown from 1953 until 1983, but still performing several weekends each and every year.

London Theatres:

Royal Strand Theatre, London, was built in 1831 by Benjamin Lionel Rayner, a celebrated Yorkshire comedian. It had a chequered history and was redesigned and added to several times during the 19th Century. By 1882 the original building was condemned. Once demolished a new theatre was quickly built and reopened under the same name. It struggled to have much success until new management established comedy plays as a popular entertainment for the theatre. The musical comedy *A Chinese Honeymoon* (1903), in which *Lily Elsie* made her name as *Princess Soo Soo*, enjoyed an enormous success, becoming the first musical to run for more than 1,000 performances in the West End. **The Royal Strand Theatre** was demolished in 1905 to make way for the Aldwych Underground Station (which sits directly on the site once occupied by the theatre) as part of the redevelopment of the area. The Aldwych Underground Station closed in 1994 and is said to be haunted by the ghost of an actress who believes she has not yet enjoyed her last curtain call.

The Gaiety Theatre was originally opened in 1864 as **The Strand Musick Hall** (sic) in 1864, only to be rebuilt and named the Gaiety Theatre in 1868. This Gaiety Theatre became known as the old **Gaiety Theatre** and eventually came under the management of impresario George Edwardes who established the 'Gaiety girls' the most famous being Gertie Millar, and his productions were more refined than the music halls and his musical shows always glorified female beauty. The old **Gaiety** was demolished in 1903 as part of the redevelopment of the Aldwych area and closed with Edwardes' musical comedy production *Toreador*—a little over four months later the curtain went up on Edwardes' musical comedy *The Orchid* at his new **Gaiety Theatre**, it's façade gazing elegantly down the Strand. The **Gaiety** remained in business until it closed in 1939. It suffered bomb damage in the blitz during WWII and stood empty for many years until it became a derelict shell, finally demolished in 1957 to be replaced by offices. The office buildings which replaced it were themselves demolished in 2006 and a new hotel—**The Silken Hotel**—is currently under construction.

Daly's Theatre, Leicester Square, London was opened in 1893 under the management of the American Augustine Daly in collaboration with the **Gaiety Theatre** impresario George Edwardes. The collaboration did not work and Edwardes dramatically took back control of the theatre one Sunday by barring the doors and locking himself in the building until Augustine Daly agreed to leave and let Edwardes take back control. Word spread and great crowds gathered in Leicester Square to watch, cheering Edwardes when he emerged in triumph. Augustine Daly returned to America disillusioned and defeated. Edwardes decided to further his 'musical comedy' ambitions by presenting more respectable and refined productions at **Daly's**, but even the Guv'nor (as he was known to many) struggled to find the right kind of show. Eventually he settled on operetta with which he established a reputation for the theatre with German composer Franz Lehar; their first presentation together being *The Merry Widow* in 1907 which made Lily Elsie an overnight star. Edwardes continued the trend with other successful operettas until the outbreak of WWI when all things German became unpopular. Edwardes died in 1915 leaving his empire in considerable debt, however **Daly's** survived and Lily Elsie made her final appearance on the stage in Ivor Novello's production of his play *The Truth Game* in 1929. The theatre closed in 1937 and was sold to Hollywood moguls Warner Brothers who demolished it and replaced it with a theatre and cinema called the **Warner Theatre**. This theatre was itself demolished in the early 1980s—apart from the façade—and Warner built a new 9 screen cinema village on the site.

The **Waldorf Theatre** (now the **Novello Theatre**), Aldwych, London, opened in 1905 and was part of the redevelopment of the Aldwych and the Strand—which had seen the demolition of the **Royal Strand Theatre** (on the site now occupied by the Aldwych Underground Station) and the old **Gaiety Theatre** (demolished 1903) among others (see *Aldwych Theatre* information). Designed by W.G.R. Sprague, it opened at the same time as its sister the **Aldwych Theatre** with the new **Waldorf Hotel** in-between the two. The **Waldorf Theatre** overlooked the new **Gaiety Theatre** (opened 1903) which occupied the corner site straddling the Aldwych and the Strand. In 1909 the name was changed to the **Strand Theatre** briefly, and in 1911 the name was changed again to the **Witney Theatre** but this name was not destined to be enduring either and in 1913 it was changed back to the **Strand Theatre** again. This name remained for the rest of the 20th century and the start of the 21st. The theatre did suffer bomb damage in WWI as a result of Zeppelin bomb raids, and again in WWII during the blitz but managed to survive relatively unscathed. To mark the 100th anniversary of the theatre the Delfont Mackintosh Group, who now own the theatre, decided on a major refurbishment and restoration programme which was completed in December 2005. They also decided to change name of the theatre to the **Novello Theatre** in recognition of Ivor Novello the actor/manager and composer of popular musicals in the 1930s and 40s who had lived and died in the flat which sits on top of the theatre (now used as offices by the Delfont Mackintosh Group). The change also served to eradicate any confusion to tourists and visitors as the name **Strand Theatre** implied it was on the Strand, whereas it is actually situated on the corner of the Aldwych and Catherine Street.

Aldwych Theatre was constructed, along with its sister the *Waldorf Theatre* (now the *Novello Theatre*) and the *Waldorf Hotel*. The *Waldorf Theatre* (now the *Novello Theatre*) on the corner of Catherine Street was opened in May 1905, and its companion. the *Aldwych Theatre*, on the Drury Lane corner in the following December. The *Aldwych Theatre* was built by Seymour Hicks in association with the American impresario Charles Frohman. It was designed by W. G. R. Sprague (who was also responsible for the *Novello Theatre* and the new block then being planned in Shaftesbury Avenue). Its builder was Walter Wallis of Balham. A Painted Act Drop remained in use into the 1930s and the theatre still retains much of its old-world appearance although in post-war years the lower stage boxes were removed and the pit absorbed into the stalls seating while the gallery was transformed into an extension of the upper circle, by the removal of the benches and the substitution of tip-up seats. In 1958 a threat to the building by a redevelopment scheme was revealed, and the London County Council rejected plans in October and again in July 1959. After much speculation, it was finally announced in July 1960, that arrangements had been concluded for the Governors of the *Shakespeare Memorial Theatre*, Stratford-upon-Avon, to take over the *Aldwych Theatre* as their London Headquarters for the next three years. When they took possession in November, drastic alterations were commenced. An apron stage with a new proscenium and lighting was constructed, similar to that at Stratford, at a cost of £75,000. The *Aldwych Theatre* has thrived and still presents plays and musicals in the 21st Century.

PRODUCTIONS

I have included productions where information is available. There was little detailed information regarding some of the early shows Elsie appeared in during her time in Salford and Manchester, other than the dates and titles, prior to her arrival in London. The shows listed below are those which were important in terms of her career progression.

THE SILVER SLIPPER : 1901

A popular musical comedy billed as an 'extravaganza' with music by *Leslie Stewart*, lyrics by *WH Risque* and libretto by *Owen Hall*. This show followed on the heels of *Stewart* and *Hall's* other popular successes for *George Edwardes—Florodora* (1899) and *The Gaiety Girls* (1893). *The Silver Slipper* turned out to be fortuitous for *Edwardes* because it brought his attention to a young actress and singer making her West End début in the production, *Lily Elsie*. It opened at the Lyric Theatre, Shaftsbury Avenue, in 1901.

Sadly there is little detailed information about this production apart froma programme held in the archive of the V&A. Lily Elsie first came to the attention of George Edwardes through her appearance in this production.

A CHINESE HONEYMOON : 1903

A musical comedy in two acts by George Dance, with music by Howard Talbot and additional music by Ivan Caryll et al, and additional lyrics by Harry Greenbank. The show opened at the *Theatre Royal, Hanley* on 16th October 1899 eventually arriving at the *Royal Strand Theatre* in the West End on 5th October 1901 for a run of 1,075 performances. *A Chinese Honeymoon* was the first musical to run for 1000 performances in the West End. The story concerns couples who honeymoon in China and inadvertently break the kissing laws—reminiscent of *The Mikado*.

London cast:
Hang Chow (Emperor of China): *Picton Roxborough*
Princess Soo Soo (the Emperor's niece): *Lily Elsie (replaced Beatrice Edwards)*
Chippee Chop: *Edward Boyd-Jones*
Hi Lung: *Percy Clifton*
Tom Hatherton: *Farren Soutar*
Mr Pineapple: *Arthur Williams*
Mrs Pineaplle: *Marie Dainton*
Florrie (a bridesmaid): *Alice Beaugarde*
Violet (a bridesmaid): *Florence Jamieson*
Millie (a bridesmaid): *Rhoda Cecil*
Gertie (a bridesmaid): *Florence Randle*
Mrs Brown (official mother-in-law): *Jenny Lowes*
Yen Yen (maid of honour to Soo Soo): *Marie Daltra*
Sing Sing (maid of honour to Soo Soo): *Fanny Wright*
Mi Mi (a waitress): *Empsie Bowman*
Fi Fi (waitress at the hotel): *Louie Freear*

For the Royal Strand Theatre:
Royal Strand Theatre: *Frank Curzon* (proprietor/manager)
Producers: *Frank Curzon & George Edwardes* et al
Musical Director: *Ernest Vousden*
Stage Manager: *Austin Hurgon*
Assistant Stage Manager: *Clarence Hunt*

Brief Synopsis:
The Emperor seeks a bride who will marry him "for himself", so he dispatches an English skipper, who has been promoted to the post of Lord High Admiral of the Chinese fleet, in search of such a woman. Returning from his quest unsuccessful he is faced with the death penalty for his failure—so he resorts to all sorts of expedients in order to avert his punishment. Some comical effects are obtained by making the Emperor believe he is betrothed to a diminutive cockney maid. To these ingredients add a cockney tradesman married to a jealous wife who insists upon her four bridesmaids travelling with her for detective and protective purposes, a pair of young lovers, and quaint (imaginary) Chinese customs.

Musical numbers:
The A-la Girl
But Yesterday
A Chinese Honeymoon
Chow-Chow's Honeymoon
Click Click
Could I But Tell You
Dolly With A Dimple On Her Chin
The Emperor Hang Chow
Follow Your Leader
He Is The Bridegroom
I Hear They Want Some More
I Knew At First Sight That I Loved Her
I Want To Be A Lidy
In Ylang-Ylang
Laughter Is Queen Tonight
The leader Of Frocks And Frills
The Maid Of Peking
A Paper Fan
That Happy Land
You Pat Me

LADY MADCAP : 1904

A musical comedy farce in two Acts by Paul A Rubens (1875-1917) with lyrics by Paul A Rubens and Percy Greenbank. The show opened in London's West End at the *Prince of Wales Theatre* on 17th December 1904. Produced by George Edwardes et al

London Cast:
Coun de St Hubert: *Maurice Farcoa*
Bill Stratford: *Paul Arthur*
Posh Jenkins: *Fred Emney*
Colonel Layton: *Leedham Bantock* (Hussar)
Major Blatherswaite: *Dennis Eadie* (Hussar)
Captain Harrington: *Edward Frasier* (Hussar)
Lieutenant Somerset: *Spencer Trevor* (Hussar)
Lord Framlingham: *Herbert Sparling*
Corporal Ham: *George Carroll* (Hussars)
Palmer (Butler to Lord Framlingham): *R. St. George*
Old Huntsman: *Richard Cavanagh*
Trooper Smith: *G.P. Bentley* (Hussars)
Gwenny Holden (a friend of Lady Betty): *Delia Mason* (replaced by *Lily Elsie*)
Susan (Lady's-maid to Betty): *Eva Sandford*
Mrs. Layton (Colonel Layton's wife): *Fred Lewis*
Lady Betty Clarridge (Lord Framlington's daughter—the 'Madcap'): *Madge Crichton*.
Ladies & Gentlemen of the chorus

During the run the cast also included *Phyllis Dare, Zena Dare* and *Gabrielle Ray. Lily Elsie* played chorus parts as well as the character part of *Gwenny Holden*.

For the Prince of Wales Theatre:
Prince of Wales Theatre: *Mr. Frank Curzon* (1868-1927) Proprietor & Manager.
Producer: *George Edwardes* et al. (Edwardes Production Manager: H.T. Brickwell).

Stage Manager: *Sidney Watson.*
Stage Director: *J.A.E. Malone* (1860-1929).
Musical Director: *Frank E. Tours.*

Brief Synopsis:
Musical comedy farce about three upper-class girls attempting to find suitable husbands. Eligible soldiers from the East Anglian Hussars fight for their attention and respective hands in marriage. For one of the girls, as a result of a dare, this entails getting a job as a servant to see if her prospects would be damaged by such a lowly position—which it wasn't as she bagged the best marriage of all.

Musical Numbers:
Her Little Dog!
I Like You In Velvet
The Beetle and the Boot
We English Maidens
Mabel and Maud and Mary!
Oh! I Am The Pet Of Mayfair.
We're Pert Little, Plump Little Page Boys!
If I Were A Soldier
One Night I Met A Dear Little Thing
See Me In A Scarlet Uniform

THE LITTLE MICHUS : 1905 *(Les p'tites Michu)*

A French operetta in three acts by Andre Messager, with a libretto by Albert Vanloo and Georges Duval. The first performance took place at Paris' *Theatres des Bouffes Parisiens*, November 1897. The English adaptation was by Henry Hamilton, with lyrics by Percy Greenbank, and was produced by George Edwardes at London's *Daly's Theatre*— opening on 29th April 1905, enjoying a run of 401 performances. It also enjoyed a Broadway run in 1907.

London Cast:
General des Ifs: *Willie Edouin*
Gaston Rigaud (Captain of the Hussars): *Robert Evett*

Pierre Michu (a provision merchant): *Ambrose Manning*
Aristide Vert (his assistant): *Louis Bradfield*
Bagnolet (soldier/servant to General des Ifs): *Huntley Wright*
Madame du Tertre: *Deborah Volar*
Madame Rousselin: *Gracie St. George*
Mlle Herpin (school mistress): *Vera Beringer*
Madame Michu (Michu's wife): *Amy Augarde*
Marie-Blanche, Blanche-Marie (The Little Michus) *Adrienne Augarde* and *Mabel Green*
Six schoolgirls (Chorus parts)
Cast also included: *Amy Fanchette, Freda Vivien, Alice Hatton, Agnes Gunn, Doris Stocker, Nina Sevening, Amy Augarde, Alice D'Orme, Emily Shepherd, Evelyn Bond, Eva Wright,* **Phyllis Dare***, Zena Dare, Morah Lister and Lily Elsie—Willie Ward, Jack Thomson, Bernard Dudley.*
Lily Elsie *took over the role of Marie-Blanche (The Little Michus) for a short period* of the run.

For Daly's Theatre:
Daly's Theatre: *George Edwardes (1855-1915)* **Acting Manager**: G.E. Minor
Producers: *George Edwardes* et al
Musical Director: *Howard Talbot (1865-1928)*
Stage Manager: *J.A.E. Malone (1860-1929)*
Choreographer: *Willie Ward (1847-1943)*

Brief Synopsis:
The Michus family are happy running their shop business, but only one of their daughters is born to them. The other is adopted. The Michus cannot remember which is which and so love each with equal passion. Complications arise when General Ifs demands the return of his daughter whom the Michus adopted, and both girls fall in love with the same man.

Act I: *The Playground of Mlle. Herpin's Scchool in Paris (1810).*
Act II: *Salon at Gneral Des Ifs.*
Act III: *Michu's Shop, Les Halles.*

Musical Numbers:
We Are Little Schoolgirls
Two Little Maids
If I Were King
When I Met A Man Like That!
How Very Like Children
So You'll Wed The General's Daughter
Look After Your P's and Q's!
Customers!
Strange How The Unexpected Should Always Come To Pass
I'm Full Of Joyful Expectation
Now Please Sit Down!
Finale: Two Little Maids (reprise)

SEE SEE : 1906

An oriental operetta in three acts which very much follows the popular style initiated with *A Chinese Honymoon*. The book was written by *George Edwardes* (1852-1915) and *Charles Brookfield* with music by *Sidney Jones* (1861-1946) and lyrics by *Adrian Ross*. Presented at the *Prince of Wales Theatre*, London (after a fairly extensive provincial tour starting in 1899!) in 1906, it proved to be another milestone in the career of *Lily Elsie* who played *Humming Bird* and again she brought 'realism' to her characterisation and thus much press attention.

London Cast:
Yen: *Maurice Farkoa*
See See: *Denise Orme*
Mai-Yai: *Amy Augarde*
Silky Lips: *Shelly Calton*
Sea of Jade: *Doris Dean*
Sly Smile: *Mabel Russell*
Tin-Kang: *Gertrude Thornton*
So-Hie: *Gabrielle Ray*
Hoang: *Fred Emney*
Mrs Hoang: *Kitty Henson*
Hang-Kee: *Huntley Wright*

Cheoo: *W.H. Berry*
Shoo-Shoo: *Lilian Hewitson*
Poo-See: *Lena Maitaland*
Miao-Yao: *Sybil Grey*
Lee: *Denise Augarde*
Humming Bird: *Lily Elsie*

For the Prince of Wales Theatre:
Lessee & Producer: *Frank Curzon*
Author/Producer: *George Edwardes*
Business Manager: *Seymour Hodges*
Musical Director: *Frank E Tours*
Stage Manager: *Sidney Watson*
Choreographer: *Willie Ward*

Brief Synopsis:
Not available, but from the character names it is fair to say it was a typical, of the time, send-up comedy of the British dealing with strange foreigners abroad. This kind of show was done with no malice and was a reflection of the colonial attitudes of the time. A jolly good jape all done in good humour, with the added ingredient of glamorous girls enchanting the audiences in typical *George Edwardes* style.

Musical numbers:
Snowflake & Rose
British Slavery et al

THE NEW ALADDIN—1906

The New Aladdin, a musical comedy in two acts, by *James Tanner* and *WH Risque* with music by *Ivan Caryll, Lionel Monckton* and *Frank Tours*. Lyrics by *Adrian Ross, Percy Greenbank, WH Risque* and *George Grossmith Jnr*. Produced by *George Edwardes* at the *Gaiety Theatre* in 1906. The production opened with *Lily Elsie* (playing the lead role of *Lally*)standing in for *Gertie Millar* who was indisposed, but she swiftly returned to take over the role. The *Aladdin* story had been dramatised extensively in England and was very popular for pantomime, but this was the first book musical on the subject.

London cast:
Genie of the Lamp: *George Grossmith, Jnr*
Cadi: *Arthur Hatherton*
Ebenezer (Lally's Uncle): *Harry Grattan*
General Ratz: *Robert Nainby*
The Lost Constable: *Alfred Lester*
The Ideal Man: *Charles Brown*
Billy Pauncefort: *Eustace Burnaby*
Reggie Tighe: *J.R. Sinclair*
Tony Cavendish: *S Handsworth*
A Tax Collector: *J.W. Birtley*
Tippin (Ebenezer's Paige): *Edmund Payne*
Laolah (the Cadi's daughter): *Olive May*
Jennie (Maid to the Princess): *Jean Aylwin*
Mrs Tippin: *Winifred Dennis*
Winnie Fairfax: *Kitty Mason*
Flo Cartaret: *Doris Beresford*
Di Tollemanche: *Enid Leonhardt*
Kit Lomax: *Tessie Hackney*
Vi Corteyon: *Gladys Desmond*
May Warrener: *Florence Lindley*
Nan Jocelyn: *Violet Walker*
Madge Oliphant: *Edna Loftus*
Millie Farquhar: *Minnie Baker*
The Charm of Paris: *Gaby Deslys*
Spirit Of The Ring: *Connie Ediss*
Lally (Ebenezer's nephew): *Lily Elsie* (replaced by *Gertie Millar*)

For the Gaiety Theatre:
Lessee: *George Edwardes*
Manager & Producer: *George Edwardes*
Stage Manager: *Herbert Cathcart*
Acting Manager: *Edward Marshall*

Acts:
Act I : *The Interior of Ebenezer's Antique Shop in Bond Street.*
Act II: *A Palace in Far Cathay.*
Act III: *The Ideal London.*

Brief Synopsis:
A reworking of the Aladdin story that remained true to the characters and general story—but contemporised it by setting it in familiar London locations for some scenes i.e Bond Street shops etc—all woven together around an original musical comedy score.

Musical numbers:
Dear Little Lady
Who Would Be A Boy
Let Us Fly Upon The Wing
Oriental Belles Languidly Reposing
When First I Looked At Your Face
Out Of The Boundless Blue
Oh, The Lamp
I'm A Maiden Who Is Rather Modest
We Have Had A Most Exciting Day
Rubbing Our Eyes In Surprise
Je suis Le Charme de Paris!
At The Close Of Night
If You Ever Go Down To A Popular Town On The Coast
When In Summertime
London, Here In London
When The Shades Of Night Are Softly Creeping
Some People
Bedtime At The Zoo
Down Where The Vegetables Grow

The Merry Widow—1907

The Merry Widow (*Die lustige Witwe*) is an operetta by the Austro-Hungarian composer *Franz Lehar*. The librettists, *Viktor Leon* and *Leo Stein*, based the story—concerning a rich widow, *Sonia*, and her attempt to find a husband—on an 1861 comedy play, *L'attache d'ambassade* (*The Embassy Attaché*) by *Henri Meilhac*.

The operetta was first performed at the *Theater an der Wien* in Vienna on 31 December 1905 with *Mizzi Gunther* as *Hanna, Louis Treumann* as *Danilo, Siegmund Natzler* as *Baron Zeta* and *Annie Wünsch* as *Valencienne*. It was *Lehár's* first major success, becoming internationally the best-known operetta of its era. *Lehár* subsequently made changes for productions in *London* and *Berlin* but the version heard today is essentially that of the original production. Well-known music from the score includes the *Vilja Song, Da geh' ich zu Maxim* (*You'll Find Me at Maxim's*), and the *Merry Widow Waltz*.

George Edwardes secured the rights to stage the production in London, at *Daly's Theatre*, as a vehicle for *Lily Elsie* (*Sonia*) and *Joseph Coyne* (*Prince Danilo*). Although *Edwardes* went through the courtesy of inviting the original librettist and lyricist to London he had already decided that its English adaptation would be undertaken by *Basil Hood*, with lyrics by *Adrian Ross*. Also that the part of *Danilo* would be non-singing (as Coyne couldn't sing—this fact he hid from *Lehar* until the very last moment) as *Edwardes* was convinced the pairing of *Elsie* and *Coyne* would be vital to its success. As it turned out he was proved right. The show became a sensation in London when it opened in 1907. Thereafter, it has played frequently in America and throughout the English speaking world, and is still frequently revived.

London cast:
Sonia (The Merry Widow): *Lily Elsie*
Prince Danilo: *Jospeh Coyne*
Visch: *W.H. Berry* (1870-1951)
Sylvaine: *Irene Desmond*
Vicomte Camille de Jolidon: *Robert Evett* (1874-1949)
Baron Popoff: *George Graves* (1876-1949)
Natalie (wife of Popoff): *Elizabeth Firth* (1884-?)
Waiter at Maxims: *Ralph Roberts*
Frou-Frou: *Gabrielle Ray*
Also in cast: *Lennox Pawle, Gordon Cleather, Fred Kaye, R. Roberts, Nina Sevening, Kate Welch, Amy Webster, Dorothy Dunbar, Dolly Dombey,*

Daisie Irving, Phyllis Le Grand, Mabel Munro, Margot Erskine, Gertrude Lester, Mabel Russell, et al

For Daly's Theatre:
Manager & Producer: *George Edwardes* (1852-1915)
Acting manager: *G.E. Minor*
Musical Director: *Barter Johns*
Choreographer: *Fred Farren*
Director: *J.A.E. Malone* (1860-1929)
Composer: *Franz Lehar*
Librettist: *Basil Hood* (after *Viktor Leon*)
Lyrics: *Adrian Ross* (after *Leo Stein*)

Act I : *An Embassy Ball in Paris*
Act II : *Garden at Sonia's House*
Act III : *Maxim's in Paris*

Brief Synopsis:
The action takes place in Paris. *Sonia* is a wealthy widow and on the death of her husband inherited his vast fortune. As she comes from a small country the powers that be are worried that if she marries an outsider she will take her fortune with her and thus plunge the country into an economic crisis. *Prince Danilo* is summoned by the ambassador and instructed to marry the widow and save their country from disaster. Instructed to attend the Embassy Ball to court the widow, he would rather spend time at Maxims and arrives late with little enthusiasm to carry out his duty. When he discovers the widow in question is *Sonia* he is horrified because they had once been lovers prior to her marriage and she was the reason he ran away to Paris—as a result he is rude and surly towards her. She is equally alarmed to find her old suitor at the Ball, as she couldn't understand why he spurned her several years before. It is obvious to all concerned they are still in love and after much intrigue and comedy, and his admission he didn't want her to think he wanted her money, and that he ran away to Paris to numb his broken heart, they reunite to the strains of the *Merry Widow Waltz*. Interwoven in the story were comedic sub plots involving a jealous older husband paranoid about his young wife flirting with younger men and other eccentric

courtiers all adding to the comedy—but this never detracted from the relationship between Sonia and Danilo.

Musical numbers:

Act I
1. Introduction—Pontevedro in Paree—"Speak for the men and the beauties"
   1a—Ballroom Music
2. Duet—A highly respectable wife—(Valencienne, Camille)—"Look now's our chance"
3. Entrance—Anna & Ensemble—"Gentlemen, no more ! I'm still a Pontevedrian"
   3a—Ballroom music
4. Solo—I'm off to Chez Maxime—(Danilo)—"My very heavy Fatherland"
5. Duet—All's one to all men when there's gold—(Anna, Danilo)—"One girl has almond eyes"
6. Finale Act I—Ladies' Choice!—(Anna, Valencienne, Danilo, Camille, St. Brioche, Carcada, Chorus)—"Ladies' choice! Did you hear the gladd'ning voice?"

Act II:
7. Intoduction, Dance and Vilia Song—(Anna & Chorus)—"No one must go yet, fellow countrymen"
8. Duet—Jogging in a one-horse gig—(Anna, Danilo)—"Gee up lassie, here we are"
9. March-Septet—You're back where you first began—(Danilo, Zeta, Cascada, St. Brioche, Kromow, Bogdanowitsch, Pritschitsch)—"It's a problem how to manage"
10. Melodrame & Dancing Scene—(Anna, Danilo)
11. Duet and Romance—Red as the rose in Maytime—(Valencienne, Camille)—"Dear friend, be calm, you know I want to get you married"
12. Finale Act II—(Ensemble)—"I wonder what it is they want"

Act III:
12a.—Entr'acte—Vilia—song
12b.—Interlude

13. The Cake-Walk
14. Ensemble—Eh, voila les belles Grisettes!—"The Grisettes of Paris greet you"
14a.—Ensemble (reprise)—(Lolo, Dodo, Jou-Jou, Clo-Clo, Frou-Frou, Margot, Danilo)
15. Duet—Love unspoken—(Anna, Danilo)—"Love unspoken, faith unbroken"
16. Company You're back where you first began (reprise)—"What to think, what to say, what to do"

A Waltz Dream—1908

A Waltz Dream (*Ein Walzertraum*) is an operetta composed by *Oscar Straus* with a libretto by *Leopold Jacobson* and *Felix Dormann*. It premiered on 3rd March 1907 at the *Carl Theater* in *Vienna*. Following this success a London production was planned with an English translation of the libretto undertaken by *Basil Hood* with lyrics by *Adrian Ross*. It opened at London's *Hicks Theatre* (formerly the *Globe Theatre* now the *Gielgud Theatre, Shaftesbury Avenue*) starring *Gertie Millar* in 1908. Due to the indisposition of *Gertie Millar*, *Lily Elsie* briefly played to role until *Miller* returned to the production.

The international success of the operetta exceeded *Straus's* expectations, and special praise was reserved for the famous waltz theme from Act II. *Straus* later arranged various numbers from the operetta and included the graceful main waltz theme into a new concert waltz. The piece made *Straus's* international reputation, touring internationally after the *Vienna*, *New York* and *London* runs.

London cast:
Franzi: *Gertie Millar*
Lieutenant Niki: *Robert Evett*
Count Lothar: *George Grossmith Jnr*
Joachim XIII: *Arthur Williams*
Fifi: *Luna Love*
Cast also included: *Vernon Davidson, Kirby Langford, Albert Kavanagh, Mary Grey, Florence Parfrey, Phyllis Beadon, et al*

For Hicks Theatre *(now Gielgud Theatre)*
Manager: *Charles Frohman* (1860-1915)
Producer: *George Edwardes* et al
Composer: *Oscar Straus* (1870-1954)
Book: *Basil Hood* (after *Felix Dormann* 1870-1928)
Lyrics; *Adrian Ross* (after *Leopold Jacobson* 1878-1943)
Stage Director: *J.A.E. Malone* (1860-1929)
Business Manager: *Oscar Barrett Jnr* (1875-1941)
Choreographer: *Fred Farren*

Act I: *Festival Hall in Prince Joachim's Castle at Flausenthum*
Act II: *Garden Salon*
Act III: *Drawing Room in the Castle*

Synopsis
The plot was very predictable for the time and involved the main characters falling in and out of love due to misunderstandings accompanied by the usual comedy elements required for such shows. The lovers would eventually be reunited for the final curtain waltzing into eternity happy at last.

Musical numbers:
Opening Chorus (Princess weds today!)
A Maiden Who Cupid Had Not Cajoled
The Trumpets Blare!
Some Men Are Born To Rule
Our Vows Exchanged
What A Misfortune
The Soft Summer Twilight
My Dearest Love
Come, Love, Don't Be Shy
Search The World Around
I Beg You Believe
I Am Seeking
Sweet Music
It Is Shameful
Oh, These Bores!

I Am An Humble Lassie
Music At Night (Thrills Of Delight).
Franzi Enchants Her Audience
The Gay Lothario

The Dollar Princess—1909

The Dollar Princess is a musical in three acts by *A.M. Willner* and *Fritz Grunbaum* (after a comedy by *Gatti-Trotha*), adapted into English by *Basil Hood* (from the 1907 *Die Dollarprinzessin*), with music by *Leo Fall* and lyrics by *Adrian Ross*. It opened at *Daly's Theatre* on 25th September 1909, running for 428 performances. The London production starred *Lily Elsie, Joseph Coyne* and *Gabrielle Ray*. In late Victorian and Edwardian England *'Dollar Princess'* was a nickname given to American Heiresses. *Playgoer and Society Illustrated* wrote: "To the average playgoer there is something very attractive in watching the antics of the vulgar when surrounded by the refinement of art which he can neither understand or appreciate . . . Miss *Lily Elsie*, as *Alice*, shows even an improvement on her performance in *The Merry Widow*.

London cast:
John Coulder (President of Coal): *Joseph Coyne*
Alice Condor (his daughter): *Lily Elsie*
Sir James McGregor: *Willie Warde*
Olga (cabaret singer): *Emmy Whelan*
Freddy Fairfax: *Robert Michaelis*
Bulger: *W.H. Berry*
Lady Dorothy: *May Hobson*
Cast also included: *Frank Hector, Basil Foster, Fred Blackman, Garnet Wilson, Paul Plunckett, Harold Deacon, Emmy Wehlen, Gabrielle Ray, Marjorie Moore,*
Gladys Cooper, Phyllis Le Grand, May Hobson, Gertrude Glyn Marion Lyndsay, Dolly Dombey, et al

For Daly's Theatre:
Manager & Producer: *George Edwardes*
Librettist: *Basil Hood*

Lyrics: *Adrian Ross*
Additional music: *Leo Fall*
Musical Director: *Harold Vicars*
Choreographer: *Fred Farren*
Director & Stage Manager: *Edward Royce Jnr* (1870-1964)

Synopsis:
A young American oil tycoon, when recruiting domestic staff, takes on a succession of impoverished members of the European aristocracy. The servants he selects are all very well connected, as indicated in the musical number: "Tho' we came here in steerage, all are members of the peerage". His sister, who has money, later follows the course of true love and takes a job in another household pretending to be impoverished. As a result she is betrothed to her hearts desire and all ends happily.

Musical numbers:

A Boat Sails On Wednesday
The Dollar Princess
Hip, Hip, Hurrah!
I Can Say Truly Rural
Insepction
Lady Fortune
Love! Love! Love!
Laove's A Race
The Marquis Of Jolifontaine
My Dream OF Love
Not Here! Not Here!
Reminiscence
The Riding Lesson
A Self Made Maiden
Tennis
Then You Go?
Typewriting

The Count of Luxembourg—1911

The Count of Luxembourg is an operetta in two acts with English lyrics and libretto by *Basil Hood* and *Adrian Ross*, music by *Franz Lehar*, based loosely on the German original *Der Graf von Luxemburg* which premiered in *Vienna* in 1909. *The Count of Luxembourg* opened at London's *Daly's Theatre* on 20th May 1911 and ran for 240 performances. It starred *Lily Elsie, Huntley Wright* and *Bertram Wallis*.

London cast:
Count Rene of Luxembourg: *Bertram Wallis*
Angla Didier: *Lily Elsie*
Registrar: *Fred Kaye*
Jean Baptiste (a waiter): *Willie Warde*
Mons. De Tresac: *Alec Fraser*
Mons. De Valmont: *Paul Plunkett*
Pelegrin: *Frank Perfitt*
Brissard: *W.H. Berry*
The Grand Duke Rutzinov: *Huntley Wright*
Juliette (a model): *Gladys Homfrey*
Mimi: *May Marton*
Lisette (maid to Angele) *Kitty Hanson*

For Daly's Theatre:
Manager & Producer: *George Edwardes*
Book: *Basil Hood*
Lyrics: *Adrian Ross*
Composer: *Franz Lehar*
Choreographer: *Fred Farren*
Musical Director: *Ernst Flecker Jnr*
Stage Manager: *Edward Royce Jnr*
Acting Manager: *T.J. Courtley*

Synopsis:
The Grand Duke may not marry Angele, with whom he is infatuated, unless she bears a title. He therefore arranges for the penniless spendthrift, Count Rene, to marry a lady whose face he is not to see,

and to agree to divorce her three months later. For this the Count receives £20,000 (half a million francs). At the wedding ceremony, the Count and his mystery bride are separated by a screen—but later they meet and fall in love. Little knowing that they are already husband and wife, they believe their romance is hopeless. But a happy ending is worked out, accompanied by Lehar's lilting music and famous waltz

Act I: *Brissard's Studio, Paris*
Act II: *Reception at the Grand Duke Rutzinov's Home, Paris*

Musical numbers:

Carnival!
Anyone Who Knows Me
Pierrot & Pierrette
Carnival! (reprise)
Lend It, Spend It, End It
A Special Bloom
I Am In Love
Someone's Here To Marry Me (I Don't Know Who)
You Will Be A Royal Highness
Your Cheque Upon Coutts
Fair Countess
Hail Angele
Once A Butterfly
Ah, The Perfume (How It Lingers)
Now If You Really Mean To Mix (In High Society)
What Are You Doing
Kukuska
Beauty Bright & Glorious
Are You Going To Dance
A Man Is A Boy
Say Not Love Is A Dream

Anything But Merry! Lily Elsie 263

MAVOURNEEN : 1915

A musical play based on the exploits at court and beyond at the time of *Charles II*. Elsie played *Patricia O'Brien* in the production but her faithful understudy was always in the shadows prepared to go on at a moments notice. It ran for 23 October 1915 to the 29th January 1916. *Elsie* made the decision to accept the offer of the part due to her husbands absence as a result of WWI.

By **Louis N Parker**
Presented at *His Majesty's Theatre*
General Manager: *Henry Dana*

Cast:

King Charles II : *Malcolm Cherry*
Buckingham: *Gerald Lawrence*
Arlington: *Gayer Mackay*
Bristol: *Roy Byford (Albert Evremond)*
Ashley: *Henry Byatt*
Berkeley: *Charles Doran*
Sidney Montagu: *Reginald Owen*
Samuel Pepys: *Edward Sass*
Father O'Rafferty: *C.V. France*
Chaffinch: *Ben Field*
Host of the Bear (Inn): *Julian Cross*
Drawer: *Vernon Crabtree*
Usher: *Donald Young/Frank Ridley*
Haffiz: *Percy Bates*
Queen Catherine: *Athene Syler*
Lady Castlemaine: *Alice Crawford*
Lady Arlington: *Violet Graham/Elaine Inescourt*
Mrs Myddleton: *Joan Chaloner*
Mrs Roberts: *Georgina Milne*
Frances Brooke: *Esme Biddle*
Margaret Brooke: *Isabel Alison*
Mrs Pepys: *Dorothy Parker*
Moyra: *Blanche Stanley*

Mercer: *Sybil Sparks*
Maid: *Irene Delisse*
Patricia O'Brien: *Lily Elsie* (understudy *Violet Graham*)

Producer & Manager: *Sir Herbert Beerbohm Tree*
Musical Director: *Percy E Fletcher*
Designer: *Percy Mcquoid*
Costumes: *Lucille et al*
Stage Manager: *Alfred Bellew*
Assistant Stage Manager: *William Abingdon*

PAMELA : 1917

A comedy, with music, in three acts with book, music and lyrics by *Arthur Wimperis* and *Frederic Norton* and Directed by *Gerald du Maurier*. Presented at London's *Palace Theatre*, 1917. Choreography by *Willie Warde*, Scenic Design by *J Fraser, Conrad Tritschler, Joseph Harker* and *Phillip Harker*. Costumes by *Lucille* and *Elspeth Phelps*.

London Cast:

Guy Tremayne: *Owen Nares*
Hughie Hickling: *Clifford Cobb*
Andy McIntosh: *George Tawde*
Sir Rupert Tremayne: *Spencer Trevor*
Le Comte de Daves: *Dare Phillips*
Huggins: *Arthur Chesney*
A Courier: *Jean Marechal*
Darval: *Fernand Leane*
A French Chef: *Lago Lewys*
Tony Woodhouse: *G.P. Huntley*
Kitty O'Malley: *Gertrude Glyn*
Tillie Wynne: *Berthe Adams*
Angele Vining: *Heather Featherstone*
A Charlady: *Pat Greene*
Pamela Durham: *Lily Elsie*

Anything But Merry! Lily Elsie 🌱 265

Musical Numbers (recordings)
I'm So Very Glad I Met You—HMV 04224 (Matrix No. HO-3046 af)
It's Not The Things You've Got (HMV 04225—Matrix No. HO-3051 af)
I Loved You So (HMV 03602—Matrix No. HO 3048 af)
Waltz theme and Cupid (Finales, Act 2). HMV 04223—Matrix No. HO 3053 af) **Cupid, Cupid** (HMV 03601—Matrix No. HO 3054 af)

Report in the Weekly Dispatch, December 16th, 1917:

"There was much talk about. The night had been an eventful one, and its great features were many. *Lily Elsie* sang never so gloriously. 'Cupid, Cupid' is the best song *Fred Norton* has written. Her silver and blue Turkish costume for that wonderful waltz, too, will be the envy of every woman . . . *Owen Nares* was very much in earnest, very sincere, of course, but I am not certain that his part in a musical play required such serious treatment . . . *Lily Elsie* looked like a princess, and when it's like that—well, there you are!"

For the Palace Theatre:
Producer & Managing Director: *Alfred Butt*
General Manager: *Maurice Volvy*
Stage Manager: *Richard Brennan*
Musical Director: *Herman Fink*

THE BLUE TRAIN : 1927

A musical comedy in three acts by *Reginald Arkell* and *Dion Titheridge*, adapted from the book by *Alfred Grunwald* and *Walter Stein*. First produced at the *Theatre Royal*, Southsea and then at the *Prince of Wales Theatre*, London, 1927. Music by *Robert Stolz*, additional numbers by *Ivy St. Helier*. Lyrics by *Reginald Arkell*. Arrangements by *Jack Hulbert* and *Paul Murray*. Directed by *Jack Hulbert*.

Act I :   *A Room in Lord Antony Stowe's House, London*
Act II: Scene 1.—*Grundelfrau, Switzerland*
           Scene 2.—*Another part of Grundelfrau*
           Scene 3.—*The Wetterhorn Chalet*
Act III: Scene 1.—*A Corridor of "The Blue Train"*
           Scene 2.—*A Terrace Resaurant on the Cote d'Azur*

London Cast:

Eileen Mayne: *Lily Elsie*
Freddy Royce: *Bobby Howes*
Ernest: *James Cameron*
Mollie Drew: *Pat Malone*
Hon. Harold Green: *Jack Raine*
Josephine Jones: *Ciceley Debenham*
Lord Antony Stowe: *Arthur Margeston*
Musicals numbers (recording)
The Blue Train (Titheradge and Gorney, Columbia 4438—Matrix No. 5661)
When A Girl Is In Love With A Man (Titheradge, Arkell, and Stolz: Duet with Arthur Margetson—Columbia 9223—Matrix No. AX 2866)
Eileen (Arkell and Stolz, Duet with Arthur Margetson, Columbia 4439—Matrix No. A 5660)
Swiss Fairyland (Arkell and Stolz, Columbia 4438—Matrix No. A 5662)
You Didn't Ask Me First (Arkell and St.Helier, Duet with Arthur Margetson, Columbia 9223—Matrix No. AX 2867)

For the Prince of Wales Theatre:
Producers: *Andre Charlot & Philip Ridgeway*
Sole Proprietor: *Miss Tonie Edgar Bruce*
Lessee & Licensee: *Andre Charlot*

THE TRUTH GAME 1928-1929

A comedy play by *Ivor Novello*. *Novello* had admired *Lily Elsie* since he had seen her in *The Merry Widow* as a boy in 1907. One of his greatest ambitions was to appear on the stage with *Elsie*—he persuaded her to appear with him in this play which he had written especially for her. In spite of her desire to retire for good (after *The Blue Train* which exhausted her voice) she agreed and it became her last public appearances on the stage. Her brief comeback had been an attempt to take her mind off her failed marriage and health. Produced by *Novello* and *Barry O'Brien* at London's *Globe Theatre* (formerly the *Hicks Theatre* now *Giulgud Theatre*), it was a great success, after overcoming initial casting and pre production disputes, when it opened on October 5th 1928. After its initial London run it went on tour where *Elsie* made her final appearance at Manchester's *Palace Theatre*, before returning to London for a second season at *Daly's Theatre* (1929). *Lily Elsie* would make her final appearance in the same theatre which had made her a star when she'd played *Sonia* in *The Merry Widow* twenty years earlier. *Novello* took the play to New York where it was successful on Broadway, but Elsie refused the offer to go and *Phoebe Foster* played her role there. The London production was Directed by Graham Browne.

London Cast:
Max Clement: *Ivor Novello*
Rosine Brown: *Lily Elsie*
Evelyn Brandon: *Lillian Braithwaite*
Lady Joan Culver: *Viola Tree*
Harris: *Doris Cooper*
James: *Frederick Oxley*
Sir Joshua Grimshaw: *Frederick Volpe*
Vera Crombie: *Mabel Sealby*
Lord Straffield: *Glen Byam Shaw*

For the Globe Theatre:
Licensee & Manager: Sir Alfred Butt
Business Manager: Charles Terry
Acting Manager: William Youngman

Full list of productions Lily Elsie appeared in including year:

1. ***Little Red Riding Hood*** *(Title role/Manchester/Queen's Theatre/UK Tour/1896)*
2. ***King Klondike*** *(Fairy/Britannia Theatre, Hoxton/1898)*
3. ***McKennas Flirtation*** *(Chorus/Play/UK Tour/1900)*
4. ***Silver Slipper*** *(Chorus/Lyric Theatre, London/1901)*
5. ***Dick Whittington*** *(Small Part/Camden Theatre, London/Xmas1901)*
6. ***The Forty Thieves*** *(Morgiana/Coronet Theatre, London/ Xmas 1902)*
7. ***Blue Beard*** *(Small Part/Coronet Theatre, London/Xmas 1903)*
8. ***Three Little Maids*** *(Hilda for a few performances only/UK Tour/1903)*
9. ***A Chinese Honeymoon*** *(Princess Soo Soo/Royal Strand Theatre/1903)*
10. ***Madame Sherry*** *(Chorus, left after few /Apollo Theatre, London/1903)*
11. ***Lady Madcap*** *(Chorus/Gwenny/Prince of Wales, London/1904)*
12. ***The Little Cherub*** *(Lady Agnes/Prince of Wales, London/1906)*
13. ***See See*** *(Humming Bird/Prince of Wales, London/1906)*
14. ***The New Aladdin*** *(Laly/Gaiety Theatre, London/1906)*
15. ***The Merry Widow*** *(Sonia/Daly's Theatre, London/1907)*
16. ***The Dollar Princess*** *(Alice Condor/Daly's Theatre, London/1909)*
17. ***A Waltz Dream*** *(Franzi/Hicks Theatre, London/ 1911)*
18. ***The Count of Luxembourg*** *(Angele Didier/Daly's Theatre, London/1911)*
19. ***The Critic*** *(Ellena/His Majesty's Theatre/1 Charity performance/1911)**
20. ***Mavourneen*** *(Title Role/ His Majesty's Theatre/Charity production/1915)*
21. ***Admirable Crichton*** *(Lady Lazenby/ Wyndnam's Theatre/1 Charity perf/1916)**
22. ***Pamela*** *(Title Role/Palace Theatre, London/1917)*
23. ***The Blue Train*** *(Eileen Mayne/Prince of Wales Theatre, London/1927)*

24. The Truth Game (Rosine Brown/Globe & Daly's Theatre/UK Tour/1928-9)

* Single performance for charity and to celebrate the coronation of King George V

Elsie also appeared in two one-night charity productions in aid of the Wounded Soldiers (WWI) 1917 and Women's Hospitals 1925

Play Pictorial—Reference/Further information:

Three Little Maids—Prince of Wales Theatre, London.
Play Pictorial, v.1, 1902, No5.
A Chinese Honeymoon—Royal Strand Theatre, London (now demolished)
Play Pictorial, v.3, 1903, No15
Lady Madcap—Prince of Wales Theatre, London.
Play Pictorial, v.5, 1905, No31
The Little Michus—Daly's Theatre, London (now demolished)
Play Pictorial, v.6, 1905, No35
The Little Cherub—Prince of Wales Theatre, London.
Play Pictorial, v.7, 1906, No43
See See—Prince of Wales Theatre, London.
Play Pictorial, v.8, 1906, No49
The New Aladdin—Gaiety Theatre, London (now demolished)
Play Pictorial, v.9, 1906, No53
The Merry Widow—Daly's Theatre, London (now demolished)
Play Pictorial, v.10, 1907, No61
A Waltz Dream—Hicks Theatre, London (formerly the *Globe*, now *Gielgud*)
Play Pictorial, v.11, 1908, No69
The Dollar Princess—Daly's Theatre, London (now demolished)
Play Pictorial, v.15, 1909, No88
The Quaker Girl—Royal Adelphi Theatre, London (now the *Adelphi Theatre*)
Play Pictorial, v.17, 1911, No104
A Waltz Dream (revival)—Daly's Theatre, London (now demolished)
Play Pictorial, v.17, 1911, No103

The Count of Luxembourg—*Daly's Theatre*, London (now demolished)
Play Pictorial, v.18, 1911, no108
The Blue Train—*Prince of Wales Theatre*, London.
Play Pictorial, v.51, 1927, No305
The Truth Game—*Globe Theatre*, London (Formerly *Hicks* Theatre now *Gielgud*)
Play Pictorial, v.54, 1929, No322

Further Reading:

Ivor: The Story of an Achievement (Novello): McQueen-Pope, W., Hutchinson & Company, London, 1951.

Fortunes Favourite (Franz Lehar): McQueen-Pope, W., Murray, D.L., Hutchinson & Company, London, 1953.

Curtain Call For The Guv'nor (A Biography of George Edwardes), Bloom, Ursula.,
Hutchinson & Company, London, 1954.

Lily Elsie appeared in only two short films—but it was never a serious attempt to develop her career in that media; a media in which she didn't feel comfortable or confident.
First, the D. W. Griffith film *The Great Love* (1918), which starred Lillian Gish. Elsie's role was a cameo. Second, *Comradeship* (1919), a black & white, silent picture. The film was very popular in its day.

Newspaper & Magazine Articles:

Listed below are the main, and identifiable sources, of press reviews and articles on Lily Elsie. There are others, but their publication/author details are not identified thus I have been unable to include them here.

Manchester Press : Review of *Nelly Power* (Nellie), 1886.
The Entr'acte Newspaper: Article on *Nelly Power's* death, 1887.

Manchester Press : Review of *The Arabian Nights*, 1895.
Manchester Herald : Review of *Little Red Riding Hood*, 1896.
Manchester Press : Review of *Little Red Riding Hood*, 1896.
The London Era : Review of *Elsie singing 'Dear Heart'*, 1899.
The London Era : Review of *A Chinese Honeymoon*, 1903.
London News : Review of *A Chinese Honeymoon*, 1903.
Illustrated & Dramatic News (London) : Article/*Interview with Lily Elsie*, 1907.
Westminster Gazette : Review of *See See*, 1906.
Play Pictorial : Review of *See See*, 1906.
London Evening News : Review of *The Merry Widow*, 1907.
The Times : Review of *The Merry Widow*, 1907.
London Pelican : Review of *The Merry Widow*, 1907.
Playgoer & Society Magazine : Review of *The Dollar Princess*, 1909.
London Herald : Review of *The Count of Luxembourg*, 1911.
London Watchdog : Article on *Elsie's marriage/retirement*, 1911.
Every Woman's Encyclopaedia : Elsie (*How o Succeed In Musical Comedy*), 1911.
The Tatler : Review of *Mavourneen*, 1915.
Theatre World : Review of *The Truth Game*, 1928.
The Times : Review of *The Truth Game*, 1928.
The Sphere : Article on the *'Gaiety Girls' reunion*, 1950.

Picture Credits

Special thanks to the following for assisting with photographs of Lily Elsie, her co stars and London theatres for inclusion in this book.

1. Mrs. Sonia Berry who has kindly allowed me to reproduce some personal family photographs.

2. **Rob Sedman** who has tirelessly documented Elsie's career on his website dedicated to her. ***Further information at:*** www.lily-elsie.com

3. **Matthew Lloyd** who has dedicated a website in memory of Arthur Lloyd which includes a vast collection of research material and images dedicated to music hall artistes and London and provincial theatre history. *Further information at:* www.arthurlloyd.com

4. **John Culme** who has dedicated a website to the history of music hall artistes and its history. An invaluable source of research information and images. *Further information at:* www.footlightnotes.tripod.com

<u>Song Lyrics</u>

The Boy I Love Is Up In The Gallery Lyrics quoted in chapters 1 & 2. Music & Lyrics by **George Ware** 1885.

George Ware wrote this music hall song for **Nelly Power** who made it famous around the country. The young **Marie Lloyd** started performing it without permission much to the annoyance of Power and Ware. As a result of Power's sudden death in 1887 Ware allowed Marie Lloyd to use it as her own and is today one of the songs she is best remembered for.

I Want To Be A Lidy! Lyrics quoted at the end of chapter 6.
Music by **Howard Talbot** and lyrics by **Harry Greenbank**.

Written for the musical comedy **A Chinese Honeymoon** (see production details) it was a very popular number in the show.

My Old Man (Said Follow The Van) Lyrics quoted in chapter 3
Music and Lyrics by **Fred W. Leigh** and **Charles Collins** circa 1912

Music hall song written for and made famous by **Marie Lloyd**. It is one of the songs for which she is best remembered.

Vitality! Lyrics quoted in chapter 14.
Music by **Ivor Novello** and lyrics by **Alan Melville**.

Anything But Merry! Lily Elsie 273

Written for the musical comedy **Gay's The Word** which opened in Manchester in 1950, then transferred to London for a West End run in 1951.

Every effort has been made to fulfil requirements with regard to reproducing copyright material. The author will be happy to rectify any omissions at the earliest opportunity.

About The Author

David was born in Oxford, England, in 1959. He graduated from London's **City University** with a BA (Hons) Degree in Journalism. In addition to this he has a teaching degree from **Lancaster University** and is currently completing an MA in Scriptwriting at the **University of Central Lancashire**. Prior to this he attended London Theatre Arts to study drama, and then worked extensively in the performing arts industry as a playwright, producer and director. His stage plays include the award winning **Forever Nineteen** and **The Post Card**—which enjoyed London and New York productions, as well as touring nationally in the United Kingdom. His involvement in adapting the libretto for Ivor Novello's 1935 musical **Glamorous Night** resulted in him directing the 50th Anniversary Concert to celebrate the life and work of Novello at the Theatre Royal, Drury Lane, in London's West End. Subsequently he has worked as the Ivor Novello Consultant on Julian Fellowes and Robert Altman's **Oscar** and **BAFTA** winning film **Gosford Park**, and contributed to the BBC Documentary on the life of Novello **The Handsomest Man in Britain.** He is the author of **In Search of Ruritania**, a biography on Ivor Novello—currently developing a screenplay based on the life of Edwardian actress Lily Elsie, and a play based on the relationship between opera composer Puccini and his wife, Elvira.

Further information available at: www.christyplays.com

INDEX Anything But Merry!

Index: Names

A
Alexandra, Queen (consort). 138, 170
Andrews, Bobbie. 185,
Asquith, Mrs. 181, N

B
Barret, Albert. 83,
Barret, Charlotte Elizabeth (Lottie). 1, 2, 3, 4, 6, 8, 9, 10, 11, 12, 13, 15, 16, 17, 18, 19, 23, 24, 26, 27, 28, 29, 45, 57, 58, 59, 60, 63, 64, 66, 67, 68, 69, 77, 83, 84, 103, 110, 111, 112, 119, 120, 121, 122, 123, 133, 134, 135, 136, 139, 141, 143, 147, 148, 171, 172, 174, 176,
Barret, Grace. 83,
Beaton, Cecil. 167, 198, 202, 204, 205, 206, 207, 208,
Berry, Sonia. v, 198, 202, 203,
Berry, WH. 124, 169,
Bloom, Ursula. ix,
Boosey, William. 82, 105, 106, 107, 108, 117,
Braithwaite, Lillian. 185,
Brown, Graham. 184,
Bullough, Ian(Sir).136, 141, 145, 147, 148, 171, 172, 174, 176, 179, 180, 188, 189, 195, 203, 205, 209, 210
Bullough, John (Sir). 148,

C
Churchill, Sir Winston. 185,
Cleather, Gordon. 124,
Cotton, Wilfred. 139, 140,
William (Billy) Charles Cotton. 1, 2, 5, 7, 8, 9, 10, 11, 12, 13, 15, 16, 17, 18, 19, 20, 23, 25, 27, 28, 48, 59, 60, 68, 69, 83, 84, 120, 139, 140, 142, 199,
Craven, Hawes. 82,
Collier, Constance. 183, 184,
Coward, Noel. 184,
Coyne, Joseph. 116, 117, 118, 122, 123, 124, 125, 126, 127, 128, 129, 130, 131, 133, 134, 145, 146, 167, 168, 176, 193,
Culme, John. v,
Curzon, Frank. 53, 67,

D
Dance, George. 67,
Dare, Phyllis. 70, 81, 131, 176, 194,
Dare, Zena. 70, 71, 72, 81, 131, 176, 194,
Darrell, Maude. 141, 147, 148,
Desmond, Irene. 124,
Dombey, Dolly. 124,

E
Earl of Dudley (2nd), William. 187,
Edward VII, King. 45, 138, 167,
Edwardes, D'Arcy. 181,

Edwardes, George. v, ix, 48, 49, 50, 51, 52, 55, 57, 58, 60, 61, 62, 63, 65, 66, 67, 70, 71, 72, 73, 76, 77, 78, 79, 80, 81, 82, 83, 105, 107, 108, 110, 111, 112, 113, 115, 116, 117, 118, 119, 120, 121, 122, 123, 124, 125, 126, 127, 128, 129, 130, 131, 136, 137, 138, 139, 142, 143, 144, 145, 146, 147, 148, 167, 168, 169, 170, 171, 172, 173, 174, 175, 176, 180, 181, 182, 188, 191, 193, 209,
Edwards, Beatrice. 56, 60, 63, 131,
Evelyn, Clara. 138, 139, 143, 144, 145,

F
Farren, Fred. 124
Fraser, Ada. 124,
Freedings, Molly. 82,
Frith, Elizabeth. 124,
Field, Mrs. 123,

G
George V, King. 167, 170, 171, 182,
Gerald Du Maurier, Sir. 183, 184,
Graham-Hodgson, Winifred. 198, 202, 208
Greenwood, Graham. v,
Gilbert & Sullivan. 49, 50, 59, 83
Glynn, Gertrude. 176,
Graves, George. 19, 20, 21, 124,
Gunther, Mitzi. 108, 112, 137,

H
Harker, Joseph. 82, 123,
Neuberger, Richard. 75, 76,
Hodder, Bert (Albert)1, 4, 6, 8, 10, 12, 13, 17, 59, 64, 68, 69, 83, 112, 119, 123, 131, 140, 141, 142, 143, 199,
Hodder, Elise [Lisa]. 198, 199, 200, 201, 203, 206, 207, 208,
Holden, Gwenny. 68,
Hood, Basil. 147, 168, 169, 170,
Howard, Tom. i,
Hurley, Alec. 10,

I
Irving, Daisy. 124,

J
Jeffires, Ellis. 184, 185,
Jones, Sidney. 81,

K
Karczag. 75, 76,
Kaye, Fred. 124,

L
Le Grand, Phyllis. 124,
Lehar, Franz. 75, 76, 106, 108, 112, 117, 123, 125, 126, 127, 130, 131, 137, 138, 143, 146, 147, 168, 169, 170, 176, 181, 193,
Lester, Gertrude. 124,
Leon, Victor. 75,
Lloyd, Marie. 11, 14, 15, 17, 18, 47, 48, 131, 176, 183,
Lloyd, Matthew. v,
Lucille (Lady Duff Gordon). 65, 123, 133,

M
Macqueen-Pope, Walter. vii, 133,
Malone, Jim. 124,
Mangan, Richard. v,
Marsh, Sir Edward. 185,
Mary, Queen (consort). 167, 170, 171, 182,
Meilhac, Henry. 106,
Miller, Gertie (Lady Dudley). ix, 51, 61, 65, 72, 76, 77, 80, 81, 103, 104, 105, 111, 112, 116, 119, 120, 121, 128, 129, 131, 134, 144, 146, 167, 176, 186, 188, 189, 194, 198,
Monckton, Lionel. 111, 116, 20, 131, 187,
Moss, Binkie. 199, 200, 201, 203, 206, 207, 208, 209,
Munn, Geoffrey. 203.
Munro, Mabel. 124,

N
Nares, Owen. 48,
Neuberger, Richard. 75, 76,
Nortcliff, Lynn. v,
Novello, Ivor [David Ivor Davies]. 136, 181, 183, 184, 185, 186, 188, 198, 204, 209

P
Phillips, Martin. v,
Pinder, Grace. 70,
Power, Nelly (Nellie). 1, 5, 7, 8, 9, 10, 11, 12, 16, 17, 18, 47, 69, 183,

R
Ray, Gabrielle. 70, 71, 118, 119, 120, 124, 131, 138, 176,
Reeve, Ada. 139,
Ross, Adrian. 81,
Rubens, Paul. 169,
Runciman, Rosy. v,
Russell, Mabel. 124,

S
Sealby, Mabel. 185,
Sedman, Rob. v,
Shaw, Glen Byam. 185,
Stein, Leo. 75

T
Taylor, Paul. v,
Theatre Royal, Drury Lane. 207, 208,
Tree, Viola. 183, 185,

V
Vicars, Harold
Victoria, Queen. 45,
Volpe, Frederick. 185,

W
Wallis, Bertram. 169, 170, 171, 176,
Walner. 75, 76,
Webster, Amy. 124,
Webster, Cecily. 209,
Welch, Kate. 124,

West, Rebecca. 209

Index: Theatres/Newspapers/Productions

A
A Chinese Honeymoon. 53, 55, 56, 60, 61, 62, 65, 66, 67, 69, 81
Adelphi Theatre, London. 138, 167,
Aldwych Theatre, London. 72, 118,
Alhambra Theatre, London. 47,
All Saints Church, Ennismore Gdns. 176,
St Andrews, Dollis Hill. 193, 200, 201, 207,
Antiques Roadshow. 203,
Argentine Widow, The. 181,

B
Blue Train, The. 182, 183,
Brittania Theatre, Hoxton. 47,

C
Caledonia Music Hall, London. 14,
Camden Theatre, London. 48,
Count of Luxembourg, The. 146, 147, 168, 169, 170, 171, 172, 173, 175,
Critic, The. 171,

D
Daly's Theatre, London. 49, 52, 53, 61, 66, 70, 71, 78, 79, 80, 81, 82, 108, 109, 115, 117, 119, 122, 123, 124, 127, 130, 131, 134, 138, 145, 146, 147, 148, 170, 179, 186, 191, 193, 204, 209,
Daily Telegraph, The. 209
Der Graf von Luxembourg. 168,
Dick Whittington. 48,
Die Lustige Witwe. 73
Dollar Princess, The. 145, 146,

E
Eades Place, Palehouse Common, Sussex. 199, 200, 207,

F
Fickle Duchess. 82, 106,
Floradora. 139,

G
Gaiety Theatre, London. 49, 50, 51, 52, 61, 65, 66, 72, 80, 82, 105, 108, 115, 116, 117, 119, 122, 123, 137, 138, 141,
Globe Theatre, London. 183, 186, 204
Gielgud Theatre, London. 204

H
Hick's Theatre, London. 146, 148,
His Majesty's Theatre, London. 171, 181,

I
Illustrated London News. 140,

K
Keep The Home Fires Burning. 181,
King of Kadonia, The. 169,
King's Theatre, Southsea. 182,

L
Lady Madcap. 68, 70,
Le' Attache! 106,
Little Cherub, The. 69, 70,
London Era Newspaper. 62,
London Evening News. 133,
London Illustrated & Dramatic News. 103,
London Herald, The. 170,
Little Michus, The. 69,
London News Newspaper. 63,
London & North Western Hotel, Salford. 25,
London Pelican Magazine. 137,
Lyric Theatre, London. 48, 53,
London Watchdog, The. 172,

M
Manchester Globe Newspaper. 27,
Manchester Guardian Newspaper. 28,
Manchester Herald Newspaper. 10, 27, 45,
Merry Widow, The. 73, 76, 106, 107, 108, 109, 111, 112, 113, 115, 116, 118, 121, 122, 123, 124, 126, 127, 128, 129, 130, 131, 133, 134, 136, 138, 140, 144, 145, 146, 147, 148, 168, 169, 170, 172, 173, 179, 180, 186, 188, 189, 191, 193, 195, 202, 204, 208, 209
Majestic Hotel, Biarritz. 144, 182,
Mavourneen. 181,
My Fair Lady. 207, 208,

N
New Alladin, The. 116, 118, 119, 120, 122,

P
Pamela. 181,
Playgoer & Society Illustrated Magazine. 146,
Prince of Wales Theatre, London. 68, 81, 103, 108, 119, 182,
Prince of Wales Theatre, Salford. 5, 7, 16, 20, 24, 25, 28, 29, 124, 140,
Princess Palace of Varieties, Leeds. 8,
Punch. 186,

Q
Queens Theatre, London. 186,
Queens Theatre, Manchester. 7, 10, 18, 26, 27, 69,
Quaker Girl, The. 167,

R
Regent Theatre, Salford. 25,
Ritz Hotel, London. 70,
Royal Strand Theatre, London. 53, 56, 62, 67, 72, 119,

S
Saint Paul's Church, Covent Garden, London. 79,

Savoy Hotel, London. 70, 76, 103, 136, 147,
Savoy Theatre, London. 49, 50, 59, 83,
See See. 81, 103, 105, 109, 110, 111, 115, 116, 122, 209,
Silver Slipper (The). 48, 53, 55
Simpsons on the Strand. 139,
Stanhope Place, 8, Hyde Park. 198, 204, 207,

T
Tatler, The. 179,
Theatre an der Wien, Vienna. 73, 75, 106, 168,
Theatre Royal, Haymarket. 183,
Theatre World. 186,
Thornton's Music Hall, Leeds. 8,
Times, The. 133, 136, 141, 186,
Truth Game, The. 179, 181, 183, 185, 186, 188, 189, 204,

V
Vienna State Orchestra. 76,

W
Waldorf Hotel, London. 72, 103
Waldorf Theatre, London. 72,
Waltz Dream, A. 146, 147, 148,

LILY ELSIE

The Last Edwardian Star
A Dramatised Documentary for Television

By
David Slattery-Christy

*Based on the Biography
'Anything But Merry!'
The Life & Times of Lily Elsie*

Draft 2 – September 2009 / 2014

© 2009 – David Slattery-Christy

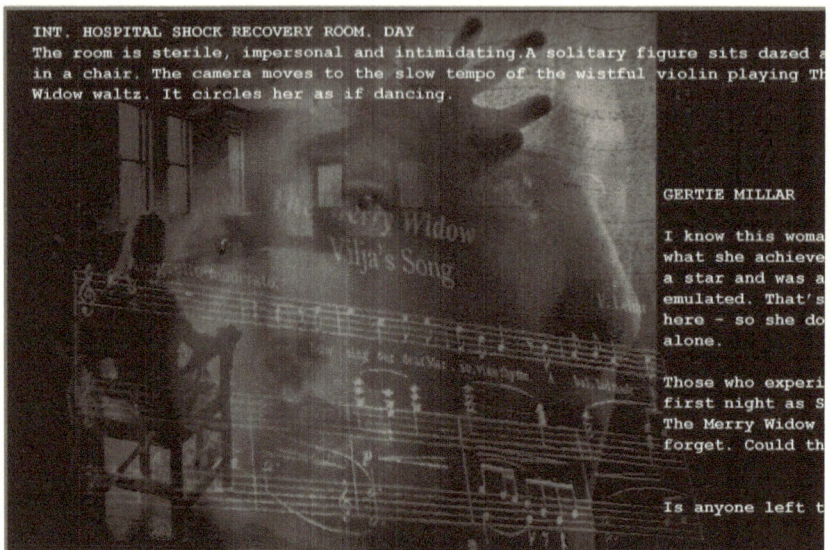

'ANYTHING BUT MERRY!'
THE LIFE AND TIMES OF LILY ELSIE

"An important contribution to our understanding of Edwardes and the Gaiety Girls, one of the most glittering periods of London's theatre history."

                                            Richard Baker – The Stage Newspaper 2008

CONTACTS:

David Slattery-Christy
Christyplays
Email. slatterychristy@aol.co.uk
Tel. 0778 8932541
Mobile. 07788 932541

Allan Bardsley
XED Films
Email: _____
Tel. 0778 8932541
Mobile. 0778 8932541

This document and the associated ideas and concepts contained within it are protected by intellectual property rights and are the property of David Slattery-Christy/Christyplays. This document has been prepared and presented in the strictest confidence and on the sole condition it is for your information only and should not be made available to any third party without express consent.

© 2009 – David Slattery-Christy

© September 2009. Lily Elsie - The Last Edwardian Star.   2.

BLACK SCREEN

                                            FADE IN:

We see an Edwardian phonograph. We hear an old wax cylinder recording of "VITALITY" the song by Ivor Novello. Listening to the music, heard through the veil of scratchy surface noise, brings alive the artists and music of a bye-gone age. It's like pulling back a curtain. Like looking at an old photograph of someone and hearing their voice. It somehow brings them to life again.

"Vitality... (Chorus)

              LYRICS
        Do you remember Gertie Millar?
        No, you wouldn't I'm afraid!
        There was Phyllis Dare and Zena
        Dare, Lily Elsie as The Widow..."

RUN TITLES:

        LILY ELSIE

        THE LAST EDWARDIAN STAR

              LYRICS (cont'd)
        Vitality, it matters more than
        personality, originality or
        topicality, it made all those top-
        liners tops!...etc

                                            DISSOLVE TO:

1   **INT. BACK STAGE. DALY'S THEATRE. EVENING.**   1

MUSIC: "Vitality" song continues - we hear the chorus again.

A stagehand is seen adjusting a stage light in the wing. He crosses to a large LX console with huge (Frankenstein like) electric pull switches. The main electric pull switch is much larger than the others. As the song reaches the part where it recalls "Lily Elsie as The Widow" he pulls the main switch down with both hands - as the contact is made a white flash fills the screen and the song ends.

                                            CUT TO:

© September 2009. Lily Elsie - The Last Edwardian Star.   3.

2   INT. ELSIE'S ROOM, DOLLIS HILL CONVENT. EVENING.   2

        CAPTION. LONDON, DECEMBER 1962.

        We see a carriage clock in close up, its movement whispers
        away time. Once established the shot opens out and we see
        the room. **THE MERRY WIDOW WALTZ** begins to play eerily in
        the background. The room is well decorated and beautifully
        furnished. Silver picture frames adorn surfaces with faces
        of stars from the past. A portrait of Lily Elsie hangs
        above the fireplace. The fire gives the room a warm glow.
        An old lady, LILY ELSIE, is lying unconscious in the bed. A
        NUN is tidying the bed. A young DOCTOR sits in a wing chair
        and is reading Elsie's medical notes and some personal
        letters written by GERTIE MILLAR.

                            GERTIE (V.O.)
                    Everybody's life should matter,
                    shouldn't it? Sometimes it is
                    hard to tell if anyone still
                    cares - has ever cared...
                    What made this woman different?
                    Special even? She was unique,
                    astonishing, but her life is
                    ending amid such loneliness. No
                    one left to mourn...
                    Some are blessed with a special
                    talent. Sometimes it seems there
                    is always a price to pay...

        WHITE ELECTRIC FLASH FILLS THE SCREEN

                                                        CUT TO:

3   INT. ELECTRIC SHOCK THERAPY ROOM. LONDON HOSPITAL DAY   3

        CAPTION. LONDON HOSPITAL, CIRCA 1950.

        (MUSIC. The Merry Widow waltz continues eerily under.)

        The room is white, sterile and clinical. A DOCTOR and NURSE
        adjust dials and equipment. A woman (ELSIE) is strapped to
        a bed and has a mouth gag and is clutching small shock
        scrolls in her hands. The NURSE places electrodes to her
        temples. We then see the DOCTOR pull down an old fashioned
        (Frankenstein like) electric switch on the wall. It
        crackles as the contacts touch. ELSIE's body convulses
        dramatically. After a few seconds pause, the whole
        procedure is repeated. We see the DOCTOR and NURSE holding
        down ELSIE's convulsing body.

© September 2009. Lily Elsie - The Last Edwardian Star. 4.

                    NARRATOR
          Mental illness was feared in all
          its forms and little sympathy or
          understanding was offered to
          those suffering from any kind of
          depression. All were subjected to
          horrendous treatments which
          reduced them to a husk of their
          former selves. Personalities
          eroded beyond recognition. Lily
          Elsie was the eminent celebrity
          of the Edwardian era, a star in
          the true sense of the word.

The doctor and nurse administer another shock on ELSIE. Her body convulses violently.

WHITE ELECTRIC FLASH FILLS THE SCREEN

                                                    BACK TO:

4   **INT. ELSIE'S ROOM, DOLLIS HILL CONVENT. EVENING.**   4

The young DOCTOR sits on the bed and holds ELSIE's hand obviously frustrated and annoyed at what he is reading in ELSIE's notes. ELSIE seems to try and grasp the DOCTOR'S hand and her eyes flicker some recognition of the comfort given.

WHITE ELECTRIC FLASH FILLS THE SCREEN

                                                    BACK TO:

5   **INT. SHOCK RECOVERY ROOM. LONDON HOSPITAL. DAY.**   5

The room is again sterile, impersonal and intimidating. Starkly white and clinical with black and white checkerboard linoleum tiles on the floor. In the centre of the room a solitary figure of a woman (ELSIE) sits dazed and slumped in a chair, her arms flopped at her side. The camera moves to the slow tempo of the wistful violin playing The Merry Widow waltz, it moves in and circles ELSIE as if dancing around her. We see ELSIE's face which seems empty and the eyes glazed, a small line of spittle is hanging from the corner of her mouth.

                    GERTIE (V.O.)
          I know this woman and what she
          achieved. She was a star of the
          stage before the First World War
          and was admired and emulated.
          Those who experienced her first
          night as Sonia in The Merry Widow
          could never forget. Could they?
                    (MORE)

© September 2009. Lily Elsie - The Last Edwardian Star.

> GERTIE (V.O.) (cont'd)
> Is anyone left to remember?

WHITE ELECTRIC FLASH FILLS THE SCREEN

BACK TO:

6 **INT. ELSIE'S ROOM, DOLLIS HILL CONVENT. EVENING.** 6

The DOCTOR is sitting in the chair still reading ELSIE's medical notes. The NUN enters with a cup of cocoa for the young doctor and places it on the side table. She crosses to ELSIE and feels her brow, then feels her hand and finds it feels colder. She looks across at the DOCTOR with concern.

> GERTIE (V.O.)
> Time waits for nobody - Elsie's time is running out.
>
> Her life began, like mine, in the music halls of northern England. There was nothing glamorous or magical about growing up amidst the squalor and the hand-to-mouth existence many encountered...

WHITE ELECTRIC FLASH FILLS THE SCREEN

BACK TO:

7 **INT. SHOCK RECOVERY ROOM. LONDON HOSPITAL. DAY.** 7

ELSIE still stares emptily across the empty room whilst slumped in the chair. She seems lifeless and defeated, her body limp. Her pleading eyes seem to try and will some slight movement of her body but none occurs.

> NARRATOR
> Her childhood performing and surviving in the music halls of Salford as 'Little Elsie' laid the foundation for her career and the manic depression and paranoia against which she fought so hard. Her mother was forever pushing her from the wings into the limelight. Her true father's identity was disputed. Billy Cotton a music hall manager and Bert Hodder a fly man were contenders. Cotton finally accepted paternal responsibility to save Elsie the shame of illegitimacy.

© September 2009. Lily Elsie - The Last Edwardian Star.   6.

The camera waltzes around ELSIE and focuses on her eyes. We see a small tear form in the corner of her eye, and then slowly begin to trickle down her cheek

                    NARRATOR (cont'd)
        By the start of the 20th Century
        Elsie was living with her mother
        in London, her father dead, and
        was poised to meet a man who
        would transform her life. George
        Edwardes.

The Merry Widow waltz swells and the camera once again takes on the eye of a waltz partner, the speed becomes faster and faster as it swirls around ELSIE and we are transported back in time to Edwardian England.

THE IMAGE BLURS.

                                                            DISSOLVE TO:

8   **INT. ELSIE'S FLAT, LONDON. NEARLY MIDNIGHT.**   8

CAPTION. NEW YEAR'S EVE, LONDON, 1905

Merry Widow music to play under to be determined.

ELSIE is standing by the bay window of her first floor drawing room looking out across the London skyline. A tear slowly trickles down her cheek. She appears tired and sad. Her MOTHER can be seen sitting asleep in a chair by the fire. An oil lamp and the flickering flames of the coal fire offer the only illumination.

                    NARRATOR
        On that cold New Year's Eve of
        1905 Elsie was distraught. She
        had successfully made her mark in
        several shows but had been
        foolish enough to anger the man
        who had helped her career so
        much. She wondered if perhaps it
        was for the best, appearing on
        the stage affected her mood and
        nerves so badly, but she felt so
        sad at letting down George
        Edwardes, and remembered fondly
        their first meeting in 1901
        backstage after a performance of
        The Silver Slipper.

WHITE ELECTRIC FLASH FILLS THE SCREEN

                                                               CUT TO:

9 **INT. LYRIC THEATRE (STAGE BOX/AUDITORIUM) SHAFTSBURY AVENUE. EVENING.** 9

CAPTION: LONDON, 1901

Music Q continues under.

GEORGE EDWARDES is an imposing man and his presence fills the stage box, which he occupies alone. He surveys the auditorium and seems impatient and somehow perturbed as if something is troubling him.

> NARRATOR
> Mr. George Edwardes was the most powerful producer and theatre owner in London's West End. An offer of a job from him meant assured success. He had helped establish the success of Gilbert & Sullivan at the Savoy Theatre, and had gone on to establish the Gaiety Theatre on the Strand - his star attraction being the beautiful Gaiety Girls. He had invested money in The Silver Slipper revue at the Lyric Theatre, and liked to check out his investment...

As the house lights fade we see EDWARDES turn his chair to watch the stage.

> NARRATOR (cont'd)
> And, instead of his usual habit of watching the audience - normally he liked to assess what the audience liked and disliked so he could suggest how changes could be made - he turned his chair to face the performers.

EDWARDES searches the chorus for the face he is seeking - when he sees her he smiles and is almost leaning out of the box to get a better view of ELSIE. His thoughts flicker across his face.

> NARRATOR (cont'd)
> Much to the surprise of many who knew him, he visited The Silver Slipper several times to watch this young girl in the chorus who had so captured his attention...

WHITE ELECTRIC FLASH FILLS THE SCREEN

                                                          CUT TO:

10   **INT. LYRIC THEATRE (BACKSTAGE) - LATER**   10

ELSIE and a GROUP OF CHORUS GIRLS are standing in the wings. The GIRLS around ELSIE are chattering excitedly. ELSIE seems nervous and quiet.

                      GIRL
            Elsie, did you see him?

                      ELSIE
            Who? The man in the box, stage
            right? No. (beat) Well yes, I
            suppose I did, he seemed to be
            staring at me a lot…

                      GIRL 2
            I'll say he was - I am surprised
            he didn't fall right out of that
            box and join us on the stage!

They all laugh which makes ELSIE blush with embarrassment.

                      GIRL
            Fancy Mr. George Edwardes taking
            a shine to our little Elsie? Do
            you think perhaps he will be
            making you into one of his Gaiety
            Girls? It'll be supper at the
            Savoy and seduction!

ELSIE turns to escape the GIRLS teasing only to find standing before her EDWARDES. She stands stock-still and looks up at him. The other girls shuffle off suddenly intimidated by his presence. EDWARDES is used to being in control and dispassionate, but suddenly finds himself a little tongue tied - which both amuses and irritates him.

                      EDWARDES
            Lily, I would like to…

                      ELSIE
            My name is ELSIE, not Lily.
            ELSIE Cotton. Lily Elsie is my
            stage name.

                      EDWARDES
            Of course, Elsie, I apologize

                      ELSIE
            There is no need.
                      (MORE)

                    ELSIE (cont'd)
          Mr. Edwardes, isn't it? You
          should be more careful...

                    EDWARDES
          I meant no offence...

                    ELSIE
          I am not offended (sensing his
          discomfort, she giggles), I was
          going to say you should be more
          careful leaning so far out of the
          stage box - I was afraid you
          would fall out!

                    EDWARDES
          Miss Lily Elsie, (he clears his
          throat and realizes she has the
          upper hand) I have come to offer
          you a position in my show A
          Chinese Honeymoon. I will arrange
          rehearsals for you and a suitable
          contract with favorable terms...

                    ELSIE
          Oh, no! I am sorry Mr. Edwardes
          and as much as I appreciate your
          kind offer I am unable at this
          time to consider working in your
          show.

EDWARDES is not a man used to hearing anyone refuse him and
is visibly aghast. ELSIE again senses his discomfort at
being wrong-footed and can't help suppressing a giggle.

                    ELSIE (cont'd)
          You see, sir, I already have a
          contract for this show and then
          just last week I signed a
          contract for pantomime over the
          coming Christmas period, so I
          won't be free until early next
          year at the soonest.

EDWARDES is so stunned he can't find any words to respond
but visibly blusters for a second or two. We see a couple
of Elsie's CHORUS GIRL FRIENDS in the background who have
been eavesdropping and are now gesticulating to ELSIE to
accept his offer. ELSIE stands smiling sweetly at EDWARDES.

                    EDWARDES
          So, you are turning me down?
          Would you allow me to speak to
          those you are contracted to so I
          could organize a release?

                    ELSIE
          I am sorry Mr. Edwardes but that
          is out of the question.
                    (MORE)

                    ELSIE (cont'd)
            A contract is a contract and had
            I signed a contract with you I
            would honour it with the same
            loyalty. I shall, however, be
            happy to consider your kind offer
            of a position in - A Chinese
            Honeymoon, wasn't it? - once I am
            available early next year, should
            your production still be running.

She smiles radiantly at him and offers her hand, which he
takes and kisses.

            It has been a pleasure to meet
            you Mr. Edwardes. Good evening.

ELSIE walks confidently into the shadow of the wing past
her two chorus-girl friends. They look as aghast as
EDWARDES. The girls scramble after her and bob a curtsey at
EDWARDES as they go. Once they have gone EDWARDES looks
around to make sure no one is around and guffaws with
laughter.

                    EDWARDES
            The little girl has definitely
            got something!

He exits laughing to himself.

WHITE ELECTRIC FLASH FILLS THE SCREEN.

Music Q - Chinese Honeymoon style

                                                CUT TO:

11 **DRESSING ROOM. ROYAL STRAND THEATRE. EVENING.**   11

CAPTION: LONDON, 1903

ELSIE is seen in her Princess Soo Soo costume, her role in
A Chinese Honeymoon. She sits looking into the mirror and
begins to prepare her hair in the oriental style, complete
with crossed sticks etc.

                                            DISSOLVE TO:
MONTAGE.

12 **INTERIOR. THEATRE.**   12

*We see brief clips and fragmented, fleeting images of Elsie
performing pieces from The Silver Slipper, Pantomime, A
Chinese Honeymoon, Little Michus, Lady Madcap, New Aladdin
& See See - all the George Edwardes shows she appeared in
prior to The Merry Widow.*

The Music and sounds from the shows attached to live-action immediately produce a curious sense of intimacy.

Intercutting shots of Elsie in different plumed hats and vivacious costumes interlaced with period photographs, posters and programme covers, newspaper cuttings.

GERTIE (V.O.)

(Under Montage and ELSIE preparing Soo Soo)

Edwardes was nobody's fool. He could have turned his back on that impudent young girl but he was shrewd. He knew she had that something special. He knew that even in a small chorus part and sharing the stage with dozens of others the audiences eye was drawn to Elsie. She had that something that neither money nor training could attain, the potential to be a star. Her singing would cause hairs to stand up at the back of his neck, it was not a powerful voice but it was pure and unforgettable.

NARRATOR

Elsie had taken over the role of Princess Soo Soo in A Chinese Honeymoon and made the part her own. She was the first actress to bring realism to her portrayal of a character and researched the Chinese costume, manners and hair style of the period to make it authentic. Edwardes indulged her at great cost, all the other actors suddenly embraced Elsie's idea of realism instead of deriding it - as they had done prior to her rave notices in the newspapers.

BACK TO:

DRESSING ROOM.

ELSIE places the wooden cross sticks into her hair, then adjusts her make up. She looks satisfied with the result and smiles at her reflection. She stands and exits the dressing room.

BACK TO:

MONTAGE.

14 INTERIOR. THEATRE.   14

We see the curtain rising, the dazzling footlights
appearing. Intercut with the brilliant slanting shaft or
ray of light from the 'follow-spot' as it tracks Elsie as
she sings.

There is George Edwardes in his private box, studying the
audience and watching Elsie.

High up above the stage in the fly-gallery, the stage hands
wave down to Elsie. Elsie smiles and waving back - blows
them kisses.

And down in the orchestra pit, we see the conductor and the
musicians playing with gusto.

Intercut with the audience applauding enthusiastically.

>   NARRATOR
> The London News reported on 16th
> March, 1903: "Miss Lily Elsie
> enchanted the audience last night
> with her portrayal of Princess
> Soo Soo in George Edwardes
> oriental fantasy farce at the
> Royal Strand Theatre. On her
> first entrance the audience were
> heard to audibly gasp not only at
> Miss Elsie's beauty but also her
> acting and singing. The fact she
> packaged her talents and
> presented herself with an
> oriental fashion added to the
> delight. Her rendition of the
> song 'But Yesterday' drew more
> gasps as the silver lined notes
> soared up to the gods
> effortlessly. Her predecessor in
> the role was Beatrice Edwards.
> 'Beatrice who?' The only name on
> the lips of patrons as they left
> the theatre for their carriages
> was 'Lily Elsie.'"
>
> A Chinese Honeymoon, as the title
> implies, was a slight musical
> comedy story of the English
> abroad who break the strict
> 'kissing laws' whilst in China,
> along with a sea captain who is
> asked by the Emperor to find him
> a true-love bride - and when he
> fails the penalty is death - and
> all the comical capers that ensue
> to escape these consequences.
>   (MORE)

                NARRATOR   (cont'd)
                Edwardians were fascinated with
                all things oriental.

THE MONTAGE CONTINUES but the images are gradually becoming
distorted as if being reflected in a broken mirror.

                      NARRATOR (cont'd)
                 But there was a dark side to
                 Elsie's temperament and Edwardes
                 knew it. She would be struck with
                 terrifying stage fright. On
                 occasion she would be so ill she
                 could not appear and seemed to
                 lose all her natural confidence.

                                             CUT TO:

15   **INT. THEATRE. BACKSTAGE.**   15

We hear the orchestra playing the overture and the audience
applauding in anticipation of Elsie's first appearance on
stage.

ELSIE IS COWERING IN THE WINGS WITH SHEER TERROR ON HER
FACE.

                                             CUT TO:

16   **INT. BACK-STAGE DRESSING ROOM. SAME TIME**   16

ELSIE is helped in by her MOTHER, only to collapse shaking
violently onto the chaise longue in tears.

                                             CUT TO:

17   **INT. DRESSING ROOM TOILET. MOMENTS LATER**   17

ELSIE is vomiting in the toilet and sweating heavily.

                                             BACK TO:

18   **INT. BACK-STAGE DRESSING ROOM. MOMENTS LATER** 18

ELSIE is raging and smashing things up. She catches her
reflection in the large mirror on the wall. Picking up a
large ashtray she hurls it. The mirror shatters into
smithereens.

                                         CUT TO BLACK:

                                             FADE IN:

19   **INT. BEDROOM. NIGHT**   19

       The room is very dark - the camera slowly circles round the
       room and moves toward the bed. ELSIE is lying curled up in
       the foetal position suffering from serious depression.

                         GERTIE (V.O.)
                    At times she would be ill for
                    days and no one could reason with
                    her or talk to her - not even me.
                    Then just a suddenly she would
                    happily appear as if nothing had
                    happened. But Edwardes held firm
                    to Elsie and her potential and
                    made sure he had her under
                    permanent contract, and also to
                    engage an understudy for her
                    always.

       Music Q, live action and montage photographs end.

       WHITE ELECTRIC FLASH FILLS THE SCREEN

                                                          BACK TO:

20   **INT. ELSIE'S FLAT, LONDON, NEW YEAR'S EVE, MIDNIGHT.**   20

       ELSIE stands alone by the window and listens to the chimes
       of Big Ben ring in the New Year 1906. She suddenly feels
       alone and a chill envelopes her. She gazes across at
       LOTTIE, her Mother who is watching Elsie with concern.

                         ELSIE
                    It's a new year. We shall have a
                    new start. A move to the country
                    would be good for us both and I
                    can forget about this life on the
                    stage, a life I never really
                    desired.

                         LOTTIE
                    You would throw it all away? We
                    have worked so hard, sacrificed
                    so much. Please, Elsie, for me,
                    make your peace with Edwardes.
                    Talk to him, explain it was a
                    mistake...

                         ELSIE
                    I feel badly letting him down
                    (beat) but his rage frightened
                    me. Nothing is worth that.

> LOTTIE
> I blame those Dare sisters - they are the ones responsible for this. If they had not led you astray none of this would have happened...

Suddenly irritated at her mother's cross word about her friends, ELSIE crosses to sit opposite her by the fire.

> ELSIE
> I will not hear a word said against Phyllis and Zena! We were having fun, I have had precious little fun or even girl friends whilst growing up. Along with Gertie, they are the best friends I have.

> LOTTIE
> Patting balloons at men in the audience, whatever possessed you? Edwardes had every right to dismiss you, it could have cost him his reputation.

> ELSIE
> I am only twenty years-old mother! Sometimes I feel ninety.

ELSIE crosses back to the window. A resentment hangs in the air between them. LOTTIE crosses to the window and nervously pulls the curtain back and peers out into the darkness as if she is expecting to see someone.

> NARRATOR
> Patting a balloon at a male member of the audience seems a slight misdemeanor today, but in 1905 it could have had serious consequences for Edwardes. His theatre license could have been withdrawn if any of his shows suggested lewd behavior, the music halls and theatres were then rife with prostitution and Edwardes had fought to make his establishments respectable.
> Fate was lending a helping hand. Unbeknown to Elsie her friend had contrived a meeting with Edwardes that very day to sort the matter out.

WHITE ELECTRIC FLASH FILLS THE SCREEN

                                                    CUT TO:

21   INT. SAVOY HOTEL, RESTAURANT, LONDON, 1905, NEW YEARS   21
      AFTERNOON.

      EDWARDES and GERTIE MILLAR are seated at a table having
      just had lunch. GERTIE is in no mood to play games and is
      direct with EDWARDES. She is one of the few people who can
      speak to him with such candor.

                              GERTIE
                    Elsie is a child, George, and you
                    should be ashamed of yourself!

      EDWARDES is nonplussed at her directness and senses he is
      in for a dressing down.

                              EDWARDES
                    I should be ashamed...

                              GERTIE
                    What on earth were you thinking?
                    (beat) Elsie needs your support.
                    Her father is dead, and she has
                    the responsibility of looking
                    after her less than reliable
                    mother. When has she ever been
                    able to just be a girl?

                              EDWARDES
                    Her behavior was inappropriate
                    and unprofessional, I had to make
                    an example...

                              GERTIE
                    Don't be so pompous, George. She
                    needs your support, not your
                    wrath! Besides, she is a rare
                    talent. In time she will eclipse
                    even me - and I will put my money
                    on that!

      EDWARDES looks at GERTIE and in his mind he knows she is
      right. GERTIE senses her job is done. She rises and waits
      for the waiter to drape her fur over her shoulders.

                              EDWARDES
                    I will speak to her...

                              GERTIE
                    If you don't, I shall never speak
                    to you again. (beat) Happy New
                    Year, George.

      GERTIE flicks the fur tail over her shoulder, gives him a
      sly wink, and exits the restaurant with a swish of silk,
      leaving EDWARDES in no doubt she means it. She smiles to
      herself as she exits with satisfaction.

                    EDWARDES
          (to himself) Why has it been my
          misfortune to have been sent the
          two most talented and
          exasperating women of the 20th
          century!

     EDWARDES chuckles to himself, exhaling a savored draw of
     his cigar.

     WHITE ELECTRIC FLASH FILLS THE SCREEN.

                                                  BACK TO:

22   **INT. ELSIE'S FLAT, NEW YEAR'S DAY. AFTER MIDNIGHT.**   22

     ELSIE sits alone gazing into the dying embers of the fire.
     She is reflecting on her life and wondering what will
     happen to them and how thy will survive.

                    NARRATOR
          Elsie had no need to worry. By
          the time she was just 21, and
          still unmarried, she was destined
          to become the most famous 'widow'
          in England, if not the world.

     WHITE ELECTRIC FLASH FILLS THE SCREEN

                                                  CUT TO:

23   **INT. THEATRE AND DER WIEN. AFTER MIDNIGHT**   23

     CAPTION: VIENNA, NEW YEAR'S DAY, 1906

     Music Cue : Vilja (instrumental & choral only) from The
     Merry Widow

     We see a young FRANZ LEHAR in close shot conducting an
     orchestra we can't see. His face expresses the ecstacy he
     feels hearing his music played by an orchestra.

                    NARRATOR
          Several thousand miles away at
          the Theatre an de Wien in Vienna
          a young composer was enjoying the
          standing ovation his new operetta
          Die Lustige Wite was receiving.
          He had fought to bring his work
          to the stage against all the
          odds.
                    (MORE)

NARRATOR (cont'd)
Franz Lehar and George Edwardes
were destined to meet and produce
the English version of his
operetta The Merry Widow at
Daly's Theatre in London's West
End.

WHITE FLASH FILLS THE SCREEN

CUT TO:

24 INT. ELLEN'S TEA ROOM. LEICESTER SQUARE, LONDON, 1906.   24
    AFTERNOON

Music Cue continues.

ELSIE and EDWARDS are seen seated in the tea rooms enjoying
afternoon tea. Their body language tells us they are
chatting happily and relaxed in each others company - like
father and daughter.

NARRATOR
Still bristling after his
encounter with Gertie, Edwardes
was as good as his word and made
peace with Elsie early in the new
year of 1906. From this point he
decided to undertake a more
paternalistic role in her life.

As they are being served, EDWARDES puts two sugar lumps in
his tea cup and stirs loudly. The spoon clunks against the
bone china. A waitress throws EDWARDES a stern look of
disapproval and ELSIE collapses in fits of giggles, in
spite of his usual reserve EDWARDES laughs too.

NARRATOR (cont'd)
Edwardes spent so much time
working he was detached from the
daily lives of his own children,
and indeed his wife. Elsie
reminded him of what he had
missed. From this point Edwardes
and Elsie's relationship was
indestructible. They could
communicate without words where a
look would do. (beat) He informed
Elsie her next show would be 'See
See' playing the part of Humming
Bird. Another populist oriental
fantasy with a similar plot to A
Chinese Honeymoon. Edwardes
decided it would keep her busy
until he found the right vehicle
to progress her career.

CUT TO:

25   **EXT. ELLEN'S TEA ROOM. LEICESTER SQUARE, LONDON, 1906.**   25
        AFTERNOON.

        GERTIE has crossed Leicester Square and is walking towards
        her carriage which is waiting. She glances in the tea room
        as she passes and notices ELSIE and EDWARDES. She smiles
        with satisfaction, glad they are united again. She enters
        her carriage and it pulls away.

        WHITE FLASH FILLS THE SCREEN

                                                        CUT TO:

26   **INT. SHOCK RECOVERY ROOM. LONDON HOSPITAL. DAY.**   26

        CAPTION: 1950

        ELSIE is seen wearing a hospital gown and sitting alone in
        the centre of the room. Her body has again been devastated
        by the electric shock therapy. Her arms hang limply at her
        side, her legs sprawled, her head slumped to one side.
        There are burns on her temples where the electrodes had
        been attached. Her eyes are clear but stunned. There is
        something of a silent scream shattering the emptiness and
        echo of the room. The camera again waltzes in and around
        her.

        Music Cue: Vilja - The Merry Widow instrumental version

        The young, glamorous ELSIE as Sonia in The Merry Widow is
        superimposed over the present day ELSIE. The camera circles
        slowly then -

        WHITE ELECTRIC FLASH FILLS THE SCREEN

                                                        CUT TO:

27   **INT. DALY'S THEATRE. DAY.**   27

        Caption: DALY'S THEATRE - LEICESTER SQUARE - 1907

        Music Cue: Vilja (instrumental) continues

        MONTAGE OF INTERLACED SHOTS:

        The atmosphere is tense - everyone's nerves are jangling.
        The assembled cast are gathered on an empty stage for the
        first read through. ELSIE is behaving like a petrified
        child. COYNE is pacing up and down cursing and muttering to
        himself.

EDWARDES glances around picking up immediately on the naked
fear in Elsie's eyes and the hostile expression on COYNE
her leading man. LEHAR and his two GERMAN LIBRETTISTS are
sat 'to attention' at the front of the stage.

>NARRATOR
>Edwardes bought the rights to The
>Merry Widow, and although he
>initially invited the original
>librettists - Viktor Leon and Leo
>Stein - to London, he had already
>decided his own team of Basil
>Hood and Adrian Ross would re-
>write the libretto for a London
>audience. Lehar was fearful
>Edwardes would tamper with his
>score, but those fears were
>unfounded.

28 **MONTAGE CONTINUED:** 28

ELSIE is standing stage centre during a rehearsal for The
Merry Widow. A single limelight illuminates her and the
camera circles her in waltz time. LEHAR is in the pit and
the orchestra are playing. EDWARDES and GERTIE are sat in
the stalls, their eyes glued on Elsie.

>NARRATOR
>Elsie feared the role of Sonia
>and initially refused to consider
>it when Edwardes first told her
>his plans. She also felt she was
>far too young to play a 'widow'
>and feared she would be laughed
>off the stage. However, she was
>eventually persuaded. The song
>Vilja terrified her as she
>believed she could not sing it as
>she lacked the opera technique.
>Edwardes insistence and belief in
>her won her over but rehearsals
>were torturous.

ELSIE misses her cue to start singing 'Vilja'. There is
panic in her eyes, the music stops playing, she looks into
the darkness of the auditorium for reassurance, then rushes
off stage in floods of tears.

WHITE ELECTRIC FLASH FILLS THE SCREEN

                                                    BACK TO:

29   **MONTAGE CONTINUED.**   29

ELSIE is distressed and is in animated discussions with
LEHAR and EDWARDES - both men are very sympathetic. Other
CAST MEMBERS, the ORCHESTRA and the MAN on the Follow-Spot
watch on in silence. High above in the fly-tower the STAGE
HANDS look down on the frightened and disoriented Elsie.
Their POV makes her look so small and vulnerable.

> NARRATOR
> Edwardes' board of directors had
> fought against Elsie being cast
> in the role, along with the New
> York actor Joseph Coyne who
> couldn't sing, and had washed
> their collective hands of the
> production. Edwardes was on the
> brink of financial ruin and
> needed a success to replenish his
> fortunes.

WHITE ELECTRIC FLASH FILLS THE SCREEN

                                                   DISSOLVE TO:

30   **MONTAGE CONTINUED**   30

EDWARDES is sat in the stalls watching COYNE and ELSIE
rehearsing a duet. LEHAR is conducting the orchestra. At
the point where COYNE should start singing, EDWARDES calls
out, "Don't sing it, Joe, just recite it!"

> NARRATOR
> Edwardes had also misled Lehar
> regarding Joseph Coyne's singing
> ability. At rehearsals he made
> great play of telling Coyne to
> just *"speak the part and save his
> voice"* - Edwardes told Lehar he
> had a throat infection. Lehar
> eventually became suspicious and
> was outraged at being duped.
> Edwardes pleaded he at least
> watch a rehearsal with Coyne talk-
> singing the part.

LEHAR is furious. He bears down on EDWARDES. LEON & STEIN
stand behind him with pinched faces. LEHAR throws his hands
in the air and briskly marches up the aisle with LEON &
STEIN in perfect Germanic military precision behind him.

                                                   DISSOLVE TO:

31   THE REHEARSALS MONTAGE CONTINUED   31

COYNE and ELSIE are on stage rehearsing a scene. GERTIE is watching from the back of the stalls. LEHAR watches and his delight at ELSIE is instantly obvious. His reservations are apparent where Coyne is concerned, but he sees the chemistry between them and his pleasure is obvious despite his leading man's inability to sing.

                    NARRATOR
          Lehar was impressed with Coyne,
          but it would have been too late
          to do anything about it anyway so
          he agreed for Coyne to stay. What
          Coyne lacked Elsie made up for,
          Lehar adored her and did
          everything he could to help and
          support her. For his part, Coyne
          hated the show and his character
          Prince Danilo and had hoped Lehar
          would insist he be replaced with
          someone able to sing the tenor
          role. Coyne was a very negative
          and strange individual offstage
          and could often be found having
          heated discussions with
          "invisible friends" on street
          corners in Covent Garden!
          Elsie found his negativity
          initially made her feel ill and
          insecure, but once they worked
          past this their partnership on
          stage was magical and Elsie loved
          performing with him. Elsie's hats
          and costumes, designed by
          Lucille, Lady Duff-Gordon,
          although exquisite, were quite
          another matter!

As GERTIE watches on she finds herself mesmerized by the music and Elsie's voice soaring through the empty auditorium.

                    GERTIE (V.O.)
          I can honestly say I'd never seen
          or heard anything like it. When
          Elsie made her first entrance
          down the staircase of the Embassy
          in full costume and with that
          enormous hat it took my breath
          away! She looked incredible. And
          at that precise moment I knew
          this was going to change her life
          forever.
                         (MORE)

> GERTIE (V.O.) (cont'd)
> It was as if The Merry Widow had been waiting for Elsie to come along all the time.

DISSOLVE TO:

32 **THE REHEARSALS MONTAGE CONTINUED** 32

ELSIE is seen struggling with the weight of her gown for Sonia's entrance scene at the Embassy Ball. Being quite small and far from robust, the heavily beaded gown swamps her and drains her of energy. The tail of the long gown scrapes on the floor behind her and she struggles to walk, never mind float down a long staircase making a glamorous entrance into the scene. The sheer weight of the gown banished any attempt at glamour! To add to her woes the matching hat, nicknamed 'The Merry Widow' by Lucille, arrived to accompany the gown and Elsie's dismay at the sight of it is palpable. GERTIE MILLAR is seen sitting in the stalls and collapses in gales of laughter. ELSIE at first seems cross at this reaction to her plight, but Gertie's laugh is infections and she begins to laugh in spite of her frustration. EDWARDES crosses onto the stage to find them both laughing so hard they are unable to speak. He exits looking cross.

> NARRATOR
> In spite of the problems Elsie persevered with the help of Gertie, until she finally mastered the art of looking elegant and glamorous in her gown and very large matching hat!

We see a montage of shots showing GERTIE helping and rehearsing ELSIE walking down the stairs in the gown and huge wide brimmed hat until she seems to float effortlessly. COYNE and other MALE CAST MEMBERS stand at the foot of the stairs to receive her. GERTIE is once again sitting in the stalls watching and admiring.

> NARRATOR (cont'd)
> Those who watched rehearsals were impressed with Elsie and Coyne - they became the characters of Sonia and Prince Danilo. Most forgot that Elsie and Coyne were their colleagues or friends. This was something quite new.

FADE OUT.

WHITE ELECTRIC FLASH FILLS THE SCREEN

33   INT. DALY'S THEATRE. OPENING NIGHT. 1907. EVE.   33

A SERIES OF INTERCUTTING SHOTS - BACKSTAGE, FRONT OF HOUSE
AND IN THE AUDITORIUM:

The atmosphere is electric with anticipation as the first
night audience arrives, filling the bars and auditorium
with excited chatter. Throngs of people are queuing for the
gallery and pit seats.

LEHAR is waiting by the pass-door adjusting his white tie
and glancing quickly at himself the full length mirror to
check he looks his best.

We hear the orchestra begin tuning up. The CAMERA pans
around the auditorium. We see elegantly dressed women with
their jewels sparkling; and men in their white tie and
tails, some in military uniform providing a bright splash
of red here and there.

BACK STAGE - The RUNNERS are rushing around banging on the
dressing room doors shouting *"Beginners stand by -
beginners stand by - this is your final call... Final call -
Beginners stand by!"*

LOTTIE is sat in a stage box with EDWARDES. The excitement
is palpable. The crimson and gold of the auditorium seems
to pulse with anticipation, the deeply polished mahogany
skirt which encloses the orchestra pit reflects a thousand
glimmers of light which bounces off the chandeliers.

The STAGE MANAGER escorts LEHAR down into the orchestra pit
where he stands waiting nervously.

The excited chatter intensifies as the orchestra finish
tuning their instruments.

LOTTIE waves to GERTIE MILLAR and her husband. The CAMERA
picks out MARIE LLOYD, PHYLLIS DARE, ZENA DARE, BEATRICE
EDWARDES and GABRIELLE RAY, all here to support Elsie.

LOTTIE is fanning herself with a programme - willing the
house lights to fade in case she faints with nervous
anticipation.

Backstage, BERT HODDER watches ELSIE talking to COYNE. They
both seemed relaxed. High up in the fly-gallery, lost in
the shadows, a crew of FIVE STAGE HANDS are signalled to
stand-by, they have a busy night ahead.

As the house lights fade there is a tingling ripple of
expectancy running through the audience.

In the gallery first nighters cheer from their bench seats
way up in the gods. Those who have left it until the last
minute rush to claim their seats.

BACK STAGE - We see the 'Beginners' cast assembled ready in
the wings. ELSIE sets herself down stage centre.

                    GERTIE (V.O.)
            The first night of The Merry
            Widow, 8th June 1907, arrived
            upon Elsie, Edwardes, Lehar and
            the cast in a flash as these
            things invariably do. Now it was
            down to the public to decide
            whether they liked this Merry
            Widow or not.

LEHAR stands on the conductors podium and turns to face the
audience. He bows and they applaud. He turns and slowly
raises his baton. Instantly a hush descends - you can hear
a pin drop. After a moment the orchestra begins. The huge
curtain slowly begins to rise.

BACKSTAGE - The ELECTRICIAN has both hands on the huge
master pull-switch. On the cue from the STAGE MANAGER he
heaves the lever down. A dazzling white flash fills the
screen as the rows of stage-lights and footlights go up and
the FOLLOW-SPOT OPERATOR picks out ELSIE with the
limelight.

ELSIE is about to make her entrance at the Embassy Ball.
Dressed in the heavily beaded gown and wearing the huge
wide brimmed hat she looks absolutely stunning. Elsie
stands elegantly at the top of the steep staircase.

GERTIE remembers the problems in rehearsal. She takes a
deep breath and closes her eyes as if offering up a silent
prayer.

ELSIE picks up her cue and gracefully and effortlessly
floats down the stairs. COYNE and other MALE CAST MEMBERS
stand ready to receive her.

                                            DISSOLVE TO:

34   **'MERRY WIDOW' - MONTAGE OF SCENES:**   34

We interlace scenes and pivotal moments as ELSIE performs
the Merry Widow. These are heightened and intensified by
cutaway shots from backstage and the auditorium. The
atmosphere is almost magical.

                    NARRATOR
            The story takes place in Paris.
            Sonia, Elsie's character, is a
            wealthy young widow and on the
            death of her husband inherited
            his vast fortune.
                        (MORE)

NARRATOR (cont'd)
As she comes from a small Balkan country, Marsovia, the powers that be are worried that if she marries an outsider she will take her fortune with her and plunge the country into an economic crisis. Prince Danilo is summoned by the ambassador and instructed to marry the widow and save their country from disaster. He duly attends the Embassy Ball to court the widow, but would rather spend his time amongst the can-can girls at Maxims Night Club so arrives later with little enthusiasm to carry out his duty.

The STAGE MANAGER and other CAST MEMBERS are watching on from the wings.

LEHAR conducts with passion and delight. On occasions there are tears in his eyes.

When he discovers the 'widow' in question is Sonia he is horrified because they had once been lovers prior to her marriage and she was the reason he ran away to Paris - as a result he is rude and surly towards her. Sonia is equally alarmed to find her old suitor at the Ball, as she couldn't understand why he had spurned her several years before.

Up in the gods, the FIRST NIGHTERS are gazing down in adoration hanging on every word and following every note.

The MUSICIANS play their hearts out

LOTTIE is sat in a stage box with EDWARDES. She is transfixed; he beams with delight.

GERTIE MILLAR and her husband, MARIE LLOYD, PHYLLIS DARE, ZENA DARE, BEATRICE EDWARDES and GABRIELLE RAY, are all watching ELSIE in various degrees of awe and admiration.

DISSOLVE TO:

Act III - ELSIE's moment of truth has arrived! LEHAR is vamping the Vilja song and looks at ELSIE intensely, but with affection, hoping she picks up her cue. He vamps the orchestra for a few seconds.

GERTIE recognizes the music and her eyes widen. Her heart is in her mouth! This is the song Elsie dreads the most, convinced her voice lacked the strength and technique it demanded.

ELSIE begins to sing - exuding confidence. Her voice soars through the theatre like a lark ascending.

                ELSIE AS SONIA (SUNG)
      THERE ONCE WAS A VILJA, A WITCH
      OF THE WOOD, A HUNTER BEHELD HER
      ALONE AS SHE STOOD. THE SPELL OF
      HER BEAUTY ON HIM WAS LAID; HE
      LOOK'D AND HE LONG'D FOR THE
      MAGICAL MAID! FOR A SUDDEN TREMOR
      RAN, RIGHT THRO' THE LOVE
      BEWILDERED MAN, AND HE SIGH'D AS
      A HAPLESS LOVER CAN...
      (chorus)
      VILJA, O VILJA! THE WITCH OF THE
      WOOD, WOULD I NOT DIE FOR YOU,
      DEAR, IF I COULD! VILJA, O VILJA,
      MY LOVE AND MY BRIDE! SOFTLY AND
      SADLY HE SIGH'D

The CHORUS SINGERS voices swell behind ELSIE as she contemplates as Sonia for a couple of beats. She then reprises the Chorus.

                ELSIE AS SONIA (SUNG) (cont'd)
      VILJA, O VILJA! THE WITCH OF THE
      WOOD, WOULD I NOT DIE FOR YOU,
      DEAR, IF I COULD! VILJA, O VILJA,
      MY LOVE AND MY BRIDE! SOFTLY AND
      SADLY HE SIGH'D

We see ELSIE from the dizzy heights of the fly gallery. HODDER, the older SENIOR FLYMAN is watching her performance intently.

                                DISSOLVE TO:

                NARRATOR
      It is obvious to all concerned
      they are still in love and after
      much intrigue and comedy, and
      Danilo's admission he didn't want
      Sonia to think he was after her
      fortune, and that he ran away to
      Paris to numb his broken heart,
      they reunite to the strains of
      The Merry Widow waltz.

The action now moves on to the Valse Duet between Sonia and Danilo at the end of Act III - "I LOVE YOU SO"

                COYNE AS DANILO (TALK-SUNG)
      THOUGH I SAY NOT WHAT I MAY NOT
      LET YOU HEAR, YET THE SWAYING
      DANCE IS SAYING, LOVE ME, DEAR!
                (MORE)

                    COYNE AS DANILO (TALK-SUNG) (cont'd)
                    EV'RY TOUCH OF FINGERS TELLS ME
                    WHAT I KNOW, SAYS FOR YOU, IT'S
                    TRUE, IT'S TRUE, YOU LOVE ME SO!

                            ELSIE AS SONIA (SUNG)
                    AND TO THE MUSIC'S CHIME, MY
                    HEART IS BEATING TIME, AS IF TO
                    GIVE A SIGN, THAT WOULD SAY, BE
                    MINE, BE MINE! THOUGH OUR LIPS
                    MAY SAY NO WORD, YET IN THE HEART
                    A VOICE IS HEARD. YOU CANNOT
                    CHOOSE BUT KNOW I LOVE YOU SO!

                            SONIA & DANILO (SUNG)
                    EV'RY TOUCH OF FINGERS TELLS ME
                    WHAT I KNOW. SAYS FOR YOU, IT'S
                    TRUE, IT'S TRUE YOU LOVE ME SO!

Danilo and Sonia waltz gently together wrapped in each
others arms as the curtain slowly begins to fall. The
thunderous roars and applause tell us all we need to know.

Back in the Fly tower - BERT HODDER looks down at his
daughter with enormous pride.

WHITE ELECTRIC FLASH FILLS THE SCREEN

                                                   CUT TO:

35   **INT. ELECTRIC SHOCK THERAPY ROOM. DAY.**   35

Sound effects: The first night roars and applause continue.

ELSIE is sitting on the wooden chair in the centre of the
room. Her temples burnt from the electrodes and spittle
dangling from the corner of her mouth. It seems there are
tears in her eyes as yet un-released to travel down her
cheeks. The camera circles her in waltz time. The applause
from years before sits oddly with her present state.

WHITE ELECTRIC FLASH FILLS THE SCREEN

                                                  BACK TO:

36   **INT. DALY'S THEATRE. EVE.**   36

We see the SUPPORTING CAST taking their respective bows.
The roar and cheers of applause continue. ELSIE is standing
breathlessly in the wing waiting her turn. COYNE enters
from the opposite wing and takes his bow. LUCILLE, the
costume designer enters and stands with ELSIE.

LUCILLE
I've never heard anything like it...

ELSIE
Do you think they enjoyed it?

LUCILLE
Enjoyed it? I don't think you can doubt that. (beat) They are cheering for you, Elsie!

ELSIE
Oh, no, it couldn't possibly be for me...

LUCILLE
Listen, they are calling your name.

ELSIE
No! They must be applauding the costumes.

LUCILLE
Go! They are calling for you...

LUCILLE practically pushes ELSIE from the wing onto the stage where she walks stage centre to take her bow. As soon as she enters the audience roar their delight and shout her name amidst the thunderous applause. EDWARDES and GERTIE are now standing next to LUCILLE in the wing.

LUCILLE (cont'd)
A new musical play has been launched, George, with an actress who will set the whole town raving over her beauty.

GERTIE
And a waltz that will set the whole world dancing to its fascinating lilt!

NARRATOR
Elsie and Coyne had to reprise the slow waltz again and again. Curtain call after curtain call was demanded by the audience who had fallen in love with Elsie as the widow and Lehar's magical waltz music.

We see ELSIE and COYNE acknowledge LEHAR in the orchestra pit - then reprise their slow Merry Widow waltz from the audience POV. Among the audience in the orchestra stalls is a handsome young man. His name is IAN BULLOUGH.

He is applauding and shouting Bravo! Up in the gallery a
YOUNG BOY of about 14 is also cheering and applauding
wildly and leaning precariously over the rail. ELSIE in the
madness of the moment, and whilst acknowledging the first
nighters in the gods, remembers seeing the young boy and
felt concerned he might fall. She had also seen the man in
the stalls and had been struck by how intently he was
watching her.

                    GERTIE (V.O.)
        The London Evening News critic
        was ecstatic. *"Lily Elsie and*
        Joseph Coyne are now taken to the
        hearts of the playgoing public
        and enshrined there for life -
        with memories to endure as long
        as anyone lives who saw them...
        the applause went across the foot
        lights like a prairie fire,
        accompanied by roars of cheers...
        the headiest stuff of all
        acclamation and it can only be
        heard in a theatre."
        It began almost immediately.
        Elsie's life was no longer her
        own. I had been in the business
        for many years, but the sheer
        obsession and attention focussed
        on Elsie eclipsed anything I or
        anyone had ever seen or
        experienced.

WHITE ELECTRIC FLASH FILLS THE SCREEN

                                                  CUT TO:

37   **INT. DALY'S THEATRE. LONDON,1907. DRESSING ROOM. EVE.**   37

After the first night triumph, ELSIE is readying herself
for the second performance. A DRESSER is fussing with her
costume for Act 1. GERTIE is sat in an armchair with a
glass of champagne. She reads out loud from a newspaper.

                    GERTIE
        "The Merry Widow last night
        consolidated reputations and at
        the topmost, dizziest peak of
        this mountain of success stood
        two people,"... it's by a young
        critic called Walter McQueen-
        Pope, for the London Evening
        News.

GERTIE puts down one newspaper only to pick up another.

                    GERTIE (cont'd)
          "*Lily Elsie and Joseph Coyne,
          almost unknown in London prior to
          the first night, but now taken to
          the hearts of the British play
          going public and enshrined there
          for life* - with memories to
          endure as long as anyone lives
          who saw them. Their first night
          was indeed remarkable. And just
          listen to this my dear..." *The
          applause went across the foot
          lights like a prairie fire,
          accompanied by roars of cheers,
          warm and glowing with pleasure
          and affection, such cheers as are
          seldom heard by players, such
          cheers, such Feeling as a few
          only encounter once in a lifetime
          - and the majority never know at
          all. Such applause is the most
          intoxicating drink, the headiest
          stuff of all acclamation and it
          can only be heard in a theatre.*"

GERTIE picks up another newspaper.

                    GERTIE (cont'd)
          And 'The Times' thinks you're
          absolutely wonderful too... "*The
          men in evening dress cheered and
          beat their hands together until
          they were sore; the women
          quivered and cheered shrilly, and
          as for the pit and gallery they
          went quite mad. Danilo and Sonia
          had the dance The Merry Widow
          waltz again and again.*"

At this point ELSIE silences GERTIE.

                    ELSIE
          Gertie - please stop it! Stop
          it!! Stop it!!! I really don't
          want to hear anymore.

                                              CUT TO:
MONTAGE

38   **INT. EDWARDES OFFICE IN DALY'S THEATRE. DAY**   38

EDWARDES is sat behind a plush desk writing and signing cheques whilst puffing on a large cigar.

NARRATOR
Edwardes was able to give himself
a well-earned pat on the back. He
could relax and pay his bills
once again.

DISSOLVE TO:

39 **INT. PUB. NIGHT.** 39

The bar is bustling with excited and enthusiastic
theatregoers fresh from the latest performance of the Merry
Widow. JOSEPH COYNE is sat unnoticed and alone.

NARRATOR
As for Joseph Coyne, he couldn't
wait to get out of the theatre on
that first night and seek refuge
in his favorite pub - which was
across the street from Daly's
stage door. He hated the show and
his part and no amount of
cheering or Bravos would make him
change his mind!

DISSOLVE TO:

40 **EXT. DALY'S THEATRE - STAGE DOOR. NIGHT** 40

We see ELSIE leaving the stage door after a performance.
The strain on her face is obvious. She notices IAN
BULLOUGH again, standing respectfully at a distance. She
also sees the YOUNG BOY, who she feared would fall off the
god's rail whilst cheering. She signs his autograph book.
IAN BULLOUGH escorts her through the crowd to her carriage
safely.

NARRATOR
Elsie on the other hand, after
the initial delight and
excitement, and as time passed,
began to find the constant
attention debilitating. She
couldn't go out or do anything
normal. The moment she did she
was mobbed by well meaning fans.
At times she would be pushed and
jostled and suffer terrible panic
attacks. In the end she didn't go
out except to travel to and from
the theatre. Inevitably Elsie
began to suffer with her nerves
and stage fright.
(MORE)

NARRATOR (cont'd)
The role of Sonia was also demanding and exhaustion began to creep up on her which made matters worse. The press began to snipe at her and call her a "*part time actress*" because she missed some performances. Her celebrity was a double edged sword.

DISSOLVE TO:

41 **INT. DALY'S THEATRE. DRESSING ROOM. EVE.** 41

ELSIE stares at her reflection in the mirror as her DRESSER places the huge Merry Widow hat on her head and secures it with a long pin.

NARRATOR
Adverts appeared in newspapers for products declaring; 'Brain Fag? Nervous Exhaustion? Try Phosferine - The Remedy of Kings.'

DISSOLVE TO:

The PHOSFERINE advertisement. It shows a weary looking Elsie extolling the virtues of the product.

ELSIE (V.O.)
"Phosferine is invaluable for nervous exhaustion and helps me to support the strain of two performances, and I think it makes the voice stronger. It is indispensable for anyone engaged in public works, and I shall always recommend it to my friends for brain-fag. You are at liberty to make use of my remarks if you desire."

CUT TO:

42 **INT. SHOCK RECOVERY ROOM. HOSPITAL. DAY.** 42

The setting is all too familiar. ELSIE is slumped in the same wooden chair staring at the wall with glazed, unfocused eyes. A NURSE walks through and calls out to her. The CAMERA slowly circles around her. Now, devoid of any emotion, ELSIE's depression is so vast she can't even respond to her own name.

GERTIE (V.O.)
Phosferine or not, it didn't stop
Elsie missing performances, but
endorsing these products was very
lucrative for her financially.
People who had waited for weeks
to see her as "the widow" were
naturally disappointed if she
failed to appear. Some took it
upon themselves to voice their
disappointment if they saw her
entering or leaving the theatre,
or whilst she was shopping. The
obsession bemused her and she
found people confused her with
the role she played.

CUT TO:

43   INT. DALY'S THEATRE. LONDON,1907. DRESSING ROOM. EVE.   43

ELSIE and LOTTIE are in her dressing room preparing for the
evening performance. There are flowers and gifts on a side
table. LOTTIE is opening each parcel as ELSIE prepares her
make-up.

GERTIE (V.O.)
She received flowers and
chocolates by the cart load at
the theatre from complete
strangers. Even jewelry, which
she promptly returned with a kind
note if an address was given -
but that was not always the case.

LOTTIE tears the wrapping off a red velvet box and opens
it. She gasps at what is inside. She hands it to ELSIE.
Inside a set comprising a ruby and diamond necklace, drop-
earings and a ring. Exact copies of the paste set she wears
in the show. These however, were real rubies and diamonds.

ELSIE
They must be returned straight
away. Are they real?

LOTTIE
They are breath-taking, aren't
they? (beat) I think they are,
Elsie!

ELSIE
Is there a note, a card,
anything?

LOTTIE
No.

(She examines the wrapping)

There's no name, no card, no address.

ELSIE
There must be something? I must return them - I wouldn't feel comfortable keeping them.

LOTTIE
It would seem you haven't a choice. Why not wear them tonight instead of the paste set - they will dazzle under the lime-lights.

ELSIE
Mother! I couldn't...

LOTTIE crosses to ELSIE and puts the necklace round her neck - they sparkle and ELSIE giggles in spite of her misgivings.

NARRATOR
The ruby and diamond set were an exception but not unique. There were diamond and gold bracelets galore. Elsie had become every man's fantasy, every woman's fashion icon with the "Merry Widow hat" selling by the thousand. All of which was very lucrative indeed for Elsie, Edwardes and The Merry Widow box office. The show ran for over two years. Coyne never missed a performance of its entire run in spite of his negative diatribes. One incident stood out for Edwardes and indeed Elsie's mother, Lottie.

DISSOLVE TO:

44 **INT. DALY'S THEATRE. LONDON,1907. EVE.** 44

ELSIE is about to perform the Vilja song. She is standing stage centre and LEHAR vamps the orchestra waiting for her to begin.

CUT TO:

| 45 | **FLY GALLERY.** | 45 |

The OLDER MAN is leaning on the rail to watch her perform - it is his favorite moment in the show. Out of the corner of his eye he sees a fly rope begin to slither and jumps to grab it. The heavy front curtain begins to descend and he is hauled up towards the metal pulleys on the roof of the stage. He knows that if the curtain falls it will hit Elsie and likely kill her. His grip remains fast and his hands are mangled in the pulleys which stops the curtain. He grits his teeth and holds in a scream that rises up his throat.

CUT TO:

| 46 | **AUDITORIUM - AUDIENCE POV** | 46 |

The heavy fringed curtain is seen dropping below the proscenium arch as ELSIE sings Vilja, it causes a draft which she feels. She doesn't notice the drips of blood splashing onto the stage behind her.

BACK TO:

| 47 | **FLY GALLERY** | 47 |

The BOYS in the fly gallery are now aware of what has happened and are holding the rope steady. When ELSIE finishes the song the House curtain closes and she is rushed off stage by EDWARDES. The BOYS loosen the rope and the FLY-MAN, who has no fingers left, lets out a blood-curdling scream and falls the two hundred feet to the stage. He dies instantly.

CUT TO:

| 48 | **WING OF THE STAGE** | 48 |

LOTTIE, Elsie's mother has rushed to the stage to see what has happened. She looks at the dead man and we see the shock on her face.

                   NARRATOR
        It was a terrible tragedy and
        sadly not uncommon for back stage
        staff to be injured or killed
        because of accidents. Elsie's
        mother was shocked because she
        thought she recognized the face
        of Bert Hodder, who had been a
        contender, along with Billy
        Cotton, as Elsie's father. She
        hadn't seen Hodder since Salford
        and the music hall years before.

DISSOLVE TO:

49 **ELSIE'S DRESSING ROOM.** 49

ELSIE is staring gloomily at her reflection in the mirror.

> NARRATOR
> Elsie's appearances grew less and less as time went by until Edwardes eventually replaced her for the last few weeks of the run. The truth was she was mentally and physically exhausted and as a result her stage fright and anxiety attacks became more frequent.

WHITE ELECTRIC FLASH FILLS THE SCREEN.

CUT TO BLACK:

FADE IN:

MONTAGE:

50 **EXT. STAGE DOOR. HICK'S THEATRE, LONDON. 1910. EVE** 50

We see ELSIE being met at the stage door by BULLOUGH who hands her a corsage and kisses her hand tenderly. He hails a taxi.

> GERTIE (V.O.)
> Elsie had at first been puzzled as to why Ian Bullough vanished from his stage door vigil in 1907 and never followed up on his invitation to take Elsie and her mother for supper.

CUT TO:

51 **INT. TAXI. SAME TIME** 51

They seem happy in each others company and Bullough takes on a protective rather than reverential role towards Elsie.

> GERTIE (V.O.)
> Until it was reported in the Times he had in fact married Maude Darrell, a Gaiety Girl. She was thoroughly disappointed but wasn't really sure why and her tears seemed ridiculous. The truth was Elsie had, for the first time in her life, found herself attracted to a young man - one she didn't feel afraid of.

52   **INT. AUDITORIUM. HICK'S THEATRE, LONDON. 1910. EVE**   52

We see ELSIE taking a bow at the Hick's Theatre after her
performance in A Waltz Dream. She sees BULLOUGH in the
stalls applauding and they smile and acknowledge one
another.

>   It was only later, whilst
>   appearing in A Waltz Dream at the
>   Hick's Theatre in 1910 that she
>   spotted Bullough in the orchestra
>   stalls once again and their eyes
>   met. It wasn't long before they
>   met and all was explained.

                                        DISSOLVE TO:

53   **INT. PALM COURT. WALDORF HOTEL, ALDWYCH. 1910. DAY.**   53

We see ELSIE and BULLOUGH having afternoon tea in the Palm
Court. It seems an elegant affair, with COUPLES WALTZING in
the background. Although Elsie is still quite shy, we can
see she enjoys his attentions. LOTTIE and GERTIE are also
with them

>   GERTIE (V.O.)
>   Bullough revealed that his wife
>   had died suddenly and tragically
>   of cancer in a matter of weeks of
>   their marriage. He explained to
>   Elsie that he was in fact engaged
>   to her when he first saw her in
>   The Merry Widow, but decided it
>   was foolish of him to offer an
>   invitation to supper as it could
>   have been seen as disloyal and
>   ungentlemanly.

LOTTIE has joined them and returns to her seat next to
ELSIE. LOTTIE is obviously wary of BULLOUGH and concerned
about her daughter's naivety where men are concerned could
see her being hurt.

>   GERTIE (V.O.) (cont'd)
>   Lottie was unsure of Bullough's
>   true intentions towards her
>   daughter. Understandable because
>   Bullough and his family, Lottie
>   confided in me, actually owned
>   the Lancashire Cotton Mills she
>   and her mother had toiled in many
>   years before. This fact always
>   seemed ironic to Lottie,
>   especially as it was obvious to
>   all they would marry.

GERTIE takes BULLOUGH onto the dance floor. ELSIE watches them waltz with delight. LOTTIE's expression is one of resignation.

> GERTIE (V.O.) (cont'd)
> Before that happened, another drama in Elsie's life would have to be played out.

CUT TO:

54 **MONTAGE: OF STILLS AND LIVE ACTION.** 54

We see a montage of photographs, programme covers and live action to represent Elsie roles for Edwardes in A Waltz Dream, The Dollar Princess and The Count of Luxembourg between 1909 and 1911.

> NARRATOR
> Elsie appeared in another three operettas for Edwardes. Teamed again with Joseph Coyne for A Waltz Dream and The Dollar Princess and with charismatic leading man Bertram Wallace in The Count of Luxembourg with music composed by Lehar. However, Elsie's next leading role would be that of a real wife to Ian Bullough. Elsie had always been fearful of men - Edwardes knew it was only a matter of time before he would lose Elsie, it was inevitable that Bullough would insist she gave up the stage once married. Before that took place another drama played out in Elsie's life.

WHITE ELECTRIC FLASH FILLS THE SCREEN

CUT TO:

55 **INT. EDWARDES OFFICE, DALY'S THEATRE, LONDON, 1911. DAY.** 55

ELSIE is seated in a winged chair by the fire. EDWARDES is sitting at his desk reading the documents given them by the SOLICITOR. GERTIE is standing by the window overlooking Leicester Square.

> ELSIE
> What does it mean?

                    GERTIE
          It means, Elsie, you are now a
          very wealthy young woman!

                    ELSIE
          But I don't understand. I don't
          even know who he is, why would a
          Lord leave me anything?

                    EDWARDES
          It would seem he lost his wife
          some years ago and he enjoyed
          your performances in The Merry
          Widow - in fact you reminded him
          of his daughter who died of
          influenza when only twenty-years-
          old.

                    ELSIE
          How terrible. The poor man.

                    GERTIE
          Be that as it may, my dear Elsie,
          but he had no-one else to leave
          his money to, so he chose you.

                    ELSIE
          But what about Ian? What on earth
          will he say about this?

There is a slight edge of hysteria in Elsie's voice. GEORGE
and GERTIE exchange concerned looks.

                    EDWARDES
          It clears up the mystery about
          who sent the ruby and diamond
          jewelry...(he chuckles hoping to
          lighten the atmosphere).

                    ELSIE
          Will it compromise my reputation?

                    EDWARDES
          No. There will be gossip, that's
          inevitable, but it's
          irrelevant...

                    GERTIE
          And it will be irrelevant to Ian
          Bullough, too. Rise above it,
          Elsie. Ignore it.

                    EDWARDES
          I will speak to Jenkins at Coutts
          Bank, ask him open a new account
          so they can transfer the funds.

>   GERTIE
>   Don't worry, Elsie, George will
>   make all the arrangements for
>   you. Do you want me to speak to
>   Ian?
>
>   ELSIE
>   No! No thank you, Gertie. I am
>   seeing him tomorrow afternoon. I
>   will tell him about it then.

ELSIE seems tired and nervous. EDWARDES looks at her with concern.

WHITE ELECTRIC FLASH FILLS THE SCREEN.

>   DISSOLVE:

56   **INT. TAXI. DAY**   56

ELSIE and IAN are together. IAN is full of beans, ELSIE is enveloped by an air of enforced jollity.

>   ELSIE
>   Where are we going?
>
>   IAN
>   It's a surprise.(beat) Trust me!
>
>   ELSIE
>   Please, Ian, where are we going?
>
>   IAN
>   What you need is to be out and
>   about... a change... away from
>   the theatre. I won't let you stay
>   at home any longer.
>
>   ELSIE
>   Where are we going!!!?
>
>   IAN
>   Elsie, please relax. We are to be
>   married soon so we can be seen
>   out without a chaperone. If you
>   must know, I am taking you to the
>   Royal Academy.
>
>   ELSIE
>   An art gallery? But I might be
>   recognized...

>   CUT TO:

57   INT. THE ROYAL ACADEMY. LONDON, 1911. DAY   57

IAN and ELSIE walk up the stairs. There are other people there but, to Elsie's huge relief, apart from one or two glances, she's almost unnoticed. As they wander amid various paintings and sculptures they talk.

                IAN
      If he chose to leave you his
      money, why would I be angry about
      it? I am pleased for you - you
      will always feel financially
      independent, which is a good
      thing.

They continue to walk looking at the paintings. They arrive at the Munch room. As they walk their footsteps reverberate from the tiled floor. ELSIE looks around. She flicks her eyes at a few of the paintings and reacts with puzzlement and unease.

The CAMERA slowly begins to move around her.

              ELSIE
      This is all new to me. Is this
      Art? Isn't art supposed to be
      beautiful?

                IAN
      It's the latest fashion - I think
      they call it Expressionism or
      something...

              ELSIE
      But this is ugly and awful... Is
      the artist mad?

                IAN
      Of course not! Well, one hopes
      not...

ELSIE is attracted to one large painting. She looks at it for a couple of beats. Then she turns to IAN.

              ELSIE
      Come here - look - its called
      'The Scream'!

IAN walks up and together they stare at the painting.

The painting shows an oppressed person with a head like an inverted pear! It clasps its hands to its ears, its mouth open in a vast, silent scream. Twisted ripples of the person's inner torment, echoes of its cry, flood out into the air surrounding it.

The person stands on a bridge - there are distant figures but they are out of reach. It is as if no one else is present. The person screams in isolation, cut off by - or despite - its outcry.

                    ELSIE (cont'd)
           How can they call this art!

                    IAN
           I don't know...

                                          FLASHBACK TO:

58   **INT. BACK STAGE - DRESSING ROOM. SCENE 18**   58

ELSIE is raging and smashing things up. She catches her reflection in the large mirror on the wall. Picking up a large ashtray she hurls it. The mirror shatters into smithereens. She stares at what's left of her reflection - her face disfigured by jagged shards of glass.

Totally distraught, Elsie collapses on her chaise longue. EDWARDES, GERTIE and LOTTIE hover over her with concern. What they are saying is echoey and incoherent but their faces have taken on a distorted, melted disfigurement reminiscent of Munch's The Scream.

WHITE ELECTRIC FLASH FILLS THE SCREEN

                                                    BACK TO:

59   **INT. THE ROYAL ACADEMY. LONDON, 1911 . DAY**   59

ELSIE has been slightly unnerved by what she has seen. As much as she derides it as ugly and therefore not 'art', she feels perturbed by it and it's reflection of her own despair.

                    ELSIE
           And you still don't think the
           artist is mad?

WHITE ELECTRIC FLASH FILLS THE SCREEN

                                              CUT TO BLACK:

                                                    FADE IN:

60 **MONTAGE:**   60

POSTERS AND POSTCARDS featuring ELSIE and WALLIS.

Music- Count of Luxembourg waltz.

                                                DISSOLVE TO:

61 **INT. DALY'S THEATRE. EVE.**   61

Music - The waltz continues

ELSIE as Angela Didier and BERTRAM WALLIS as The Count of Luxembourg are dancing the waltz from the final act. The CAMERA swirls around them.

                                                DISSOLVE TO:

The AUDIENCE receive the curtain call with tumultuous applause.

                    NARRATOR
        The Count of Luxembourg opened
        at Daly's Theatre on 8th May,
        1911, and was an instant hit with
        press and public alike describing
        Elise as *'enchanting and in sweet
        voice'* and declaring the slow
        waltz as *beautiful, guaranteeing
        not a dry eye in the house for
        many a night to come!*

        Bullough wasted no time in
        getting Elsie to agree a date for
        their marriage. Almost
        immediately, gossips had started
        to spread so many rumors about
        Elsie's betrothal and possible
        retirement from the stage.

                                                DISSOLVE TO:

62 **INT. ELSIE'S DRESSING ROOM. EVENING**   62

ELSIE is staring bleakly at her reflection in the mirror. Far from being happy, she is slipping into the gloomy world of her own. A place devoid of colour and instead washed in tones of black and grey.

                    NARRATOR
        The London Watchdog reported
        tartly *"Is she going to retire
        and marry or not?"*... *"She's a
        mediocre talent anyway"*.
                    (MORE)

                    NARRATOR (cont'd)
              "If she is retiring from the
              stage then why doesn't she go as
              soon as possible?!"

Fragments of sentences overlap and echo around in Elsie's
mind again and again.

                    OVERLAPPING VOICES
              Is she going to retire?... she's
              only a mediocre talent... why
              doesn't she go?.... A part time
              actress... There really is far
              too much Lily Elsie!

                                             DISSOLVE TO:

63   **MONTAGE:**   63

NEWSPAPERS - FRONT PAGE HEADLINES SPIN ONTO THE SCREEN.

"Miss Lily Elsie's Hats!, Miss Lily Elsie's Trousseau!,
Miss Lily Elsie's Wedding Dress?, Will Miss Lily Elsie
Leave The Stage?, Miss Lily Elsie To Retire!, Miss Lily
Elsie Not To Retire!, Miss Lily Elsie's Wedding Day Fixed!"

                    NARRATOR
              The situation became even more
              aggressive...

                    CRITIC 1 (V.O.)
              "London has hardly simmered down
              after its great excitement. For
              weeks its jaded appetite has fed
              on..."

                                             OVERLAP WITH:

                    CRITIC 2 (V.O.)
              "For months London has hung on
              every gracious word of it's
              popular favorite..."

                                             OVERLAP WITH:

                    CRITIC 1 (V.O.)
              "... licked up the crumbs of her
              smallest confidences - gone wild
              over the question would she
              retire or not..."

                    CRITIC 2 (V.O.)
              "... and above all - WHEN WOULD
              IT BE?

                                             OVERLAP WITH:

CRITIC 1 (V.O.)
"...it is a strange, mad world,
my masters!"

BACK TO:

64   INT. ELSIE'S DRESSING ROOM. EVENING   64

ELSIE stops powdering her face and puts down the make-up.
She stares at her the reflection in the mirror.

GERTIE (V.O.)
Elsie was outraged by these terse
headlines and hurtful, vicious
comments and became very upset.
She had always been the last
person to court publicity and had
shied away from it. She became
exhausted and depressed, her
anxiety attacks had returned and
she began to miss performances.

There is a knock on the door accompanied by a loud voice.

RUNNER (O.S.)
Your five minute call Miss Elsie -
five minutes... five minutes!

ELSIE
Thank you Freddie - thank you.

She looks at herself in the mirror and sighs gently. A tear
trickles down her cheek.

GERTIE (V.O.)
Elsie was now looking forward to
October when she could leave the
show, perhaps find some peace and
contentment out of the glare of
the spotlight and concentrate on
her coming wedding.

DISSOLVE TO:

65   INT. EDWARDES OFFICE IN DALY'S THEATRE. DAY   65

ELSIE is perched nervily on the seat of a large leather
armchair. EDWARDES puts a few more lumps of coal on the
fire.

ELSIE
George, there is something I must
tell you and there is a favour I
need to ask.

EDWARDES senses Elsie's nerves and turns to look at her. He gives her a smile.

> ELSIE (cont'd)
> We've agreed that I'll be leaving in just a couple of weeks. The wedding is planned for November after which I shall be retiring from the stage - we hope to start a family. I hope you can understand.

EDWARDES eyes drop, his face tinged with sadness. He takes a deep breath and recovers.

> EDWARDES
> So - the stage will finally be losing Lily Elsie - its brightest star. It will sadden me but at least you will be going whilst at the height of your success and we will always keep our friendship. We have come a long way together my dear.

ELSIE moves over to him. She embraces him and gently kisses him on the cheek.

> EDWARDES (cont'd)
> And the favour?

> ELSIE
> Will you do me the honour of giving me away at the wedding? You have always been like a father to me and as my father is dead... it would mean a lot to me if you would consider it.

EDWARDES catches his breath and smiles tenderly. Then he turns and looks out of his office window. His eyes are full of tears and he doesn't want Elsie to see. She senses this.

> ELSIE (cont'd)
> (Brightly)
> Good - I will take that as a yes! So that's settled then. Now I must fly because Gertie is expecting me.

DISSOLVE TO:

66 ALL SAINTS CHURCH, ENNISMORE GARDENS, LONDON. 1911. DAY 66

EDWARDES is seen escorting ELSIE down the aisle. They glance round at the smiling faces of the congregation as they walk to the altar. Stars like GERTIE, COYNE, WALLIS, the DARE SISTERS, GABRIELLE RAY and MARIE LLOYD are all assembled in celebration.

> GERTIE (V.O.)
> 7th November 1911 was the day Edwardes escorted Elsie down the aisle. She looked so fragile and etherial in the gown especially designed for her by Lucille, Ian Bullough seemed a tall and powerful young man by comparison. For Elsie her marriage to Bullough was also an escape from the stage and all the problems she considered it had brought her. She was still only 25 years-old.

The camera circles EDWARDES and ELSIE in waltz time as they make their way down the aisle. Happy faces surround them and then they start to transform into a distorted Munch like image.

CUT TO:

67 INT. SHOCK RECOVERY ROOM. HOSPITAL, CIRCA 1950. DAY. 67

The camera is circling ELSIE very fast in Waltz time. It begins to slow down. ELSIE is again slumped on the simple wooden chair in a white hospital gown. The burns on her temples from the electrodes are more intense than previously seen. This time she seems more lucid than before, although she is still not recovered enough to physically move her body - she stares ahead and life flickers in her eyes.

> ELSIE
> (talk-sing)*VILJA, O VILJA! THE WITCH OF THE WOOD (beat) WOULD I NOT DIE FOR YOU, DEAR, IF I COULD! (beat) VILJA, O VILJA, MY LOVE... SOFTLY AND SADLY HE SIGH'D*
> Ian, is that you? Do you remember Gertie Millar? No, you wouldn't... I'M AFRAID! Everybody dead... dead... dead!
> Please, don't touch me. I don't like being touched... Leave Me...
> (MORE)

ELSIE (cont'd)
leave Sonia alone. Where is
George? George, are you there?

A NURSE stands in the corner of the room in a crisp, starched uniform. She appears cold and dispassionate and is observing ELSIE as she rambles. She scribbles notes on her clipboard.

ELSIE (cont'd)
Girls whom I know are continually asking me questions about the world of the stage, and they all want to know if it is easy to get on it! Is Joseph in his dressing room? Ivor, darling, is that you?

WHITE ELECTRIC FLASH FILLS THE SCREEN

CUT TO:

68 **INT. ETON SQUARE HOUSE. BEDROOM. 1911. DAY** 68

ELSIE is seen laying in bed. She is tense and terrified. IAN is laying with his back to her. He takes a swig of whiskey from a glass on his bedside table. The whisky bottle is half empty. The atmosphere is thick with disappointment.

GERTIE (V.O.)
From the very start there were problems. Elsie, in spite of being 25, was still quite naive to the physical and intimate side of married life. She found it painful and humiliating. Ian resigned himself to Elsie's frigidity. Their marriage was in fact doomed - after a frightening miscarriage Elsie discovered she was unable to carry a child full-term. Ian didn't know how to cope - he instead concentrated his energies on the family business and hoped that in time things would work out better.

CUT TO BLACK:

FADE IN:

69 **EXT. DALY'S THEATRE. LEICESTER SQUARE, LONDON,1929. DAY.** 69

ELSIE is seen looking up at the theatre. She then gazes at the posters and marquis advertising *'THE TRUTH GAME - starring LILY ELSIE and IVOR NOVELLO'*

                    NARRATOR
          After her marriage it was
          inappropriate for her to work or
          make public appearances. However,
          by the time the Great War had
          broken out, her marriage was
          over. Divorce was out of the
          question, so Bullough and Elsie
          mostly led separate lives. They
          would appear at functions
          together and at charity events.
          War work occupied them, and
          separated them completely.

ELSIE briskly walks towards the side of the building and
enters the stage door.

                                        DISSOLVE TO:

MONTAGE:

**LIBRARY SHOTS: THE HUSTLE AND BUSTLE OF LONDON'S WEST END.
SHAFTESBURY AVENUE, LEICESTER SQUARE AND PICCADILLY CIRCUS.**

Music - we hear ELSIE singing

                                        DISSOLVE TO:

INT. HMV RECORDING STUDIO. DAY.

ELSIE is in the middle of a recording session. Standing at
a microphone she sings the song, 'Pamela' from the musical
comedy of the same name.

                                        SUPERIMPOSE:

CUE - HMV 78 record spinning round.

Elsie's song continues

                                        SUPERIMPOSE:

CUE - 1920's Radiogram

The song continues.

                                        DISSOLVE TO:

**LIBRARY SHOTS: STREET SCENES - SHAFTESBURY AVENUE,
LEICESTER SQUARE AND PICCADILLY CIRCUS.**

Crowds queuing at cinemas to watch the latest Hollywood
Movies: *"Applause"* *starring Helen Morgan and Joan Peers.*

"The Virginian" starring Walter Huston and Gary Cooper and Oscar winning, *"The Broadway Melody"* starring Bessie Love, Anita Page and Charles King.

BACK TO:

INT. HMV RECORDING STUDIO. DAY.

ELSIE is still recording her songs. We hear her singing 'Cupid Cupid'

SUPERIMPOSE:

POSTERS, PHOTOGRAPHS AND PROGRAMME COVERS SPIN ONTO THE SCREEN.

THE MUSIC CONTINUES...

          NARRATOR
Elsie made an appearance in the musical play Mavourneen in 1915. It was a light entertainment set among the court intrigues of Charles II. In 1917 she agreed to appear in the successful musical play Pamela, a frothy musical comedy farce, taking on the title role of the same name. Critics from the Weekly Despatch enthused:

          CRITIC 1 (V.O.)
"Lily Elsie never sang so gloriously. 'Cupid Cupid' is the best song... Her silver and blue Turkish costume for that wonderful waltz, too, will be the envy of every woman...Lily Elsie looked like a princess, and when it's like that - well, there you are!

OVERLAP WITH:

          CRITIC 2 (V.O.)
"How the stalls shouted and 'the gods' roared when they welcomed back their old favorite, Lily Elsie."

THE MUSIC FADES

DISSOLVE TO:

© September 2009. Lily Elsie - The Last Edwardian Star. 52.

INT. DRESSING ROOM. NIGHT.

A familiar setting. ELSIE is staring blankly at her reflection in the mirror. MOLLIE, her Dresser, is fussing with hats and costumes.

                NARRATOR
        Elsie struggled with her voice
        and the demands of so many
        performances a week. She had
        assumed her stage fright, anxiety
        and depressions would end once
        she retired from the stage, but
        this never happened. In fact her
        anxiety and paranoias had
        increased.

                                                        CUT TO:

70   INT. DALY'S THEATRE. LONDON,1929. DAY.   70

ELSIE enters the stage door and acknowledges the DOOR MAN with a smile. She makes her way back stage and then crosses to the pass door which leads to the auditorium. She goes through the door and walks through the empty stalls and then sits on a familiar aisle seat a few rows back.

The atmosphere is thick with ghostly voices and memories.

Echoes of past applause can be faintly heard and the glittering Edwardian audiences are but a breath away in the flickering shadows.

                NARRATOR
        Elsie found it hard to believe so
        many years had passed and life
        had changed so much since she
        last worked in this theatre. The
        Edwardian era was long past, now
        just a faint memory for most.

WHITE ELECTRIC FLASH FILLS THE SCREEN.

                                                        CUT TO:

71   MONTAGE: OF STILLS AND LIVE ACTION.   71

ARCHIVE SHOTS: HUGE ARTILLERY BOMBARDMENTS INTERCUT WITH TRENCH WARFARE, WOUNDED SOLDIERS BEING TREATED.

Newspaper spins onto the screen with 'BRITAIN AT WAR WITH

GERMANY' HEADLINE.

MUSIC - 'Keep The Home Fires Burning' CHORUS

          NARRATOR
The horrors of the Great War looming like a colossal monster blocking the way to that other world she had known so well.

MUSIC - 'Your King and Country Want You.'

    OH, WE DON'T WANT TO LOSE YOU
BUT WE THINK YOU OUGHT TO GO.
FOR YOUR KING AND YOUR COUNTRY
BOTH NEED YOU SO.
WE SHALL WANT YOU AND MISS YOU
BUT WITH ALL OUR MIGHT AND MAIN
WE SHALL CHEER YOU, THANK YOU,
BLESS YOU,
WHEN YOU COME HOME AGAIN.

ARCHIVE MONTAGE CONTINUES.

NEWSPAPER SPINS ONTO THE SCREEN WITH 'EDWARDES IMPRISONED BY THE HUN' HEADLINE.

          NARRATOR (cont'd)
George Edwardes had the misfortune to be in Germany at the outbreak of war, as ever he was looking for the next operetta he could transform into a London hit. He was imprisoned by the Kaiser for several months as an enemy alien. After everything he had done to promote German music, it seemed so unjust. Lehar petitioned for his repatriation in the summer of 1915. Edwardes spirit was broken by his ordeal when he returned to England. He died of heart failure on 4th October 1915 aged just 60.

NEWSPAPER SPINS ONTO THE SCREEN WITH 'GAIETY GIRL IMPRESARIO' EDWARDES IS DEAD AT 60!

          NARRATOR (cont'd)
Elsie's own mother had died at the start of the 1920s and was finally at peace after suffering from cancer.

THEATRE PROGRAMME FOR 'THE BLUE TRAIN' SPINS ONTO THE SCREEN.

MUSIC: We hear a montage of song recordings

DISSOLVE TO:

MONTAGE.

72   INT. STAGE. DAY   72

A PHOTO-CALL. ELSIE IS SURROUNDED BY JOURNALISTS AND PRESS PHOTOGRAPHERS. SHE SMILES BRAVELY AND GRACIOUSLY POSES FOR THE CAMERAS.

               NARRATOR
As 1927 approached Elsie found herself agreeing to a divorce. She also found herself increasingly lonely. Working on the stage alleviated that loneliness for a time. The Blue Train, a musical comedy, was offered to her and she accepted it the hope it would restore her spirits and equilibrium. Her role as Eileen Mayne was fun and she was honoured when, on it's transfer to the West End, George V and Queen Mary came to see her perform. However, she resigned herself to never singing again - her voice was no longer up to the strains of eight shows a week.

BACK TO:

73   **INT. DALY'S THEATRE. LONDON,1929. DAY.**   73

ELSIE has moved from her seat and walks down the centre aisle to the orchestra pit. She runs her hands along the mahogany skirt of the pit, feeling its silky, highly polished surface. She pictures Lehar standing there looking so proud on that Merry Widow first night half a lifetime ago. She then turns and takes in the empty auditorium. Looking up at the gods she remembers a young boy.

FLASHBACK TO:

74   **(SCENE 36) INT. DALY'S THEATRE. LONDON,1907. EVE.** 74

Elsie takes her curtain call after a performance of The Merry Widow.

Up in the gallery a YOUNG BOY of about 14 is also cheering and applauding wildly and leaning precariously over the rail.

FLASHBACK TO:

75 (SCENE 40) DALY'S THEATRE. STAGE DOOR. 1907. EVE. 75

Elsie is leaving the stage door for her carriage. The YOUNG BOY, who she feared would fall off the god's rail whilst cheering, is waiting with his autograph book. She signs it with a smile.

                BOY
      Thank you, Miss Elsie!

His reply is so earnest and star struck she can't help giggling.

BACK TO:

76 **INT. DALY'S THEATRE. LONDON, 1929. EVE.** 76

Elsie is smiling at these memories. She continues walking through the auditorium imagining past audiences. They seem alive in her mind and, unlike the black and white images of the films, they are vibrant with colour and life.

              CRITIC 1 (V.O.)
     "Lily Elsie and Ivor Novello are
     the most picturesque pair..."

              NARRATOR
     That young boy up in the gods
     would grow up to become Ivor
     Novello. Elsie would make her
     final performance in his play The
     Truth Game which he wrote
     especially for her. By chance her
     character, Rosine Brown, is that
     of a wealthy widow! Novello
     played her love interest Max
     Clement. She falls in love with
     Max only to discover he is a
     distant relative, so if they
     marry she would lose her
     inherited fortune. Many said it
     was a reflection of Novello's
     memories of Sonia and her plight
     in The Merry Widow. The critic
     from Theatre World Magazine
     declared:

                    CRITIC 1 (V.O.)
          "Complete satisfaction with the
          entertainment is practically
          guaranteed..."

                    NARRATOR
          The Times was less gushing in its
          praise.

                    CRITIC 2 (V.O.)
          "The play is shallow and
          scattered in its conclusion, but
          the trimmings are often very good
          fun."

ELSIE walks up the steps by the orchestra pit and onto the
stage. She stands centre stage. There is a sadness about
her, a sadness because she has today made a decision about
her future.

                                             CUT TO:

77   **INT. DALY'S THEATRE. DRESSING ROOM. 1929. EVE.**   77

Elsie enters her dressing room. A huge arrangement of
Lilies are awaiting her. She looks at the card which simply
says "Darling Elsie. Love Ivor." She smells their heady
scent as Molly, her dresser, helps her to remove her coat,
she then sits at her dressing table and looks at her
reflection and begins to ready herself for the performance.

MOLLY notices Elsie's wistful expression and is concerned.

                    MOLLIE
          Excuse me but... is everything
          alright Miss Elsie?

Elsie doesn't respond.

                    MOLLIE (cont'd)
          Miss Elsie... is everything
          alright?

ELSIE catches MOLLIE'S worried look.

                    ELSIE
          Yes - thank you Molly.
          Everything's fine. I'm just a
          little tired that's all - nothing
          to be concerned about...

                    NARRATOR
          Elsie had decided tonight's would
          be her very last performance.
                         (MORE)

                    NARRATOR (cont'd)
          Novello had asked her to go to
          New York with the play, but she
          had decided she didn't want
          to.(beat) Gertie was coming to
          see her perform tonight, which
          she was looking forward to.

WHITE ELECTRIC FLASH FILLS THE SCREEN

                                        CUT TO:

78   **INT. SHOCK RECOVERY ROOM. HOSPITAL. 1950. DAY.**   78

ELSIE is laying on a hospital trolley unconscious. TWO
DOCTORS are reviewing her case and discussing her therapy.
Referring to Elsie's medical notes, their demeanor is cold
and dispassionate.

                    DOCTOR 1
          This patient has undergone an
          intensive course of shock therapy
          in the hope it would alleviate
          the manic depression, anxiety and
          paranoia.

                    DOCTOR 2
          As the treatment thus far has
          been less than successful, I can
          only recommend a Lobotomy.

                    DOCTOR 1
          The quality of life is so
          diminished, a frontal lobotomy is
          really the last resort...

                    DOCTOR 2
          It certainly won't make matters
          any worse...

The DOCTOR's faces dissolve and distort like a 'Munch
painting. The CAMERA closes in on ELSIE. It begins to
circle her in Waltz time, getting faster and faster.

WHITE ELECTRIC FLASH FILLS THE SCREEN:

                                        DISSOLVE TO:

79   **INT. DALY'S THEATRE. LEICESTER SQUARE, LONDON,1929. EVE.**   79

We see GERTIE in close shot watching the performance of The
Truth Game. We can hear the audience laughing and
responding to Elsie and Ivor's performances. Gertie's face
is beaming with delight.

GERTIE (V.O.)
I watched Elsie's performance and was pleased this success had come her way. She had lost none of her talent for delivering comic dialogue and her timing was superb - and was a very good actress, one who could carve herself a whole new career working in straight plays.(beat) She still looked so youthful and slim!

GERTIE adjusts her ample figure in her seat as she joins in the applause.

WHITE ELECTRIC FLASH FILLS THE SCREEN

CUT TO:

80 **INT. DALY'S THEATRE. LONDON,1929. LATER** 80

The AUDIENCE are cheering and applauding. ELSIE and IVOR take their curtain call. Ivor then leads Elsie forward to receive her own applause. He stands back and applauds with the rest of the cast. ELSIE spots GERTIE in the orchestra stalls and smiles an acknowledgement to her.

NARRATOR
Elsie would try and remember this night always. She was determined to fade into a dignified obscurity. This time her retirement would be done quietly and certainly not through the ever intrusive newspaper industry spreading malicious and hurtful gossip.

IVOR embraces ELSIE and kisses her on the cheek. He holds her hand as the house curtain falls for the last time.

WHITE ELECTRIC FLASH FILLS THE SCREEN

CUT TO:

81 **INT. DALY'S THEATRE. ELSIE'S DRESSING ROOM. 1929. EVE** 81

GERTIE and ELSIE are sharing a glass of champagne after the performance. They are in good humour and happy in each others company.

ELSIE
'Lady Dudley', how kind of you to visit me backstage...

GERTIE
It's Gertie to you miss! Well, I played enough make-believe countesses in my life, so I thought I might as well be a real one!

ELSIE
Do you love him - the Earl of Dudley?

GERTIE
William, I adore him! He's flirted with me for years, even when Lionel was alive.

ELSIE
I am happy for you, Gertie. Did you hear anything about Ian? I was upset when I knew he'd remarried, but I am resigned to it now.

GERTIE
He didn't waste time did he?

ELSIE
In what way?

GERTIE
His new wife delivered him a son yesterday...

ELSIE looks shaken at this news. GERTIE realizes her mistake. ELSIE forces a smile and raises her glass to Gertie.

ELSIE
Here's to us and the future.

GERTIE
To George and his Gaiety Girls! The ones still here anyway...

They laugh and clink their glasses. Behind the smile, Elsie's eyes look haunted.

WHITE ELECTRIC FLASH FILLS THE SCREEN

CUT TO:

82 INT. ELSIE'S ROOM 34, DOLLIS HILL CONVENT. BEFORE DAWN 82

The carriage clock on the mantlepiece is seen in close up whispering away time. It is just after 2.30am. The shot opens out and we see the YOUNG DOCTOR reading Elsie's notes.

>   GERTIE (V.O.)
>   Elsie was true to her word. She
>   never performed again after that
>   night at Daly's Theatre. Her
>   divorce had a terrible effect on
>   her health and then Ian died
>   suddenly of a heart attack in
>   1936. In spite of everything, a
>   part of her would always love
>   Ian. It was then she started to
>   receive the initial electric
>   shock therapy - a supposed
>   miracle cure...

ELSIE cries out the name "Gertie" followed by "Ian" which makes the young doctor jump and also alerts the nun who enters and crosses to Elsie.

>   GERTIE (V.O.) (cont'd)
>   In 1939 she moved to Bournemouth
>   for the duration of World War 2 -
>   unable to cope and happy to lose
>   herself in her garden and
>   occasional charity work. By the
>   late 1940s her health had
>   deteriorated markedly.

                                                  CUT TO:

83 INT. GAIETY GIRLS REUNION. PATHE NEWS. STRAND. LONDON 1946 83

ARCHIVE NEWSREEL - VISION & SOUND:

We see a clip of ELSIE and some of the old GAIETY GIRLS in a Pathe news reel.

THE SOUND TRACK RUNS UNDER:

>   GERTIE (V.O.)
>   I was unable to attend the Gaiety
>   Girls reunion but remember Elsie
>   telling me she was to have a
>   lobotomy, a surgical procedure on
>   the brain, which might, her
>   doctors had assured her, help to
>   cure her depressions.
>   (MORE)

GERTIE (V.O.) (cont'd)
She began to look so frail, and
suffered excruciating anxiety
attacks, it seemed that anything
was worth trying to improve her
quality of life.

WHITE ELECTRIC FLASH FILLS THE SCREEN

SOUND: THE PATHE NEWS CLIP OF THE GAIETY GIRLS REUNION
PLAYS UNDER, THEN SEGUE'S INTO THE MERRY WIDOW WALTZ.

CUT TO:

84   **INT. OPERATING THEATRE. DAY**   84

The room is white, sterile and clinical. A NURSE in a crisp
white gown is preparing an array of surgical instruments
for the lobotomy operation. Among them is one that looks
just like an ice-pick with a curled end.

CUT TO:

85   **INT. HOSPITAL CORRIDOR. SAME TIME**   85

ELSIE is wheeled along the corridor and into the treatment
room.

BACK TO:

86   **OPERATING THEATRE.**   86

TWO DOCTORS and another NURSE are preparing for the
operation. ELSIE is wheeled into position under an intense
bright light and strapped down securely. One DOCTOR
attaches a thick leather belt with two electrodes around
Elsie's temples. A mouth gag is inserted. The wires are
connected to the electric shock machine. The dials that
control the electric current are set to maximum.

                    DOCTOR
          Ready everyone? Okay then -
          charge please!

The other DOCTOR flicks the switch. The electrodes crackle.
The DOCTOR and NURSES hold down ELSIE's convulsing body.
The procedure is repeated four times.

The convulsions subside and ELSIE falls unconscious. The
NURSE removes the electrodes and places a surgical towel
over Elsie's nose and mouth.

                    DOCTOR (cont'd)
          Single-end explorer and hammer
          please...

A NURSE passes the ice-pick to the DOCTOR who then peels back each eyelid. He inserts the 'explorer'.

> DOCTOR (cont'd)
> Now... we simply insert the probe above the eyeball and level with the plain of the nose... up into to the back of the orbit and tap it through to locate the frontal lobes.

He taps the probe with the hammer and wiggles it about to sever the frontal lobes and withdraws it.

> DOCTOR (cont'd)
> And there we are... All done. Just over three minutes - that's very good!

WHITE ELECTRIC FLASH FILLS THE SCREEN

CUT TO:

INT. ELSIE'S ROOM 34, DOLLIS HILL CONVENT. DAY.

CAPTION: DOLLIS HILL CONVENT. 1959

ELSIE is sitting alone in a wing chair with a blanket over her legs. The camera slowly circles. SISTER MARIA enters and places a cup of tea and a biscuit on the side table next to ELSIE. She is going to say something but thinks better of it.

> NARRATOR
> There was never a coherent response from Elsie - her brain too scrambled to respond in any normal way. The damage was irreparable. By the late 1950s there was no one left to care. Elsie's friends, including Gertie, Novello and Coyne were all dead. She would spend her final years lost inside herself, where no one could reach her anymore.

WHITE ELECTRIC FLASH FILLS THE SCREEN

CUT TO:

INT. ELSIE'S ROOM 34, DOLLIS HILL CONVENT. NIGHT

MUSIC: The Merry Widow Waltz

CAPTION: 1962

ELSIE is lying unconscious in her bed. The DOCTOR is sitting holding ELSIE's hand. SISTER MARIA wipes Elsie's forehead and straightens the bed clothes. She smiles at the DOCTOR and leaves. Looking across at her face he can't help thinking she looks quite lovely and it is hard to believe she is 76 years old, she has an elegance about her even under these circumstances. An ominous rattle is heard coming from Elsie's throat and chest. The DOCTOR looks at his watch, realizing that there is not much time left.

> GERTIE (V.O.)
> Elsie can't understand why she doesn't recognize the faces coming into her mind...whether she dreaming or awake...nothing makes sense to her anymore... That's why I'm here, so she doesn't die alone.

FLASHBACKS

A MONTAGE OF SHOTS ARE OVERLAID AND SUPERIMPOSED IN A GHOSTLY, ETHERIAL WAY:

ELSIE is seen waltzing slowly with JOSEPH COYNE.

DISSOLVE TO:

GERTIE is seen reciting the line from 'Vitality'

> "Do you remember Gertie Millar? No you wouldn't I'm afraid."

DISSOLVE TO:

ELSIE patting a balloon into the audience.

DISSOLVE TO:

ELSIE as Princess Soo Soo in a Chinese Honeymoon giggling.

DISSOLVE TO:

GEORGE EDWARDES appears and looks straight into the CAMERA

> EDWARDES
> "Elsie, the one and only Merry Widow. It is unnecessary to say more."

DISSOLVE TO:

We see IAN watching ELSIE gracefully walking down the aisle at their wedding.

DISSOLVE TO:

LOTTIE appears with GERTIE at her side.

BACK TO:

88 INT. ELSIE'S ROOM. LATER   88

The young DOCTOR has been joined by SISTER MARIA, they are startled when ELSIE suddenly opens her eyes and attempts to sit up, holding out her hand as if trying to grasp someone's hand. She smiles in recognition of someone the Doctor and Sister Maria can't see.

In her mind's eye, ELSIE sees LOTTIE and GERTIE smiling brightly, they are beckoning her to join them.

WHITE ELECTRIC FLASH FILLS THE SCREEN

TIME LAPSE
DISSOLVE TO:

89 INT. ELSIE'S ROOM. LATER   89

MUSIC: The Merry Widow Waltz continues under.

The young DOCTOR checks for a pulse, he then exchanges a sad look with SISTER MARIA, then the doctor shakes his head. ELSIE has passed away. SISTER MARIA gently places ELSIE's arms under the bedclothes and then covers her face with the sheet. The DOCTOR writes out the death certificate and SISTER MARIA witnesses it.

                    NARRATOR
          A tragic end to a life which had
          promised so much. There were
          those who concluded that for all
          her success and celebrity, Lily
          Elsie's life had, in many ways,
          been anything but merry.

SISTER MARIA walks across and draws back the heavy curtains. At once the room is flooded with soft, shimmering, almost incandescent, rays of sunshine.

DISSOLVE TO:

FLASHBACK:

THE MUSIC SWELLS and ELSIE and JOSEPH COYNE are seen gently waltzing on the first night of The Merry Widow.

And as they dance, the audience cheering their delight is heard in a ghostly way - an echo of the past. As the curtain slowly begins to fall. The thunderous roars and applause tell us all we need to know.

                                              FADE TO BLACK.

CREDITS

                            THE END

www.ingramcontent.com/pod-product-compliance
Lightning Source LLC
Chambersburg PA
CBHW030109240426
43661CB00031B/1346/J